AMERICAN DECLARATIONS OF LOVE

American Declarations of Love

Edited by
Ann Massa

MACMILLAN

First published 1990

Published by
THE MACMILLAN PRESS LTD
Houndmills, Basingstoke, Hampshire RG21 2XS
and London
Companies and representatives
throughout the world

Typeset by Vine & Gorfin Ltd, Exmouth, Devon
Printed in the People's Republic of China

British Library Cataloguing in Publication Data
American declarations of love.
1. English literature. American writers.
Special subjects. Love. Critical studies
I. Massa, Ann, 1940–
810.9'354
ISBN 0–333–44112–5

Contents

Notes on the Contributors

Richard Brown teaches English and Anglo-Irish literature at Leeds University, and is himself a poet. He is the author of *James Joyce and Sexuality* (1984), founding co-editor of the *James Joyce Broadsheet*, and has written widely on modern literature and sexuality.

Brian Harding is Senior Lecturer in American Literature at the University of Birmingham, where he teaches in the American Studies Programme and the English Department. He is the author of *American Literature in Context II, 1830–1865* (1982) and of articles on the American Transcendentalists. His edition of *Young Goodman Brown and Other Tales* was published by Oxford University Press in its World's Classics series in 1987. He is currently preparing a World's Classics edition of Hawthorne's *The Scarlet Letter*.

Ann Massa studied and has taught American Studies and American Literature at various universities in the United States and England; she currently teaches in the School of English at the University of Leeds. Her main publications include *Vachel Lindsay, Fieldworker for the American Dream* (1970); *The American Novel since 1945* (1975); and *American Literature in Context, 1900–30* (1982), a collection of fourteen essays. Her articles include a body of work on Harriet Monroe and the Chicago Renaissance. She is currently researching the changing image of England and the English in the work of Henry James.

John McCormick, Professor of Comparative Literature at Rutgers University, has most recently published *George Santayana: a Biography* (1987) and is preparing an edition of Santayana's 'Marginalia'. Professor McCormick's earlier publications include *Catastrophe and Imagination: an Interpretation of the Recent English and American Novel* (1957) and *Fiction as Knowledge: the Post-Romantic Novel* (1975).

Elsa Nettels is Professor of English and Mildred and J. B. Hickman Professor of Humanities at the College of William and Mary. She has written on a range of nineteenth and early twentieth century writers, in journals and in her *James and Conrad* (1977) and *Language, Race and Social Class in Howells America* (1988).

Robert J. Scholnick, Dean of Graduate Studies and Professor of English at the College of William and Mary in Williamsburg, Virginia, is the author of *Edmund Clarence Stedman* (1978) and numerous articles on nineteenth century American literature and culture. His most recent publication on Walt Whitman is ' "The Password Primeval": Whitman's Use of Science in "Song of Myself" ', which appeared in *Studies in the American Renaissance*, 1986. He is editing a collection of original essays on American literature and science and completing a book on Whitman and science.

Judy Smith is Professor of American Literature at Kenyon College. She has published widely on nineteenth century materials and is at work on a deconstructionist study of a range of Hawthorne's fictions.

Robert Viscusi, Professor of English and director of the Humanities Institute at Brooklyn College, City University of New York, has recently published *Max Beerbohm, or the Dandy Dante: Rereading with Mirrors* (Johns Hopkins University Press, 1986). He has written and lectured widely on British literature of the nineteenth and twentieth centuries, on literary and psychoanalytic theory, on Italian-American writing, and on Anglo-Italian literary relations. Professor Viscusi is associate editor of *Browning Institute Studies* and a member of the advisory board of *Differentia: Review of Italian Thought*. He spent the 1986–87 year in Italy on a fellowship from the National Endowment for the Humanities writing a book on the relationship between Italy and English literature.

John A. Ward is Chairman and Professor in the English Department at Kenyon College and President of the Midwest Modern Languages Association. His articles and papers have focused on Boswell, Johnson, Fielding, Dickens, Lawrence and Anthony Burgess, as well as on Faulkner, Hemingway, Lindsay and Robert Lowell.

T. Daniel Young is Gertrude Conaway Vanderbilt Professor of English, Emeritus, at Vanderbilt University. Among the twenty-eight books he has published are *Gentleman in a Dustcoat: A Biography of John Crowe Ransom* (1976); *The Past in the Present: A Thematic Study of Modern Southern Fiction* (1981) and *Fabulous Provinces: A Memoir* (1988).

1

Introduction: The Pursuit of Love

ANN MASSA

American Declarations of Love sets out to take provocative issue with one of the unchallenged clichés of American literary criticism: that there's been something odd about the way in which American literature has or hasn't approached the subject of love. The conventional wisdom runs thus. First, that love has been morbidly linked with death and curiously identified with violence. Second, that some aspects of love – child/adult, man/nature and man/man relationships, for instance – have been dealt with *ad nauseam*. Third, that adult, heterosexual love – though beautifully defined by Emerson: 'A private and tender relationship of one to one, which is the enchantment of human life'[1] – has been embarrassing and even alien to the American literary consciousness.

One set of explanations advanced to support this oddness or absence of love has been grounded in the American Experience. The American writer, weighed down with the responsibility of being spokesman, prophet and Jeremiah for a society striving to be better than most, has consequently gone beyond everyday relationships. The New World's Utopian, Edenic connotations have implied an unfallen America; thus the literature's curious choice of female roles (reformed and sexless or the old Eve and dangerous) and the compulsion to create self-reliant male characters. D. H. Lawrence's image of a race of 'masterless' men[2] and Leslie A. Fiedler's depiction of the women of American fiction as 'monsters of virtue or bitchery, symbols of the rejection or fear of sexuality'[3] have helped engender the conviction that American literature casts men and women in idiosyncratically stereotypical roles and evades the subject of adult, heterosexual love. Typically, a recent biography of F. Scott Fitzgerald has Fitzgerald's heroines and Zelda, too, as types of 'the true American Eve, who refuses to be prey, who turns

1

huntress and defeats men on their own ground'. The biographer, André Le Vot, creates his own stereotype, too. With *The Great Gatsby* and *Tender is the Night*, 'the woman-idol took the place of the traditional bestiary in American Literature's coat-of-arms'. Classically, Le Vot grounds his thesis in such arguably dominant phenomena as the frontier, the West and the continent itself :

> From *Moby Dick* to *Huckleberry Finn*, from James Fenimore Cooper to Jack London, the American imagination rejected women and the subtleties of amorous intrigue. Rootlessness and violence were the only legitimate ways for its solitary heroes to know and affirm themselves.

Thus 'a resolutely masculine, action-orientated fiction, in which male friendship took the place of apprenticeship to love'.[4]

Certainly there is much in the American experience which makes for differences in the literature. Why not write of the frontier rather than the drawing room when the frontier and not the drawing room is the reality? Why shouldn't the literature of a self-consciously test-case society ask cosmic questions rather than everyday ones: Ahab's 'Is it I, God, or who, that lifts this arm?'[5] Not to ask such questions would have been inexplicable; not to be curious about love would have been just as extraordinary. For America, perhaps more than most societies, was given to formulating questions and answers about the human condition as well as American destiny. To be an immigrant was to seek; to be an American was to define. America itself posed the question: what *was* life about? Relationships, the earliest, covenant theories said; relationships between God and man, church and state, pastor and congregation, individual and individual, individual and society. And, as revolutionary America indicated, that society was preoccupied with another series of relationships: King and subject, empire and colony, federalism and states rights. America was, by definition, people looking radically at relationships. 'Oh brave new world that hath such *people* in it' (italics mine) says Miranda in *The Tempest*, Shakespeare's American play. There was nothing in the life of American people nor in that country's theory to suggest that adult heterosexual relationships were not a significant part of that world. The Declaration of Independence, an ardent document, surely said so. It claimed as inalienable rights 'Life, Liberty and the Pursuit of

Happiness'. At that time and in that context happiness implied well-being, wholeness, achievement; but it was not a term so abstract as to exclude love or to deny that for some love and happiness could be and would be synonymous. Wasn't love as well as liberty an appropriate goal for the inhabitants of the New World?

Not, it has been argued, if those New World men and women were Puritans or their irretrievably conditioned heirs. H. L. Mencken's not unserious definition of Puritanism – 'the haunting fear that someone, somewhere, may be happy'[6] – runs directly counter to the letter and the spirit of the Declaration. Literary criticism continues to argue for the pervasive influence of Puritanism on American writers: William H. Shurr's *Rappaccini's Children* (1981), for example. Its subtitle is 'American Writers in a Calvinist World' and its thesis that the Calvinist perception of God and of good and evil has shaped writers as diverse as Eugene O'Neill and Edward Albee, Robert Frost and Wallace Stevens, Mark Twain and Henry David Thoreau. For them and for many others, argues Shurr, the legacy of the Puritan fathers has been an obsessive sense of sinfulness in a violent and unforgiving universe dominated by a wrathful God. Similarly, Samuel H. Coale's *In Hawthorne's Shadow* (1985) perceives Manichean dilemmas in the work of Faulkner, McCullers, Styron, Updike, Cheever and Gardner. The crucial relationship in this neo-Gothic literature is still between the guilty and God and not between guys and dolls.

There are dissenting voices. *The American Puritan Imagination: Essays in Revaluation* (1974) edited by Sacvan Bercovitch is important for its refreshing emphasis on the aesthetic dimensions of the Puritan mind and for its analysis of Puritan literary taste as flexible enough to accommodate pagan models, scatology and erotic ambiguity. If there is still the Puritan plain style, there is also passionate allegorising. Karl Keller's essay on Edward Taylor shows that poet's preoccupation with writing as process and as art; Robert Richardson demonstrates that the Puritan was always trying to achieve a balance between the good world God had made and His heavenly world; and Richardson finds in Anne Bradstreet's poetry the suggestion that

> earthly love, the best of this world, is . . . an emblem of what awaits the saved. . . . This world and the next validate each other. Love is the way to heaven and the best image of heaven is a realm of eternal love.[7]

But in general, literary criticism either ignores the subject of love (indeed, thematic approaches seem inappropriate to current linguistically focused theorists) or advances traditional readings of a culture which produced writers who produced a literature that is chary of adult heterosexual love and wary or dismissive of women.

The texts themselves, it is argued, yield and support such conclusions. D. H. Lawrence spoke to this persuasively in *Studies in Classic American Literature* (1923). The romance theory of American literature, briefly articulated in the mid-nineteenth century by Nathaniel Hawthorne and elaborated by Richard Chase in 1956, remains influential, and alternative theses seem less potent.[8] Chase detected

> a tendency towards melodrama and idyl; a more or less formal abstractedness, and, on the other hand, a tendency to plunge into the underside of consciousness, a willingness to abandon moral questions or to ignore the spectacle of man in society, or to consider these things indirectly or abstractedly.[9]

Jonathan Baumbach's *The Landscape of Nightmare* (1965) follows on from Chase; so does Robert Scholes' *The Fabulators* (1967) and Michael Davitt Bell's fine recent study, *The Development of American Romance: The Sacrifice of Relation* (1980). But of this school it is the brilliant Leslie Fiedler who stimulated this collection of essays, which is part reaction and part supplement to his *Love and Death in the American Novel* (1960; a revised edition appeared in 1966). *American Declarations of Love* sets out to offer a modest and necessary response to the largely unanswered challenge of Fiedler's arresting assertion that American writing[10] is either evasive or perverse in its treatment of love; or both.

Shortly after the publication of *Love and Death in the American Novel* I remember a lecture in which, with serio-comic intent, I used a passage from Saul Bellow's *Henderson The Rain King* to illustrate Fiedler's assertion that what heterosexual encounters there were in American literature were odd indeed. In the passage, Henderson, middle-aged American, encounters Willitale, old African chief. Willitale is a woman 'whose flesh of the arm overlapped the elbow'; with 'not many teeth'; with atrophying white hair. As a mark of her favour, she allows – she insists – that Henderson kiss her belly.

> I kissed, giving a shiver at the heat I encountered. My face . . .

sank inward. I was aware of the old lady's navel and her internal organs as they made sounds of submergence. I felt as though I were riding in a balloon above the Spice Islands, soaring in hot clouds while exotic odours arose from below. My own whiskers pierced me inward, in the lip.

How did I come to emphasise such a passage and to overlook the relationship between Eugene Henderson and his wife Lily? Who enjoy each other physically. Who do disagree – about good and evil, life and death, reality and illusion – but who hate to disagree. They recognise that there are profound imbalances between them. Lily, says Henderson, 'wanted us [in marriage] to end each other's solitude. Now she was no longer alone. But I still was and how did that figure?'[11] By the end of the novel it doesn't. Henderson learns a giving love. That makes him whole, and makes Henderson and Lily philosophically as well as physically one.

How did Fiedler make me misread this novel? It is something to do with his zest, his panache, his élan. The apparently formidable command of cultures and literatures and disciplines overwhelms. And those of us who have been overwhelmed by Fiedler are perhaps the kind of scholars who have such relish for that rare thing, provocative, living criticism, that we find it hard not to be grateful for it, and swayed by it, too. It's a breath of fresh air. If nothing else – and it's a considerable 'nothing else' – Fiedler sets cats among pigeons. He forces revaluations. We have to confront his thesis before we can rest in another or offer our own. Paradoxically, the most effective rethinking so far has come from feminist critics who might be expected to make their own case if not Leslie Fiedler's for the 'maleness' of American literature. In *The Madwoman in the Attic* (1979), Sandra Gilbert and Susan Gubar have shown how a number of Emily Dickinson's techniques – the exploitation of gender which undermines literary, social and moral conventions, the deliberate withholding of the sex of the speaker – serve to assert Dickinson's own powerful and complex sexual identity. And in *The Resisting Reader* (1978), Judith Fetterley offers a characteristically fine reading of Ernest Hemingway's *A Farewell to Arms* as a surface idyll ironically undercut by a bleak vision of the radical and inevitable limitations of love.

To a degree, Fiedler's own scholarly techniques undermine his work. He simply assumes that the best fiction has at its centre 'the passionate encounter of a man and woman which we have the right to expect at the centre of the novel' (24) (*Pride and Prejudice* and *Vanity Fair* are two of the unconvincing examples of such great and therefore non-American love stories.) Where it suits his purposes, Fiedler will read texts with blinkers on. If Hawthorne describes Arthur Dimmesdale's movements as 'resembling the wavering effort of an infant', then Fiedler, who sees Dimmesdale as desexed by the monstrous Hester, has discovered evidence of a literal regression to childhood (221). Fiedler's choice of texts is arbitrary, too. Dashiell Hammett is made to seem as important as William Faulkner. *Uncle Tom's Cabin* is cited and used as a major work of art. The deliberate omission of Sinclair Lewis, John Dos Passos and Thomas Wolfe is compensated for by the inclusion of William Hill Brown, Oliver Wendell Holmes and George Lippard (whose *The Quaker* is seen as a more important rendering of adult hetero-sexuality than Theodore Dreiser's *Sister Carrie*).

The omission of *Wuthering Heights* and *Jane Eyre* and of *Persuasion* too raises the question of the basis on which Fiedler selects texts and organises arguments. Is he detecting or implanting in literature his own reservations about heterosexuality and women? He writes of Richardson's 'terrifyingly acute' 'insight into the complexities of the female mind' (60–1). This insight? Women are liars. But Fiedler would seem to be speaking of himself as well as attempting to speak for Sam Clemens when he says that 'For a good American like Twain, all offences are offences against the woman' (276). Leslie Fiedler thinks he finds in literature the types he believes exist in life. Saints and liars. Virgins and whores. Fair and dark women. Who look so and are so. Thus he makes James's good Isabel Archer – 'her hair . . . was dark even to blackness' – a blonde; and Mme Merle, her blonde rival, a brunette (284). He is torn between wanting to believe that American men and American writers idealise good women and regretting that 'the heroine in our classic books is almost invariably a dull and embarrassing figure, a monster of virtue' (71).

Fiedler's sexism, his unsupported assumptions, his random examples, his perversions of texts and characters and his ultimately unconvincing forays into comparative literature make it impossible for him to support his case convincingly. But does that disprove his thesis? Can we, for instance, deny that the central relationship in many American texts is homoerotic? Or that *The Scarlet Letter*, for instance, may properly be read as a religious horror novel, even though Hester and Dimmesdale gave a great deal, perhaps all for love (Hester's feeling for Dimmesdale makes 'a joint futurity of endless retribution' acceptable, even desirable to her; he dies fearing, above all, that 'it may have been vain to hope that we could meet hereafter'.)[12] If we can so righteously disagree with details of Fiedler's interpretations, can we provide an alternative reading of American literature's treatment of love?

Not readily; both because Fiedler's bravura reading is as right as it is wrong and because of the inherent difficulties of the subject. How to define love? Fiedler tried.

> What is called "love" in literature is a rationalization, a way of coming to terms with the relationship between man and woman that does justice, on the one hand, to certain biological drives and, on the other, to certain generally accepted conventions of tenderness and courtesy. (30)

But in attempting to be specific he achieves a ridiculous and exclusive rigour. He seems to argue for a love literature which is judicious, thorough and realistic; always the same and never imaginative. His definition suggests a norm; it proposes an average experience. The literature of American popular song challenges such assumptions. It is less exclusive of mood and individuality and offers a cumulative definition of a volatile and varied emotion. Love is: 'The Greatest Thing'; 'A Many Splendored Thing'; 'Here to Stay'; 'For Sale'; 'Just One of Those Things' (one of those 'crazy' things). Ambrose Bierce, who compiled a dictionary of American definitions, adopted yet another stance.

> *Love,* n. The folly of thinking much of another before one knows anything of oneself.
> *Love,* n. A temporary insanity curable by marriage or by removal of the patient from the influence under which he incurred the disorder. This disease, like *caries* and many other ailments, is prevalent only among civilized races living under artificial conditions; barbarous nations breathing pure air and eating simple food enjoy immunity from its ravages. It is sometimes fatal, but more frequently to the physician than to the patient.[13]

While not typical of American thought and writing, these entries in Bierce's *Devil's Dictionary* identify concepts which have informed the critical perception of love in American literature and, to a degree, its creative portrayal. It is antithetical to the individual and therefore to be shunned. It is not natural but artificial and so must be denounced. It fails because women are undifferentiatedly unworthy vehicles for men's hopes.

The writers considered in *American Declarations of Love* have attempted to explore and define the nature of love in ways that defy both Fiedler and Bierce. But the thrust of this volume is not dogmatically to deny other ways of reading American literature; it is to add to them and on occasion to temper. The moonlight tones and techniques of Hawthorne's romance theory are not necessarily incompatible with Judy Smith's reading of *The Marble Faun*, while the discussion of Arthur Miller testifies to the continuing presence of what William H. Shurr calls 'the dark moon' of Calvin and of America. But present too in this volume is the moon that is rhymed with spoon and which is dark and light, half and full, deceptive and illuminating: an appropriately complex image for love as Henry James beautifully demonstrates in *Portrait of a Lady* as Isabel Archer looks at the ways in which lovers present and inevitably misrepresent themselves to each other.

> If she had not deceived him in intention she understood how completely she must have done so in fact. She had effaced herself when he first knew her; she had made herself small, pretending there was less of her than there really was. It was because she had been under the extraordinary charm that he, on his side, had taken pains to put forth. He was not changed; he had not disguised himself, during the year of his courtship, any more than she. But she had seen only half his nature then, as one saw the disk of the moon when it was partly masked by the shadow of the earth. She saw the full moon now – she saw the whole man. She kept still, as it were, so that he should have a free field, and yet in spite of this she had mistaken a part for the whole.[14]

Henry James, as Elsa Nettels reminds us, called love 'the great relation', and love, she argues, is the main preoccupation of his characters and the primary subject of his fiction. For each of the twenty novels that follow *Watch and Ward* (1878) centres on a love relationship in which different elements – sexual desire, adoration, infatuation, sympathy, frustration, jealousy – are mixed, and in which other kinds of love – homoerotic, incestuous, vicarious, necrophilic, may evoke feelings as powerful as those generated by socially sanctioned heterosexual love. She argues too that James did as much to transform the love story's traditional types and motifs as he did to transform the novel form, and that he defined artistic principles to inform the portrayal of love. And since James portrays love as a process, a development unfolding in time, it is of necessity more than or other than sexual hunger. It is the growth of passion that perhaps by definition cannot be fulfilled; 'an inner fire of the imagination that is fed more by unsatisfied desire than by emotional fulfilment'.[15]

In his essay on Emerson, John McCormick quotes Henry James's regretful assessment that in Emerson's genius, 'Passions, alternations, affairs, adventures had absolutely no part'. McCormick reveals a man who in his private life and writing exhibited intense and physical emotion but who in public spoke and wrote of heterosexual love only to diminish it. Emerson knew what it was to love and to be in love; but philosophical consistency and the loss of his first wife led him to reduce love to a temporary and minor phenomenon in the history of the soul. 'Our affections are but tents of a night', but 'the soul may be trusted'.[16] What McCormick has to say about Emerson adds depth to the portrait and resonance to the voice of the whole man.

'Some Kind of Love Story', the essay on Arthur Miller, also argues that the life informs the art. In spite of elaborate and reiterated theories which suggest that relationships are at the centre of his work, Miller initially avoided placing adult heterosexual love or a woman at the centre of plays which are concerned less with this imaginary man and that imaginary woman and their unique or typical relationship, than with Man. In the early Miller plays characters are the embodiments of issues; they stand for aspects of the human condition or parts of the social structure. But with *After the Fall* (1964), and thereafter, there is an increasing and major treatment of love and of women. For all his disclaimers about the degree to which that play is autobiographical and for all the need to respect the privacy of Miller's relationship with Marilyn Monroe, she, the Maggie character in *After the Fall*, is perhaps the catalyst in his work. She has caused the shift in the Miller oeuvre from studies of representational relatedness to the exploration of adult heterosexual relationships.

For fifty years Italian-American novelists have been debating the important question America freshly poses to the children and grandchildren of Italian immigrants: What is the meaning of love? the central theme of Italian poetry, religion, and folklore. 'Debate in the Dark: Love in Italian-American Fiction' addresses the effect of social and cultural experience on a community's perception and experience of love: love under pressure – patriarchal, matriarchal, priestly and immigrant. To the already extraordinary interplay of youthful desire and parental ambition have been added the complications of a world of bewildering social heterogeneity and racial nuance. Consequently, in Italian-American fiction love presents itself as a dilemma. And dilemmas do not only make victims; they make heroes. Robert Viscusi looks at the heroic fictions of Pietro di Donato and introduces a range of fine writers unfamiliar to most readers: Helen Barolini, Gilbert Sorrentino, Joseph Arleo and Carol Maso. It is in their work, Viscusi argues, where strategies are developed by those who resist material and racial encirclement, that love in Italian-American literature really becomes interesting.

Brian Harding refreshingly argues that Hemingway's tales resist any attempt to find sexual chauvinism in them. He assesses Hemingway as 'a wonderfully acute observer of human inter-actions and a remarkably responsive listener who devised an aesthetic that allowed him to suggest emotions and states of mind ignored or despised by complacent believers in sexual stereotypes'.[17] Hemingway's gift was for conveying a sense of the power, complexity and strength of adult heterosexual love by the minimal techniques of an art that could select moments of loss and failure.

Another ambitious narrative strategy – Hawthorne's – is analysed by Judy Smith in her essay, on *The Marble Faun*. In that novel Hawthorne explores the frightening loss attendant upon our refusal to accept our full humanity, and his illuminating and complex vision is at challenging odds with the rigid divisions of the characters. Judy Smith demonstrates how Hawthorne works with two dynamically interactive texts. The consciously constructed surface text includes moralistic authorial intrusions and models itself after the convention of casting its characters in roles that are light and pure or dark and suspect. The consciously deconstructed text, which includes the decidedly untraditional use of nineteenth century botanic imagery, insists on the need to revise our reading of human nature and of human love.

For those who would wish to argue that unless the relationship between a man and a woman is consistently at the centre of a novel, it isn't a love story, William Faulkner's *Put Out More Flags*, which can be read as part of the Sartoris family saga, may not seem to be significantly about love. But T. Daniel Young shows how, in that text and in *Sanctuary* and 'There Was a Queen', Faulkner undertakes a study of the emotional and physical complexity of the marvellously named Narcissa Benbow. He explores her attempts and capacities to find fulfilment in romantic love, in sexual experience, in marriage and motherhood. The pattern that emerges is of achievement and disappointment; the pattern will be repeated hopefully, hopelessly. 'I wouldn't advise anybody to marry', says Miss Jenny to Narcissa. 'You wont be happy, but women haven't got civilized enough yet to be happy unmarried, so you might as well try it'.[18]

Perhaps there has been too much written about Whitman as homosexual poet. Robert Scholnick approaches Whitman's phallic language, his changing emotional landscape and the 'Calamus' sequence of poems in particular for what they tell us as adults of both sexes about the terrible pains and almost inexpressible ecstasies which come with love. Diagnostically and passionately Whitman charts the discovery and loss of love, the release and the anxiety, the reassurance and the despair. Who else conveys so well what it is to ache with amorous love, and who suggests more effectively that 'sex contains all', that 'out of dimness opposite equals advance, always substance and increase, always sex / Always a knit of identity, always a distinction, always a breed of life'.[19]

Two other poets are considered in this collection. In an essay which looks back to Robert Lowell's earlier love poetry, John Ward sees the poet of *The Dolphin* using techniques which are less effective than his former work precisely because the authenticity of erotic and loving experience is beginning to escape him or has become too fragile and ironic to capture in verse. The volume of sonnets shows us Lowell 'trying to supply in artful lines a version of loving experience that proves love is powerless to save him, lost in life and writing'. Indeed, *The Dolphin* may show that Lowell 'knew and wishes to demonstrate that love is and was powerless to save: a powerful revision of the tendency of a sequence of sonnets on love'.[20] Bob Dylan's love lyrics, argues Richard Brown, fall into five phases. In his middle period, between 'Nashville Skyline' and 'New Morning' (a period coinciding with his marriage), Dylan adopts the conventional language of love with an extravagance that seldom seems far short of self-parody. But in early and late lyrics he sets against the clichéd '"I love you" that most incontrovertible of modern realities, the reality of sexual desire'. Then, suggests Brown, Dylan, 'as determined to penetrate to truths behind the romantic myths of love as he is to expose the social truths disguised behind myths generated by self-interest and corrupt power', writes at his vigorous and subtle best.[21]

There is, then, a good case to be made for the existence of a rich and varied American love literature, for writing which does not curiously evade but which remarkably confronts. *American Declarations of Love* has not set out to offer pat generalisations, but the permutations and combinations of this particular collection of essays inevitably generates some speculation about tendencies and trends. The argument for realism in love, for instance, stretches at least from Hawthorne to Miller. Henry James and Ernest Hemingway are probably not alone in making crucial use of the structured silence when they write of love. The evolving Italian-American novel and the verses of Bob Dylan are surely only two examples of fresh contributions to the literature and language of love. Sometimes the originality is of degree rather than kind, for American writers seem prone to adopt extreme stances. Emerson denies love in favour of the soul; Whitman indulges in epic and lyric affirmations of the primacy of sex; Lowell is merciless in the use of private material in his love poetry, while Faulkner employs an almost case-study approach to the subject.

Other collections of essays on love would generate other ideas; and judging by the essays which this volume was, regretfully, not able to accommodate, there is no shortage of alternative tables of contents. One such might well include an examination of Chapter 132 in *Moby Dick*, where Melville advances a heterosexual ideal, a balance and fusion of masculine and feminine elements which is not accessible to the exclusively masculine Ahab, who as a result makes the wrong choice – to chase the whale rather than return to Nantucket.

It was a clear steel-blue day. The firmaments of air and sea were hardly separable in that all-pervading azure; only, the pensive air was transparently pure and soft, with a woman's look, and the robust and man-like sea heaved with long, strong, lingering swells, as Samson's chest in his sleep.

Hither, and thither, on high, glided the snow-white wings of small, unspeckled birds; these were the gentle thoughts of the feminine air; but to and fro in the deeps, far down in the bottomless blue, rushed mighty leviathans, sword-fish, and sharks; and these were the strong, troubled, murderous thinkings of the masculine sea.

But though thus contrasting within, the contrast was only in shades and shadows without; those two seemed one; it was only the sex, as it were, that distinguished them.

Aloft, like a royal czar and king, the sun seemed giving this gentle air to this bold and rolling sea; even as bride to groom. And at the girdling line of the horizon, a soft and tremulous motion – most seen here at the equator – denoted the fond, throbbing trust, the loving alarms, with which the poor bride gave her bosom away.

Tied up and twisted; gnarled and knotted with wrinkles; haggardly firm and unyielding; his eyes flowing like coals, that still glow in the ashes of ruin; untottering Ahab stood forth in the clearness of the morn; lifting his splintered helmet of a brow to the fair girl's forehead of heaven.[22]

Melville provides material for any number of *American Declarations of Love*. In the compelling incestuous love which is at the heart of *Pierre* he seems to deny sexual norms; so, among others, does Edith Wharton. The relationship between artistic and sexual power which American literature posits deserves study. Willa Cather, for instance, is pre-occupied with women whose strong sexual desires seem to threaten their creative integrity. The realists and naturalists have written about love with an unexpected and challenging divergence. William Dean Howells, in *Their Wedding Journey*, undercuts romantic illusions; and in *A Modern Instance* explores both marital incompatibility and the desirability of divorce. But Frank Norris, in *The Octopus*, is unequivocally romantic. Love transforms, Annixter tells Hilma.

"Just loving you has changed my life all around. It's made it easier to do the straight, clean thing. I want to do it; it's fun doing it. Remember, once I said I was proud of being a hard man, a driver, of being glad that people hated me and were afraid of me? Well, since I've loved you I'm ashamed of it all. I don't want to be hard anymore, and nobody is going to hate me if I can help it. I'm happy and I want other people so. I love you," he suddenly exclaimed; "I love you, and if you will forgive me, and if you will come down to such a beast as I am, I want to be to you the best a man can be to a woman."[23]

There is, too, an important idiomatic literature of love in those lyrics of American musicals and of classical popular song which combine the casual and formal properties of American speech: 'Of Thee I Sing, Baby'. Has any other body of lyrics managed to render poetic such unattractive sounds as the names of the boroughs of New York City? ('We'll have Manhattan, the Bronx and Staten Island too'). Is there anything to compare with a love song which comically and magically incorporates references to Edison and sound, Marconi and wireless, Whitney and his cotton gin, Wilbur and his brother, Fulton and his steamboat, Ford and his Lizzie, Hershey and his chocolate bar? And Rockefeller Center? And Christopher Columbus?[24]

Ogden Nash has, on occasion, caught this idiom; so have the erotic and tender sonnets of e. e. cummings, whose uniquely punctuated texts reproduce the rituals and actions of intercourse. These sonnets might bear comparison with Lowell's. And with Anne Bradstreet's? Edward Albee's dark rendering of love and marriage – 'Why have we invented the word love in the first place?' he asks in *Zoo Story*, and in *All Over*, adds, 'Selfless love? I don't think so. We love to be loved'[25] – echoes Scott Fitzgerald's rendering of Dick Diver. 'He had made his choice . . . chosen the sweet poison and drunk it. Wanting above all to be brave and kind, he had wanted, even more than that, to be loved. So it had been. So it would ever be.'[26] Alice Walker could well figure as a twentieth century Emersonian; for at the end of *The Color Purple*, Celie and Albert have conquered their sexual desire for Shug Avery and are a contented part of an ever expanding circle of soul people. In true transcendental spirit Celie addresses her last letter to 'Dear God. Dear stars, dear trees, dear sky, dear peoples. Dear everything. Dear God.' 'And us so happy', she declares.[27]

Benn Crader, in Saul Bellow's most recent novel, *More Die of Heartbreak*, wonders why the pursuit of love goes on. Because

the hardest items of all [in life] have to do with love. The question then is; So why does everybody persist? If love cuts them up so much and you see the ravages everywhere, why not be sensible and sign off early?

His nephew, a University Professor who teaches a seminar on 'The Meaning of Love' has an answer which denies the connection between love and death and which is difficult to improve on. ' "Because of immortal longings," I said. "Or just hoping for a lucky break." '[28]

Notes

1. Ralph Waldo Emerson, 'Love', in *The Selected Writings of Ralph Waldo Emerson* (New York: Random House, 1950) p. 219.
2. D. H. Lawrence, *Studies in Classic American Literature* (London: Mercury Books, 1965) p. 5. First published 1923.
3. Leslie Fiedler, *Love and Death in the American Novel* (London: Paladin, 1970) p. 24. Page references are to this, the second edition.
4. Andre Le Vot, *F. Scott Fitzgerald*, tr. William Byron (Harmondsworth: Penguin Books, 1983) pp. ix, xi. Scott Donaldson, *Fool for Love* (New York: Congdon & Weed, 1983) also advances the traditional argument that love 'was not a subject close to the mainstream of American literature' (p. 99), though he cites James and Dreiser as exceptions. Although the book is primarily a biographical portrait it offers a fine reading of the ways in which the war imagery in *Tender is the Night* reinforces that novel's projection of the war between the sexes.
5. Herman Melville, *Moby Dick* (New York: W. W. Norton, 1967) p. 445.
6. H. L. Mencken in *The American Mercury* for 1925, quoted in Marcus Cunliffe, *The Literature of the United States* (Harmondsworth: Penguin Books, 1981) p. 23.
7. Robert D. Richardson Jr., 'The Puritan Poetry of Anne Bradstreet', in Sacvan Bercovitch (ed.), *The American Puritan Imagination* (New York: Cambridge University Press, 1974) p. 113.
8. Alfred Habegger, for instance, in *Gender, Fantasy and Realism in American Literature* (New York: Columbia University Press, 1982), speaks for those authors of 'works of criticism and literary history that, opposing Chase, regard the realistic novel as a principal type of American fiction' and he further 'attempts to make a case for seeing realism as the central and pre-eminent literary type in democratic society' (p. vii). But Habegger reduces the writer to an unimaginative cultural and autobiographical spokesperson; and in his aggressive and defensive preoccupation with the inevitable and rightful (because realistic) masculinity of American literature, finds fault with, for example, *Portrait of a Lady*'s defective view of men. A more useful and less dogmatic counter to Chase (and to Perry Miller and F. O. Matthiesen, to whom the book is dedicated), is employed in Sacvan Bercovitch (ed.), *Reconstructing American Literary History* (Cambridge, Mass: Harvard University Press, 1986): 'It will be the task of the present generation to reconstruct American literary history by making a virtue of dissensus' (p. viii).

9. Richard Chase, *The American Novel and its Tradition* (London: G. Bell and Sons, 1958) p. ix.

10. Fiedler's examples are from fiction, but his generalisations concern the American writer (p. 15 and *passim*).

11. Saul Bellow, *Henderson the Rain King* (London: Weidenfeld & Nicholson, 1959) pp. 71, 74, 80.

12. Nathaniel Hawthorne, *The Scarlet Letter* (Edinburgh: William Paterson, n.d.) pp. 94, 307.

13. Ambrose Bierce, *The Enlarged Devil's Dictionary* (London: Victor Gollancz, 1967) p. 180 (first published 1906).

14. Henry James, *The Portrait of a Lady* (Harmondsworth: Penguin Books, 1983) p. 426.

15. See p. 70 quoting Philip Sicker, *Love and Quest for Identity in the Fiction of Henry James* (Princeton University Press, 1980) p. 19.

16. See p. 44.

17. See p. 114.

18. See p. 103.

19. Walt Whitman, *Leaves of Grass* (New York: New American Library, 1960) p. 105 ('A Woman Waits for Me'), p. 51 ('Song of Myself').

20. See p. 141.

21. See pp. 177, 181.

22. Melville, op. cit., p. 442.

23. Frank Norris, *The Octopus* (New York: New American Library, 1981) p. 284.

24. Ira Gershwin, 'They All Laughed,' *George Gershwin's Greatest Hits* (n.p.: Warner Bros. Publications, 1976) pp. 101–5.

25. Edward Albee, *The Zoo Story* (New York: New American Library, 1961) p. 36; *All Over* (London: Jonathan Cape, 1972) p. 109.

26. F. Scott Fitzgerald, *Tender is the Night* (Harmondsworth: Penguin Books, 1982) p. 325.

27. Alice Walker, *The Color Purple* (London: The Woman's Press, 1983) pp. 242, 246.

28. Saul Bellow, *More Die of Heartbreak* (New York: William Morrow, 1987) p. 11.

2

Fall into Human Light: Hawthorne's Vision of Love

JUDY SMITH

'Love is the true magnetism'
Hawthorne to Sophia, 1841

As Hawthorne articulates his love for Sophia Peabody, whom he called variously his Dove and his Sophie, he adopts the conventional division of maiden from temptress, but he does so to subvert such division, reminding us that human nature – and human love – is a wonderful commixture of opposites. Hawthorne delights in holding her 'divided' character in an exquisitely unified love:

> There is an unaccountable fascination about that Sophie Hawthorne – whatever she chooses to do or say, whether reasonable or unreasonable, I am forced to love her the better for it. Not that I love her better than my Dove; but then it is right and natural that the Dove should awaken infinite tenderness, because she is a bird of Paradise, and has a perfect and angelic nature – so that love is her inalienable right. And yet my wayward heart will love this naughty Sophie Hawthorne; – yes, its affection for the Dove is doubled, because she is inseparably united with naughty Sophie. I have one love for them both, and it is infinitely intensified, because they share it together.[1]

Here Hawthorne embraces the ambiguous mixture of human nature; he allows himself the freedom to combine the angelic and the wayward parts of himself and his beloved into an inseparable whole. He knows well, however, the destructive tendency of his age to insist upon rigid division, to separate human life and love into reductive absolutes. In his fiction, Hawthorne explores the terrible

17

loss attendant upon our refusal to accept our full, complex humanity. We commit a crime against human nature as we sacrifice ambiguous reality to a rigid ideal.

Hawthorne's illuminating and complex vision, which is at provocative odds with the rigid division of his characters, is nowhere more apparent than in the ambitious narrative strategy of *The Marble Faun*. Here Hawthorne works with two dynamically interactive texts, a tension often noted but wrongly attributed to his evasive ambivalence or his inability to shed his modest, moralistic vision.[2] The consciously constructed surface text includes moralistic authorial intrusions and models itself after the convention of assigning its characters into roles that are light and pure or dark and suspect. The consciously deconstructed text, which includes botanic imagery and ironic manipulation of character, argues against such division and insists on the need to revise our reading of human nature and of human love.

Such revisioning occurs as Hawthorne makes clear his separation from Kenyon, whose is the central sensibility in the novel. It is Kenyon, not Hawthorne, who assigns the love of Donatello and Miriam to the 'lurid glow' of the underground and his own love for Hilda to the 'celestial light' of the heavens. It is Kenyon, not Hawthorne, who transforms Miriam from a passionate flower to a cold gem and Hilda from an icy snow-drop to a warm posy. Through authorial irony and botanic imagery, Hawthorne uncovers the sterility and destructiveness of an insistent purity of vision; he will ironically reduce Kenyon to an impotent, whitened 'statue'. Kenyon is sprayed with lime from a toy gun at a carnival, the visual realisation of the effects of his absurd rejection of flesh for marble, his determination that Hilda be inhumanly pure. Kenyon may insist on worshipping a 'household saint', but Hawthorne insists on a vision of love which needs neither angel nor demon but which affirms that we are midway between them, partaking of both and being neither. *The Marble Faun* is no less than Hawthorne's attempt to warn us against a fall from human light by reducing human love into heavenly or infernal components, or banishing what is natural from our human constructions.

I

The chastening implications of separating human construction from nature is made clear in Hawthorne's rendering of setting. At the entrance to Miriam's studio is a fountain which

> brims over from one stone basin into another, or gushes from a Naiad's urn, or spurts its many little jets from the mouths of nameless monsters, which were merely grotesque and artificial when Bernini, or whoever was their unnatural father, first produced them; but now the patches of moss, the tufts of grass, the trailing maiden-hair, and all sorts of verdant weeds that thrive in the cracks and crevices of moist marble, tell us that Nature takes the fountain back into her great heart, and cherishes it as kindly as if it were a woodland spring.[3]

That our entrance to Miriam's studio and our introduction to her is framed by this reminder that our 'grotesque and artificial' constructions can be reclaimed and naturalised by 'verdant weeds' and the sexually suggestive maidenhair,[4] reinforces Hawthorne's intent. Miriam's residence is a mirror of her character: she is an amalgam of the artificial and the natural, a hybrid mixture of innocence and experience. A potential balance between these polarities is the inviting possibility placed on her doorstep for those who can enter and contain such plurality. As we will see, Kenyon rejects this offer; though capable of far more, he will insist on seeing only the grotesque and artificial, pronouncing that the urn is irreparably cracked.

Hawthorne invokes Miriam's hybrid nature not to damn her but to highlight the inability of those around her to contain it. Well before the dramatic murder of her model, and the question of her involvement in the crime, she is on her way to being condemned in Kenyon's sight. Hawthorne carefully details the transformation of Kenyon's belief in her innocence to his insistence on her guilt, a transformation begun with the speculation allowed by revealing a particular aspect of her hybridism: 'one drop of African blood' may run in her veins. She is not 'pure'; she may not even be a maiden.

Her ambiguous racial history is complemented by her equally ambiguous demeanour. She gives the appearance of being the proverbial full-blown rose that promises it will not 'difficult to develop a casual acquaintance into intimacy' (21). Coupled with her 'freedom of thought, and force of will', these attributes invite those around her to penetrate her mystery. Despite her appearance and suspicious history, Miriam complicates the expected response; far from inviting intimacy, she reservedly 'kept people at a distance'. It is this mixture, as it were, of whore and virgin, flower and bud, that is the text Kenyon encounters and which thwarts his attempts to read her as stained or pure.

Initially Kenyon responds to Miriam in the best spirit of friendship, 'taking her good qualities as evident and never imagining that what was hidden must be therefore evil' (24). But when he hears the 'rumors', visits her studio and observes her with her model, Kenyon begins to make the equation between secrecy and evil. He approaches Hilda to reveal his doubts; she upbraids him for his suspicions. Despite his rueful admission that Hilda the good is, of course, Hilda the right, he adds in frustration his revealing declaration that Miriam 'is such a mystery!' (109). Unable to accept that a woman who adopts such 'freedom of intercourse' also keeps herself from revealing to him her secret, Kenyon begins his move toward damning her for not allowing him that cherished peep beneath her petals. He will remove the mystery; he will reread the given text. Dismissing the natural maidenhair, his version of Miriam will be cast into a stony, cold assessment that her secret must be grotesque; it must be to provide a perfect antithesis to his transformation of Hilda, a copyist from New England, from a fair maiden into a celestial presence, a transformation designed to keep himself safe from the 'lurid glow' of hybrid textuality.

Hawthorne underscores his ironic portrait of Kenyon by prefacing the scene in the studio where Miriam does offer to reveal her secret (she is rebuffed by Kenyon's cold suspicion) with a discussion about 'womanhood' in general and Kenyon's sculpting of Hilda's hand, and of Cleopatra in particular. And prior to these scenes Hawthorne has carefully framed the portrait with Kenyon's self-limiting perception of Hilda and the role into which he casts her: ' "Dear Hilda, this is a perplexed and troubled world! It soothes me inexpressibly to think of you in your tower, with white doves and white thoughts for your companions, so high above us all, and with the Virgin for your household friend"' (112). Kenyon has constructed a perfect foil to Miriam's complexity and the mirror it creates for his own human condition; he erects a 'celestial clarity' in its place. Kenyon insists on one kind of picture; Hawthorne deliberately unveils another.

In his studio, Miriam provides Kenyon with the last piece of ammunition he needs for her deflation. As Miriam assesses his sculpture of Hilda's hand, she claims that he 'must have wrought it passionately, in spite of its maiden palm and dainty finger-tips'. In response to Miriam's observation that this art contains a mixture of the passionate and the pure, Kenyon vehemently denies Hilda's complicity; he was, we are told, 'anxious to vindicate his mistress's maidenly reserve' (121). Kenyon is too anxious here, leaving us to speculate that he is becoming ensnared by the text he is creating. He maintains Hilda's innocence by casting himself into the role of a thief. Hawthorne presses home the irony; as Kenyon lays the hand back in its ivory casket, 'He dared not even kiss the image he had himself made; it had assumed its share of Hilda's remote and shy divinity' (122). By elevating Hilda to the heavens, he consigns himself to the regions of shame, and truncates the natural balance of passion and purity.

Next they discuss his Cleopatra, a work described as passionately complex; depending on the angle from which it is viewed, 'softness and tenderness' coexist with a revelation of a woman as 'implacable as stone, and as cruel as fire' (127). Miriam marvels at Kenyon's ability to capture such complex 'womanhood' and wonders who the model is. Hawthorne's descriptions hint that it is Miriam herself:

> The sculptor had not shunned to give the full Nubian lips, and other characteristics of the Egyptian physiognomy. His courage and integrity had been abundantly rewarded; for Cleopatra's beauty shone out richer, warmer, more triumphantly, beyond comparison, than if, shrinking timidly from the truth, he had chosen the tame Grecian type. (126)

Kenyon's speculations about Miriam, her drop of African blood, her dark secret, seem to constitute the model for this sculpture. Sensing that Kenyon's can be a 'large view' capable of containing such multiplicity, Miriam asks him to hear her secret. We should not be surprised that Miriam senses a coldness that compels her to withdraw; Hawthorne has prepared us for Kenyon's transformation. His refusal to be intimate 'resulted from a suspicion that had crept into his heart and lay there in a dark corner' (129). It is not so much a suspicion about Miriam's involvement with her model as it is his earlier equations and polarizations that come into play and cause him to renounce the full vision afforded by 'courage and integrity' for the fragmented, partial sight of the hand alone. Miriam senses that the only intimacy Kenyon can allow is with the disembodied hand; she knows that her secret, her 'dark red carbuncle – red as blood – is too rich a gem to put into a stranger's casket' (130). In Hawthorne's fiction, the fierce vitality of Cleopatra is no match for the power of that delicate hand. Kenyon has chosen his version of the text. Substituting a fragment for the whole, he, as well as Miriam, will become the victim of his own unnatural constructions.

Miriam is in as much danger from Donatello, who is the apparent incarnation of an innocent Faun, as she is from Kenyon; both insist on casting her into a role of their own making. This is made manifest in the scene with Miriam and Donatello at the Villa Borghese, where the garden's 'beauty lies in the neglect that leaves Nature so much to her own ways and methods'. Hawthorne is careful to add that 'there is enough human care', however, 'to prevent wildness from growing into deformity' (72). Like the fountain in front of Miriam's studio, the Villa Borghese is the medium between human construction and nature that wins Hawthorne's approval. In this balanced state, Miriam and Dona-tello sport among the paths and flowers, the anemones and the violets, those flowers usually associated with the fair maiden. At first glance, this scene may seem an evocation of a prelapsarian unity with nature. A closer look reveals that human construction has intruded far into this woodland; the violets become the token of corruption and an instrument of bondage.

Their play becomes mock violent; 'They pelted one another with early flowers, and gathering them up twined them with green leaves into garlands for both their heads.' (The ritual violence associated with flowers, which we will see again at the Carnival, is underscored by the symbolism of the garland; in addition to its use for victorious adornment, the garland was ritually applied to victims being prepared for sacrifice.) Their increasingly flawed idyll is all too easily interrupted:

"Hark!" cried Donatello, stopping short, *as he was about to bind Miriam's fair hands with flowers, and lead her along in triumph;* – "there is music somewhere in the grove!"
"It is your kinsman, Pan, most likely," said Miriam, "playing on his pipe. Let us go seek him, and make him puff out his rough cheeks and pipe out his merriest air! Come; the strain of music will guide us onward like a gayly colored thread of silk."
"*Or like a chain of flowers,*" responded Donatello, *drawing her along by that which he had twined.* (84; my italics)

She is being bound by 'a chain of flowers', chained by the flower of the mind to conform to its 'grotesque and artificial' model. 'By that which he had twined', Miriam and the unsuspecting reader are drawn further towards doom.

Donatello and Miriam are caught in an imprisoning ideal of animal innocence. Miriam doubts seriously Donatello's likeness to the mythic Faun; indeed, she perceives something intelligently savage about this woodland spirit, 'whose faithful watch was no more to be eluded than that of a hound' (159). Hawthorne repeatedly characterises Donatello as a dog, but the absurdity lessens as we discover that Donatello hounds Miriam as surely as her model does. She tells Hilda that she wishes he 'would not haunt my footsteps so continually' (18). Despite her numerous warnings that he should leave her alone, Donatello persists, declares his love and refuses to be driven off. As Donatello insists on the part of 'a faithful hound', compelled to follow – and to obey – his beloved mistress, Miriam is cast into the role of responsible keeper.

Like Hilda's, such innocence can be dangerously deceptive. And, like most of the characters, we are quick to believe that what we witness is finally Miriam's crime; a closer look, however, finds Hawthorne carefully painting a picture that is more clouded, less certain. Miriam is uncertain of her actual participation in the crime. It was all like a 'dim show' and 'she could not well distinguish what was done and suffered; no, not even whether she were really an actor and sufferer in the scene' (171). She does declare her guilt, but she does so because Donatello threatens suicide. When he says that her eyes bade him do it, she is not convinced; it is not until he threatens to end his life that Miriam acquiesces. Donatello warns her: ' "Say that I have slain him against your will, – say that he died without your whole consent – and, in another breath, you shall see me lying beside him." ' (173) Whether she willed it or not is uncertain; what is clear, however, is that she must assume the role, be bound by that which he had twined, be made to conform to the text that has been spun out to erase ambiguity.

It is Hilda, however, who becomes the judge of Miriam's guilt, a role created by both herself and those around her. Just prior to and directly after the murder, Hilda's religious qualities are stressed. She is elevated beyond a simple kinship with humanity; 'There is certainly a providence on purpose for Hilda, if for no other human creature' (180). All 'religiously believe' this, to use the words of Coverdale, for not to believe and enforce this celestial clarity would rob her of her function. This gentle maiden, this proverbial shrinking violet, usurps a traditionally masculine role; held aloof and superior, she is the judge, the instrument of Providence. To be in the circle of those virgin skirts ironically imparts a measure of their divinity; this is what makes them so attractive and what demands that they remain intact. Like Kenyon with the sculpted hand, all fall into believing that their self-constructed images are the truth itself.

As Miriam approaches Hilda's tower, Hawthorne emphasises this need. 'Had she been compelled to choose between infamy in the eyes of the whole world, or in Hilda's eyes alone, she would have unhesitatingly accepted the former, on condition of remaining spotless in the estimation of her white-souled friend' (202). It is not so much for the fair maiden's sake that we keep her unblemished; it is rather for our own. Despite evidence to the contrary, Miriam accepts Hilda's version of the story, complying with the text that insists upon clear divisions of guilt and innocence. Miriam acknowledges the threat she now poses to Hilda's virginity, and rather than be guilty of deflowering the ideal, chooses to withdraw, stained and guilty, having accepted, as Hawthorne ironically points out, 'a sentence of condemnation from a supreme tribunal' (210). The irony increases as we remember that we too witness the scenes and are prone to accept the sentence of a version constructed to truncate the whole truth.

II

From this point on, the separation of Hilda and Miriam into the fair maiden and dark temptress becomes more pronounced. They become symbolic figureheads whose influence is seen largely in the characters they influence. Kenyon, 'a young man, and cherishing a love which insulated him from the wild experiences which some men gather', visits Donatello in his Apennine home, straying amid 'its vineyards and orchards, its dells and tangled shrubbery'. In his insulating virginity, Kenyon grapples with his uncompensated love for his cherished ideal, Hilda, while he attempts to restore the now complex Donatello to his former simplistic self. In Kenyon's perception of the tangled vegetation that surrounds him, Hawthorne reveals both the sculptor's non-virginal thoughts and the rigid restraints that must be put on them. The 'enchanting nooks' are,

To the sculptor's eye . . . rich with beauty . . . in that sweetly impressive way where wildness, in a long lapse of·years, has crept over scenes that have once been adorned with the careful art and toil of man; and when man could do no more for them, time and nature came, and wrought hand in hand to bring them to a soft and venerable perfection. There grew the fig-tree that had run wild and taken to wife the vine, which likewise had gone rampant out of all human control; so that the two wild things had tangled and knotted themselves into a wild marriage-bond, and hung their various progeny – the luscious figs, the grapes, oozy with the Southern juice, and both endowed with a wild flavor, that added the final charm – on the same bough together. (242)

The oxymoronic quality of this passage reveals Kenyon's difficulty and at the same time it provides Hawthorne with an excellent cover for his ironic comments. The sculptor's eye pronounces the scene 'sweetly impressive' and 'soft'; yet the ensuing description denies these qualities, challenges the sweet virginity he professes to see and with which he is supposed to see. Kenyon's propensity to deny the oozy and violent sexuality amidst these sylvan groves by overlaying it with the reductive vision he has sculpted is consistent with his predilection for interpreting Hilda's severity and stubbornness as marks of her 'gentle decision and independence'. In order to live up to the ideal of his own creation, he must rid himself of the provocative associations of such tangled, oozy nature.

To this end, Kenyon begins to mould himself into an image that will fit into the virginal hand of his cherished Hilda. He upbraids himself for any ideas he has about Hilda that hint at sexual anticipation and pronounces that all of Hilda's words and actions must be absolutely correct. So, when he next meets Miriam, at Monte Beni, Kenyon remarks directly on her beauty (Hilda has praised Miriam), a remark which causes Miriam to ask if her 'lack of feminine modesty' has shocked his 'delicate sensibility'. Her question provokes a telling response. Though Kenyon admits that he does not know what passed between her and Hilda, he has nevertheless interpreted the event and is ready with his reading of the text. He deems, without question, Hilda right, and enforces this reading by declaring Hilda's typical ascension above common humanity: 'The white shining purity of Hilda's nature is a thing apart; and she is bound, by the undefiled material of which God molded her, to keep that severity' (287). The irony nearly overwhelms; she is bound, as well, by the 'defiled material' with which they have moulded her. The conflation of the divine and the human, the substitution of a personal interpretation for an absolute text, becomes yet more pronounced when Kenyon begins to elevate himself and adopt a severity toward Miriam and Donatello. Hilda's apotheosis firmly established, it is but a short step for Kenyon to assume a similar role: his aspirations toward the ideal, his association with a godly creature of his own making, infuse him with a priestly function.

At the statue of Pope Julius, Kenyon assumes his role as priest, interpreting the ways of God to humanity. Appropriating the words of a marriage ceremony, Kenyon warns them that although the 'bond betwixt you . . . is a true one and never – except by Heaven's own act – should be rent asunder', they must 'Take heed; for you love one another, and yet your bond is twined with such black threads, that you must never look upon it as identical with the ties that unite other loving souls' (321–2). Kenyon voices his warning, we are told, because he is 'anxious not to violate the integrity of his conscience'. But he violates the integrity of divinity; like the minister in *The Scarlet Letter* who dares say he knows the limits of Heaven's mercy, Kenyon pronounces that they can never know earthly happiness; even to think of it will result in there being 'no holy sanction on your wedded life' (322). No, absolutely not, because all holy sanction must be preserved for Hilda and her mate. To enforce this severe sentence, Kenyon usurps the words spoken to Adam and Eve: 'for mutual elevation and encouragement towards a severe and painful life, you take each other's hands' (322). To the sculptor's celestially clear vision, the wedding/sacrifice is complete. The entire cast has been fitted into a script of purity.

Hawthorne addresses the error of constructing such a text in a lengthy authorial intrusion in which he reminds us that our knowledge of evil in the world often 'takes substance and reality from the sin of some guide, whom we have deeply trusted and revered, or some friend whom we have dearly loved'. This knowledge and the confusion it brings occur because we have invested this person with an unduly elevated status, 'that one friend being to us the symbol and representative of whatever is good and true'. When the disillusionment sets in, 'We stare wildly about us, and discover – or, it may be, we never make the discovery – that it was not actually the sky that tumbled down, but merely a frail structure of our own rearing (328–9). Kenyon, who will be brought again to the brink of this recognition, will sacrifice it for the frail but powerful structure of his own rearing. Like Milton's Adam and Eve, he rests too secure in his choice of a guide, too secure in his own ability to interpret text.

Kenyon has prepared himself well for receiving the 'Snow-drops and Maidenly Delights' of his little dove. The lore which surrounds both the snow-drop and the dove enforce the hidden, murderous quality of these symbols of love and peace.[5] His love, described as "the amaranthine flower" furthers this intertwining of love and death,[6] the exchange of the crimson rose for 'snow-drops and sunless violets' (374). These images form an appropriate warning of the coming death of Kenyon's passionate art, of the sacrifice of his vision of the complexity of human love. As Hawthorne uncovers Kenyon's Cleopatra for our view, he reminds us that she is the 'fossil woman of an age that produced statelier, stronger, and more passionate creatures than our own' (377). With Kenyon lay the potential for resurrecting this age in our own.

In the next chapter, appropriately entitled 'Reminiscences of Miriam', Kenyon gives voice again to the compassionate complexity of vision that allowed the creation of his Cleopatra. He admits to Hilda that alongside his view that Miriam and Donatello are guilty – probably of murder, certainly of too much freedom – is another that calls them heroic. Hilda, 'looking at the matter through the clear, crystal medium of her own integrity', (384) declares severely that there can be no intermixture of right and wrong. Alas, it is Hawthorne's age, and in it men like Kenyon yield to the 'gentle steadfastness' of such 'alpine soils'. He will sacrifice his uneasy, multiple vision for the safe simplicity of his white ideal. His dishonesty here – and Hawthorne has reminded us that Kenyon does possess the capacity for honesty and integrity – will be the basis of Hawthorne's extended irony and the 'act awry' which leads to the fall that Hawthorne documents. As Kenyon claims Hilda's 'clairvoyant' vision as his own, he falls from the wholeness of his nature. He falls from an honest, ambiguous notion of life and love to the dishonest, fragmented but clear wedding with an ideal.

III

The transformation is nearly complete. No longer simply a fair maiden, Hilda has been given a celestial grace, clothed by Kenyon's insistence that she be above mercy. Miriam, likewise, is no longer simply a dark temptress; as Kenyon looks at her, she is transformed into a 'gem . . . that glittered with a clear, red lustre. . . . Somehow or other, this colored light seemed an emanation of herself, as if all that was passionate and glowing, in her native disposition, had crystallized upon her breast' (396). The 'somehow or other' is not so mysterious; these women not only hold the deposits of Kenyon's sculpted text, but they also become the very text itself, completing the transformation of life into art. One shines with white light, the other with a lurid glow; these lights, however, seem artificial and grotesque, unreclaimed by the softening of nature. Kenyon has fitted 'womanhood' into a jewel so that it may fit into his ivory casket; in so doing, as Hawthorne makes clear, he has truncated 'manhood' to fit there as well.

Before Kenyon can be allowed to claim his ideal, Hawthorne submits him to a final test, a test that includes both a renunciation of art and sexual humiliation. Before he can be admitted fully to the shrine-like bedroom of his creation, he must reverently denounce anything that might stain the purity of the ideal. He sets off in search of Hilda only to uncover instead the buried Venus. 'Kenyon beheld the fingers of a marble hand'; further searching shows that 'the poor, fragmentary woman forthwith showed that she retained her modest instincts to the last' (423). Kenyon's outburst ' "I seek for Hilda, and find a marble woman!" ' is overtly ironic. Less obvious, however, is how carefully Hawthorne has controlled the irony, how he has prepared us to read his text here.

After Kenyon hears Hilda's confession to the priest, he is 'stung into irreverence' by her 'misapplied veneration' for St. Peter's; in retaliation he attempts to deflate the sanctity she finds there. Reflecting on the 'delicate' people living in this 'ever mild and tranquil air', he remarks that then 'These architectural tombs of the Pope might serve for dwellings and each brazen sepulchral door-way would become a domestic threshold. Then, the lover, if he dared, might say to his mistress, "Will you share my tomb with me?" – and, winning her soft consent, he would lead her to the altar, and thence to yonder selpulchre of Pope Gregory, which should be their nuptial home. What a life would be theirs, Hilda, in their marble Eden!' (369). Ever fond of framing, Hawthorne provides us once again with a threshold through which to view the scene with the Venus. The irreverent power of Kenyon's reductive vision of St. Peter's is coming back to haunt him; he in fact will choose the 'tranquil' air of a marble woman – or, more correctly, a woman he has cast into a marble image – and entomb himself within a marble Eden. Kenyon is unable to take an inspired interest in his newest discovery; the real discovery is ours as Hawthorne uncovers once again Kenyon's need to see only in extremes. Because of the 'strength of a human affection, the divine statue seemed to fall asunder again, and become only a heap of worthless fragments' (424). This utter fragmentation, this extreme devaluing is the result of Kenyon's inability to appreciate what Hawthorne describes as a rare sculpture 'in which we recognize Womanhood, and that, moreover, without prejudice to its divinity' (424). Kenyon will not allow himself to accept this discovery; he explains his response of indifference with his oft-quoted declaration that ' "Imagination and the love of art have both died out of me" ' (427). Hawthorne has pronounced sentence. The price of Kenyon's refusal to accept multiple reality is the death of his ability to see it.

Having dismissed the passions of art and imagination, Kenyon arrives at the carnival where he will be pelted by Hawthorne's ironic barbs. Kenyon encounters sportive battle with flowers used as weapons. 'The sport of mankind, like its deepest earnest, is a battle', Hawthorne tells us, 'so these festive people fought one another with ammunition of sugar-plums and flowers' (439). Knights and ladies pelt each other with 'fragrant bunches of sentiment' which, instead of being 'fresh and virgin blossoms' gathered from the countryside as in times past, are now 'venal and polluted flowers', tied together by 'sordid hands'. They are 'miserably wilted' so that, at best, they make only flaccid ammunition: everything that surrounds Kenyon at this point verges on impotence. Kenyon is making a *rite de passage* in reverse: he is regressing from manhood to sterility.

Kenyon becomes a martyr to the people at the carnival. 'His sad and contracted brow' invites ridicule and derision, a fate Hawthorne claims is his just due. With art and imagination declared dead, his sexuality remains to be humiliated, a duty effectively carried out by the giantess who assaults him:

There came alone a gigantic female figure, seven feet high, at least, and taking up a third of the street's breadth with the preposterously swelling sphere of her crinoline skirts. Singling out the sculptor, she began to make a ponderous assault upon his heart, throwing amorous glances at him out of her great goggle-eyes, offering him a vast bouquet of sunflowers and nettles, and

soliciting his pity by all sorts of pathetic and passionate dumb-
show. Her suit meeting no favor, the rejected Titaness made a
gesture of despair and rage; then suddenly drawing a huge pistol,
she took aim right at the obdurate sculptor's breast, and pulled
the trigger. The shot took effect, . . . covering Kenyon with a cloud
of lime-dust, under shelter of which the revengeful damsel strode
away. (445–6)

'Obdurate' in his refusal to accept her 'bouquet of sunflowers and
nettles', Kenyon is converted into an impotent replica of marble; he
has become the symbolic marble man to complement his marble
woman. The 'gigantic female figure' couples sunflowers, ever the
symbol of 'lofty and pure thoughts', with nettles, the emblem for
slander.[7] Threatened by the slanderous threat to his own 'lofty and
pure thoughts' that this towering hulk of femaleness represents,
Kenyon rejects her entire bouquet, depriving himself of its intermixture. His fictive covering is so tightly in place that he will soon
dust off the shot from his obdurate heart. But the damage has been
done; like Miriam's jewel, his breast mirrors the reality of his
choosing.

Hawthorne does not even let Kenyon receive the one missile he is
capable of accepting without a delicious bit of irony. Kenyon is
ready to receive the final shot at his heart, the 'single rosebud'
which Kenyon has identified as his love, his self, that Hilda throws
at him. But along with that missile of maidenly love comes another;
at the very instant the rose-bud alights on him, 'we are ashamed to
say, a cauliflower . . . flung by a young man from a passing carriage,
came with a prodigious thump against his shoulder'. (451).
Composed of the white buds, the cauliflower head is a thumping
reminder of the dual sting and caress of the celestial maiden. I
cannot help but wonder if Hawthorne envisioned himself as that
young man in the carriage, throwing one final ironic barb, and
leaving Kenyon standing naked, as it were, in the barren sunshine –
the light produced by his refusal to accept a mature definition of the
nature of men and women.

As Kenyon and Hilda declare their engagement, Hawthorne slips
in hints that this upcoming marriage may be woven of threads as
dark as that of Miriam and Donatello. 'The poor speculative
sculptor' utters his final questioning of Hilda's 'clear, crystal'
division of right from wrong as he wonders if the Fall might have
been a fortunate one. Hilda is 'shocked', she says, 'beyond words'.

Kenyon silences his questioning; he denies voice to that which threatens his role as not unsaintly bridegroom of his self-made angel. He now appeals to Hilda to keep him safe in his role: ' "Were you my guide, my counsellor, my inmost friend, with that white wisdom which clothes you as a celestial garment, all would go well" ' (460–1). Hilda accepts his proposal, but not without a sobering reminder that her garments may be the illusion of his own making. She tells him that she is 'a poor, weak girl' and that she has 'no such wisdom' as he fancies she has. Underneath the celestial fictive covering that Kenyon and, to a degree, Hilda herself puts in place there may be, Hawthorne warns, an irreparably cracked urn.

Hilda, we are told in our final glimpse of the bridal couple, 'had a hopeful soul', but her optimism is balanced beautifully by the wedding gift Miriam presents. That Etruscan bracelet, 'characterized by a seven-fold sepulchural gloom' and endowed with the voice of art – Miriam had given to each gem its story – becomes a powerful reminder of Hawthorne's text. This bracelet will go home with the couple, will have a glow of its own at their fireside. As Hilda sits 'enshrined and worshipped as a household saint, in the light of her husband's fireside' (461), her light may be softened, darkened, rendered more complete by Miriam's gift. Unreal absolutes should be, can be modified by a recognition of the way people are. Even now, 'happy as Hilda was, the bracelet brought tears into her eyes, as being, in its entire circle, the symbol of as sad a mystery as any that Miriam had attached to the separate gems' (462). Hawthorne presents this bracelet as a gift to us, too: not only that we may be reminded of the voice, the art behind it but also so we may remember the sad mystery of the circle. Finally, Hawthorne leaves us on a threshold through which we may see the circular nature of human life and love. The linear division of opposites may insulate us for a time, but the circle we have attempted to exclude haunts our journey, threatens to reclaim and soften the white light of artificial constructions.

Hawthorne carefully casts this ambiguous light upon the union of Kenyon and Hilda, a union dependent upon their exclusion from the larger circle of 'poor, speculative' humanity. He provides one text which tempts us to fall into the clarity of rigid divisions; he also proffers another text through which we may avoid this fall from full humanity and remember that love is an intermixture of the white and the red, the soul and the body, the pure and the passionate. Hawthorne's very definition of his genre[8] insists upon the mixture of these lights; so too does his definition of human life and love. Unlike Kenyon, Hawthorne had little difficulty accepting the mixed nature of his own love for his 'dove', Sophia:

> True it is, that I never look heavenward without thinking of you, and I doubt whether it would much surprise me to catch a glimpse of you among those upper regions. Then would all that is spiritual within me so yearn towards you, that I should leave my earthly incumbrances behind, and float upward and embrace you in the heavenly sunshine. Yet methinks I shall be more content to spend a lifetime of earthly and heavenly happiness intermixed. So human am I, my beloved, that I would not give up the hope of loving and cherishing you by a fireside of our own, not for any unimaginable bliss of higher spheres. Your influence shall purify me and fit me for a better world – but it shall be by means of our happiness here below. In my present state of spiritual life, I cannot conceive my bliss without the privilege of pressing my lips to yours – of pillowing my head upon your bosom. (333)

Far from being completely identified with Kenyon, Hawthorne stands apart, viewing his character's creations with a critical eye. It is an author fully aware of and in control of his character who announces Kenyon's inability to envision a sexual intimacy with his celestial angel: 'He was authorized to use little freedom towards that shy maiden, even in his visions; so that he almost reproached himself when sometimes his imagination pictured in detail the sweet years that they might spend together' (275–6). 'Authorized', of course, by Hawthorne as his creator, but 'authorized' more by the authority of his own created text. That Kenyon's text has such powerful authority over his 'life' is one more reminder of the dangers of insisting on inhuman ideals, on fragmented vision.

Hawthorne, whose imagination had 'been irreverent enough' to imagine the love between Hester and Arthur, is also 'irreverent enough' to challenge the popular stereotypes of love, to subvert the division of fair maiden from dark temptress, and to correct the separation of spiritual and earthly. By so doing, he attempts to capture a human light in which we will no longer be driven to consign ourselves and our loves to the 'celestial light' of the heavens or the 'lurid glow' of hell. His courage and integrity prompt him to a narrative experiment in creating a fiction which may help us make real the vision voiced in *The Scarlet Letter*, of a time and a place that would put the relations between men and women on a more sure footing – a more human footing in which we accept each other as mixed, ambiguous beings instead of rigid, one-dimensional symbols of our own allegories.

Notes

1. *The Letters 1813–1843*, The Centenary Edition of the Works of Nathaniel Hawthorne (Columbus: Ohio State University Press, 1984), xv, p. 400. All subsequent references in the text will be to this edition. Leland S. Person, Jr, 'Hawthorne's Love Letters: Writing and Relationship', *American Literature*, 59 (May 1987) pp. 211–27, agrees that the love letters provide evidence that Hawthorne did not reduce women to a single image.
2. For representative arguments see David Downing, 'The Feminine Ideal and the Failure of Art in *The Marble Faun*', *Recovering Literature*, 9 (1981) pp. 5–14; Jonathan Auerbach, 'Executing the Model: Painting, Sculpture, and Romance Writing in Hawthorne's *The Marble Faun*', *ELH*, 47 (1980) pp. 103–20; Philip Rahv, 'The Dark Lady of Salem', *Partisan Review*, 8 (1941) pp. 362–81; Nina Baym, 'Thwarted Nature: Hawthorne as Feminist', *American Novelists Revisited: Essays in Feminist Criticism* (Boston: G. K. Hall, 1982) pp. 55–77; and Frederick Crews, *The Sins of the Fathers: Hawthorne's Psychological Themes* (New York: Oxford University Press, 1966).
3. *The Marble Faun*, The Centenary Edition of The Works of Nathaniel Hawthorne (Columbus: Ohio State University Press, 1968), iv, p. 38. All subsequent references in the text will be to this edition.
4. Crews, p. 234.
5. The dove, symbol of peace, is also known as cruel and pugnacious and as 'an omen of coming death'. See Maria Leach (ed.), *Funk & Wagnalls Standard Dictionary of Folklore, Mythology, and Legend* (New York: Funk & Wagnalls, 1972) p. 322. Ernest Ingersoll, *Birds in Legend, Fable and Folklore* (New York: Longmans, Green, 1923) p. 141, remarks that the dove 'discloses a curiously double and diverse symbolism . . . for this bird serves as an emblem of purity and conjugal affection in one association; and in another suggests the familiar epithet "soiled" '. The snow drop, in spite of its divine association with the coming of spring, is considered unlucky for 'it looks for all the world like a corpse in its shroud'. See T. F. Thisellon Dyer, *The Folklore of Plants* (1889; reissued Michigan: Singing Trees Press, 1968) p. 274. The intertwined qualities of peace and violence, life and death reinforce the ambiguous nature of Kenyon's alliance with Hilda.
6. Judith Fryer, *The Faces of Eve* (New York: Oxford University Press, 1976) pp. 89–91, argues that 'pale maidens deprive men, who enshrine them and declare them objects of their affection, of a necessary vitality (like the amaranthine flower)'.

7.　Mrs. Sarah Josepha Hale, *Flora's Interpreter* (Boston: Marsh, Capen & Lyon, 1838) p. 205; Hale, p. 134 and Leach, p. 788.

8.　In 'The Custom House' Hawthorne defines the medium for romance writing as one which combines the warm light of a fire with the 'cold spirituality of the moonbeams', creating a place 'where the Actual and the Imaginary may meet, and each imbue itself with the nature of the other'. *The Scarlet Letter*, The Centenary Edition of the works of Nathaniel Hawthorne (Columbus: Ohio State University Press, 1962), I, pp. 35–6.

3

'The Heyday of the Blood': Ralph Waldo Emerson

JOHN McCORMICK

Henry James's review-essay 'Emerson' established an interpretation of Emerson's character that the passage of a century has
changed slightly if at all.[1] Reviewing James Elliot Cabot's 'official'
biography, *A Memoir of Ralph Waldo Emerson* (1887), James found in
Emerson's life and work a man of genius, but 'paleness' too, 'a lack
of colour', a life in which 'Passions, alternations, affairs, adventures
had absolutely no part . . .' (2). In the course of considering
Emerson's lack of enthusiasm for the paintings in the Louvre and
the Vatican, together with his hostility to such as Shelley, Dickens,
Jane Austen, Cervantes, Dante and Aristophanes, James remarked
darkly, 'There were certain complications in life which he never
suspected' (31). Seventy-five years after James's essay, Waggoner
virtually echoed James's summary, writing that Emerson 'platon-
ized' love and 'armored' himself against grief at the death of his
wife and his son, for 'he could not afford to think about love with all
the power of his mind and heart as he could think about most other
subjects'.[2]

Despite the continuing prevalence of James's view, it is now
possible to believe that Emerson indeed belongs in a collection
entitled *American Declarations of Love*; that beneath his published,
public, quasi-philosophical surface lay a pulsing, emotional and
often torn spirit, chafing at restraint and refusing the bland blanket
of transcendental uplift at least until well into middle age. Over the
decades, materials which were not available to Cabot or which he
chose to omit from his *Memoir* indicate a much more human figure
than that of the official portraits, an Emerson who fell passionately
in love, even as other men, and one in whom his times, his
antecedents and his own nature produced a complexity of response

that reinforces twentieth-century suspicions of saints and moral martyrs.

One might seem to play the voyeur by directing attention to the record of Emerson's responses to what he called, quoting Hamlet, 'The heyday of the blood',[3] but it is precisely that record that is missing from the common conception of the man. First is the fact that the aridity of the Calvinist tradition to a descendant of New England clergymen born in 1803 was fierce enough to inhibit any slightest surrender to a very young man's concupiscence. From both conviction and convention, the adolescent Emerson resisted the sexual in favour of the celestial, not without a struggle. The history of his struggle has been preserved in previously censored or ignored journals, notes, and letters.

His first recorded skirmish with passion, if that is not too strong a word, occurred in his third year at Harvard, when he was seventeen. The object of his attention was male, whose surname Gay has a more or less appropriate ring in a later day. Emerson noted in his journal for August 8, 1820, 'There is a strange face in the freshman class whom I should like to know very much. He has a great deal of character in his features & should [be] a fast friend or bitter enemy. His name is Gay I shall endeavour to become acquainted with him & wish if possible that I might recall at a future period the singular sensations which his presence produced at this.'[4] In the event, Martin Gay became neither friend nor enemy, nor did the two ever exchange more than a few words, yet for the next eighteen months, journal entries sketch the course of Emerson's reactions. On 24 October 1820, he records visions by day and night of young Gay, who had 'cold blue eyes ... We have had already two or three long profound stares at each other. Be it wise or weak or superstitious I must know him' (39). Six months later, however, Emerson decided that he had idealised Gay, imagining him as poetic, solemn, given to friendship and having a fund of 'rich sober thought'. Emerson's change of attitude resulted from his discovery that Gay had been involved in the gutting of the freshman dining hall and had been suspended and rusticated for his part in the affair. One result of the flirtation was some dreadful verses (to Gay, so assume Emerson's most recent editors), beginning, 'Perhaps thy lot in life is higher / Than the fates assign to me' (40). Emerson resolved to abandon his illusions, but as late as 28 February 1822, he wrote in Latin a purposefully ambiguous passage seeming to indicate his attraction to Martin Gay (94–5).

It would be mistaken to conclude that Emerson had set out on the road to Sodom before his twentieth birthday. He simply did not know any young women during his undergraduate years, and if modern cant is to be credited, sexual ambivalence in the very young is normal and to be expected. At least one reader of the journals, however, interpreted the material according to Freud, discovering that Emerson feared incipient homosexuality, but transferred his fear from sex to food and its consumption: Evelyn Greenberger quotes Emerson in 1832. '"One would think that the hog, that walking sermon upon Gluttony, was enough to turn the stomachs of all men from intemperate eating. Then was ever the full feeder ready for religion"' Evelyn Greenberger further claims that aversion to eating accounts for Emerson's disapproval of communion, which heterodoxy led to his resignation from his pastorate and to his subsequent lay career as writer and lecturer.[5] The essay concludes with the notion that Emerson was 'bi-sexual' and cites a journal entry concerning human inability to say all that we intend: '"What a little of all we know is said! . . . Hence the oestrum of speech: hence these throbs & heart beatings at the door of the assembly to the end, namely, that the thought may be ejaculated as Logos or Word"' (52–3). 'Oestrum' according to this unsubtle reading equals female, 'ejaculation' equals male, and the two together equal bi-sexuality.

Possibly. But if one prefers to root about in the conscious rather than in the unconscious, Emerson emerges straight as an arrow. The record shows an Emerson who fell deeply in love, who went courting the young woman as soon as he could afford to do so, and married her at age twenty-six. In December 1827 Emerson travelled to Concord, New Hampshire, to preach to the Unitarian Society. On Christmas Day he first saw Ellen Louisa Tucker, a pretty, voluptuous girl of sixteen. One year later the two became engaged and in September 1829 they were married. Seventeen months later, in February 1831, Ellen Tucker Emerson died of tuberculosis.

As young lovers conventionally then did, Mr Emerson and Miss Tucker exchanged verses, Emerson writing a dozen or so.[6] Because their verses are relentlessly conventional, it is the letters and journals that indicate the reality and profundity of the emotion involved. Emerson praised Ellen's beauty and elegance of manner to his brothers,[7] while Ellen declared an 'ocean of love to Ralph Waldo's pint' (22). In Ellen's company, the dreadfully serious Emerson became happy and relaxed, calling her variously Elind,

Nelly, Ellinelli, Grandma, his Queen of Sheba, his Phoenix bird, or 'mon amie'; she called him 'King' or 'Grandpa'. In Ellen's album, he wrote of his undying love for her in French, a language that his puritanical aunt Moody hoped Miss Tucker could not read.[8]

Emerson's journals during the time of his engagement and brief marriage abound in invocations to Ellen and declarations of his love. That was the period in which he was writing his first sermons, already struggling to reassure himself of his orthodoxy, but now Ellen often triumphed over theology: among reflections on history and religion (1829), he abruptly changed pitch with 'Oh Ellen, I do dearly love you—'.[9] A month before the marriage, Emerson and Ellen made a visit to the Shaker community at Canterbury, New Hampshire, in the course of which one of the elders, he wrote to his brother Charles, 'Mother Winkley or Sister Winkley hath given Ellen and I [sic] a long & earnest sermon on the beauty of virginity and striven to dissuade us from our sinful purpose of "living after the way of manhood and womanhood in the earth" but I parried her persuasion & her denunciations as best I might & insisted we were yoked together by Heaven to provoke each other to good works so long as we lived.' Perhaps indignation caused him to describe the Shakers, 'excepting a shrewd handful of male and female oligarchs' as 'a set of clean, well disposed, dull & incapable animals'.[10]

Abruptly the journals of the brief year and a half marriage to Ellen change; the yearnings and playfulness of the engagement are absent. The entries become notes for sermons or abstract meditations on abstract subjects. The change, we may readily infer, was owing not to Emerson's having become emotionally cold but to his awareness of his wife's illness and his inevitable knowledge that she was doomed. By January 1831 Ellen was exceedingly ill, and Emerson was soon to write, 'Ellen Tucker Emerson died 8th February. Tuesday morning 9 o'clock.' Then followed a long prayer addressed in turn to Ellen and to heaven, praising her bravery and piety.[11] To his aunt Mary Moody he wrote, in the lugubrious idiom of his day, 'My angel is gone to heaven this morning & I am alone in the world and strangely happy. Her lungs shall no more be torn nor her head scalded by her blood nor her whole life suffer from the warfare between the force & delicacy of her soul & the weakness of her frame'.[12]

Emerson's grief, firmly allied to his love for Ellen, remained acute for at least two years after her death, while her memory would remain vivid for the remainder of his fifty-one years of life. His grief assumed Poesque and Baudelairian dimensions five days after

Ellen's death as he wrote in his journal, 'O willingly, my wife, would I lie down in your tomb.'[13] A journal entry of a year later reads, 'I visited Ellen's tomb & opened the coffin.' That entry may be the record of a dream, but Rusk among others believes that he recorded reality, not dream.[14] One of the distracted and incoherent fragments of verse that Emerson wrote after his wife's death is hardly the work of an unfeeling, abstracted man:

> Teach me I am forgotten by the dead
> And that the dead is by herself forgot
> And I no longer would keep terms with me.
> I would not murder, steal, or fornicate,
> Nor with ambition break the peace of towns
> But I would bury my ambition
> The hope & action of my sovereign soul
> In miserable ruin . . .[15]

Ellen's death contributed, I think, to Emerson's break with the organised church. In September 1832 he resigned as pastor of the Second (Unitarian) Church of Boston and began a *Wanderjahr* in Europe, returning to renewed intellectual activity, determined not to 'affect' to suffer.[16] In 1834 he inherited from Ellen's estate sufficient capital to assure an annual income of $1200, a circumstance that doubtlessly aided his disposition to re-marry. In that same year he proposed marriage to Lydia Jackson of Plymouth, Massachusetts, where he had given occasional sermons. Lydia, whom Emerson re-named 'Lydian' (to avoid the hiatus of Lydia Emerson?) was eight months older than Emerson, an intelligent, astringent woman of highest principle. In his first extant letter to her, Emerson called her 'my Lydian Queen' (American nineteenth-century lovers were royalists), assuring her that he was not 'a metaphysical lover. I am a man & hate & suspect the over refiners, & do sympathize with the homeliest pleasures & attractions by which our good foster mother Nature draws her children together'. His long letter concludes, 'Dearest forgive the egotism of all this letter. Say they not 'The more love the more egotism'. . . . Write, write to me. And please dear Lydian take that same low counsel & leave thinking for the present & let the winds of heaven blow away your dyspepsia'.[17] Lydian's chronic dyspepsia derived from her habit of starving herself: anorexia in our jargon.

Emerson's second marriage lacked the *élan* of his first. There can be no doubt the second marriage was based in respect and love, but reading both on and between the lines of the record, one finds an atmosphere quite different from that between the younger man and his child-bride. Lydian was a mature woman, her religion was intense and conventional, her intelligence acute and her outlook often incompatible with her husband's. Perhaps the tenor of the marriage was set in 1836, when after buying a house in Concord, Massachusetts, Emerson 'suffered the usual fate of the newly married man by being elected a hog-reeve'.[18] It is hardly feasible to think of Ellen's husband assessing fines against the owners of marauding swine. Lydian disliked housekeeping and cooking; she offended Emerson's aunt Mary Moody by serving her lamb nine days consecutively. Lydian had other quirks. When she began keeping chickens, she worried about their feet being cold in the Massachusetts winter and wrapped their feet in wool. The chickens did not like that because it prevented them from scratching in the garden. Lydian's good friend Henry Thoreau therefore made the chickens 'some neat little cowhide shoes', tied about their slender ankles. But the Emersons finally gave up keeping chickens because they were incapable of killing and eating them.[19]

It is significant that Lydian's daughter was baptised Ellen Tucker. In her biography of her mother, Ellen Emerson wrote that 'Mother asked father questions about his first wife. In one of his journals he says "I had a long long remembering talk with Lidian [sic] about Ellen, which brought back that delicious relation".' The biographer adds that her father gave Lydian all his first wife's letters to read (77). In addition, Ellen Emerson says that 'For five years Mother said she and Father were getting more married all the time, they were as happy as it was possible to be'. The intensity of their happiness changed, however, as it dawned on Lydian that her husband was not a Christian in her sense of the word; 'a most bitter discovery'. Family prayers ceased (79). A light frost descended, one may conclude.

Not all was frost. Ellen Emerson writes, 'I saw in one of [father's] journals, "A man needs a wife to be silly unto" and he fully enjoyed the privilege himself'. She thought that he was 'very sportive and poetical always when he was upstairs with mother'. 'I remember he once broke forth

> How beautiful in the morning is the human race
> Getting up to breakfast—

but couldn't go on. Lydian finished it with

Head foremost tumbling
Out of bed, grumbling
They wash their face and neck first.' (91)

Sportive or not, in cooler moments Emerson's expressions of love to
Lydian in his letters became progessively more formal and conventional. An early letter of 4 March 1835 addresses Lydia [sic] 'o
magnet mine', and closes with 'Your lover, Waldo E'.[20] By 1848
Emerson's signature had become 'I commend myself to your
wonted kindness'.[21] His heavy irony might support Pommer's
suggestion that by 1848 Emerson had become weary of domesticity,
preferring to give fullest attention to his career as writer and
lecturer.[22] It is hard to disagree. Emerson's equivocal view of
marriage may best be seen in his two journal entries citing a
quotation from Landor: ' "Love is a secondary passion in those who
love most; a primary in those who love least." '[23]

Various women found Emerson attractive, and he them, although
no evidence whatsoever exists to indicate that Emerson was ever
anything but faithful to Lydian. The most interesting of his female
admirers was that extraordinary woman, born out of her time,
Margaret Fuller. Their ten-year acquaintanceship began in 1835,
when at twenty-five she was already formed in intellect and
temperament, but believed that in Emerson she had met the
counsellor and friend she was seeking. In her capacity as first editor
of *The Dial* (1840), the journal of the American transcendentalists,
she edited Emerson's wandering contributions with professional
objectivity. She tutored him in German pronunciation and urged
Goethe upon him. She introduced him to George Sand's novels, in
which he found 'authentic revelations of what passes in man &
woman'.[24] At first Emerson found Margaret Fuller ingratiating, but
she soon got on his nerves. She was overly familiar, he noted, and
her nasal voice, her plainness, her habit of blinking 'all repelled; & I
said to myself, we shall never get on'.[25] In a long letter of 1840,
Emerson showed something between embarrassment and fright at
her pushing manner: 'There is a difference in our constitution . . . It
seems as if we had been born and bred in different nations. You say
you understand me wholly. You cannot communicate yourself to
me' (589). Again to Margaret Fuller, 'You would have me love you.
What shall I love? Your body? The supposition disgusts you. What
you have thought and said? Well, whilst you were thinking &
saying them, but not now. I see no possibility of loving any thing

but what now is, & is becoming; your courage, your enterprize, your budding affection, your opening thought, your prayer, I can love – but what else?'[26]

With time the relationship became stable, but it always retained a varnish of regret. Margaret Fuller wrote in her journal, 'Waldo and I have good meetings, though we stop at all our old places. But my expectations are moderate now; it is his beautiful presence that I prize, far more than our intercourse.'[27]

Emerson's essay on 'Love', published in 1841, is the main source of misapprehension about his true attitude to the subject. Because it is one of his least competent efforts, it supports the notion of his emotional frigidity. Now he could write that a man will 'shrink and moan' as he remembers in maturity the joys of his youth. 'Alas! I know not why, but infinite compunctions embitter in mature life the remembrances of budding joy, and cover every beloved name.'[28] Now he defines love as 'the dawn of civility and grace in the coarse rustic' (212), seeming never to have rubbed elbows with coarse and rustic lovers. The greater part of the essay is an episode in Emerson's transcendentalism, with unacknowledged Platonic and Wordsworthian overtones. Beauty matters because of its divine origin: 'the Deity sends the glory of youth before the soul, that it may avail itself of beautiful bodies as aids to its recollection of the celestial good and fair; and the man beholding such a person in the female sex runs to her, and finds the highest joy in contemplating the form, movement, and intelligence of this person, because it suggests to him the presence of that which indeed is within the beauty, and the cause of the beauty'. Again, 'Divinity in beauty cleanses love of the gross' (216–7). The argument becomes fully transcendental with 'things . . . cannot step backward from the higher to the lower relations . . . Thus even love, which is the deification of persons, must become more impersonal every day . . . Little think the youth and the maiden who are glancing at each other . . . with eyes so full of mutual intelligence, of the precious fruit long hereafter to proceed from this new, quite external stimulus' (i.e. transcendence). With marriage, 'The soul is wholly embodied, and the body is wholly ensouled' (218).

While Emerson's essay argues that physical passion is merely an adolescent phase on the way to spiritual maturity, it also seems to lament the kind of physical and emotional relationship he had with Ellen. There are frozen moments of nostalgia in this frigid essay.

But be our experience in particulars what it may, no man ever forgot the visitations of that power to his heart and brain, which created all things anew; which was the dawn in him of music, poetry and art . . . when a single tone of one voice could make the heart bound, and the most trivial circumstance associated with one form is put in the amber of memory; when he became all eye when one was present, and all memory when one was gone; when the youth becomes a watcher of windows and studious of a glove, a veil, a ribbon, or the wheels of a carriage (213).

There are words of warmth and passion imprisoned in this cold medium. If Emerson's youthful feelings were 'fancies' they were also 'delicious'; and 'delicious' too were the carnal relationships which he was apparently so eager to have give way to spiritual ones. If those climactic joys which await lovers are joys of the soul, the introduction to that 'felicity' is described by Emerson in a fine definition of love: 'a private and tender relationship of one to one, which is the enchantment of human life' (210). Whilst Emerson feels intellectually and perhaps experientially obliged to deny them as ephemeral, he sketches the stages of courtship and infatuation and commitment in ways that are tender and touching. When alone lovers

> solace themselves with the remembered image of the other. Does that other see the same star, the same melting cloud, read the same book, feel the same emotion, that now delights me? They try and weigh their affection, and adding up costly advantages, friends, opportunities, properties, exult in discovering that willingly, joyfully, they would give all as a ransom for the beautiful, the beloved head. . . . For it is the nature and end of this relation, that they would represent the human race to each other (219).

Emerson knows what it is to love, and to be in love, but he reduces these experiences to temporary and minor phenomena in the history of the soul. 'Give All To Love', proclaims a poem probably written to Ellen after her death. 'Obey your heart', he continues; 'follow it utterly'; 'leave all for love'. But the next word in the poem is 'yet'; and the adjuration is to

> Keep thee to-day
> Tomorrow, forever,
> Free as an Arab
> Of thy beloved.

Thus Emerson falls back on a prudent self-reliance and a doctrinaire transcendentalism, too.

> Though thou loved her as thyself,
> As a self of purer clay,
> Though her parting dims the day,
> Stealing grace from all alive;
> Heartily know,
> When the half-gods go,
> The gods arrive. (774–5)

The heart, like the mind, must fix itself on what is 'beyond'.

Emerson concludes 'Love' with 'we are often made to feel that our affections are but tents of a night', but 'the soul may be trusted to the end. That which is so beautiful and attractive as these relations must be succeeded and supplanted only by what is more beautiful, and so on for ever' (220–1). That 'and so on for ever' lacks conviction; but it served to affirm to his public that he had become the 'metaphysical lover' he had once denied being, even while his private notes continued to indicate love and grief for Ellen. If the heyday of the blood had passed, the intensity of his private emotion – and love was a *private* and tender relationship – had not. Emerson public and Emerson private wore different faces. Taken together, they add depth to the resulting portrait and resonance to the voice of the whole man.

Notes

1. First published in *Macmillan's Magazine* (1887), then in James's *Partial Portraits* (London and New York: Macmillan, (1888) 1899. References are to the reprint of 1899.
2. Hyatt H. Waggoner, *Emerson as Poet* (Princeton University Press, 1974) p. 200.
3. In the Essay 'Love', and out of context. Hamlet (III, iv) reproaches his mother for marrying Claudius: 'You cannot call it love, for at your

age / The heyday of the blood is tame, it's humble, / And waits upon the judgement . . .'

4. *The Journals and Miscellaneous Notebooks of Ralph Waldo Emerson*, eds. William H. Gilman, George P. Clark, Alfred R. Ferguson, and Merrell R. Davis (Cambridge, Mass.: Belknap Press of Harvard University Press, 1960–1978), I, p. 22. Henceforth cited as *Journals*.
5. Evelyn Barish Greenberger, 'The Phoenix on the Wall: Consciousness in Emerson's Early and Late Journals', in *Ralph Waldo Emerson, New Appraisals, A Symposium*, ed. Leonard Nick Neufeldt (Hartford: Transcendental Books, 1973) pp. 47–8.
6. Thus the count in Henry F. Pommer, *Emerson's First Marriage* (Carbondale: Southern Illinois University Press, 1967) p. 33. *Poems* (Boston and New York: Houghton Mifflin, 1904), contains five verses specifically addressed to Ellen; 'Give All to Love' is perhaps the best of the erotic verse. Two verses of Ellen Tucker, 'Lines' and 'The Violet', are also included.
7. Pommer, p. 9.
8. Ralph R. Rusk, *The Life of Ralph Waldo Emerson* (New York: Charles Scribner's Sons, 1949) p. 131.
9. *Journals*, III, p. 153.
10. *The Letters of Ralph Waldo Emerson*, ed. Ralph R. Rusk, 6 vols., (New York: Columbia University Press, 1939), I, pp. 175–6.
11. *Journals*, III, pp. 226–7.
12. *Letters*, I, p. 318.
13. *Journals*, III, p. 226.
14. Rusk, *Life*, p. 150.
15. *Journals*, III, p. 228; undated Fragment 48.
16. Pommer, p. 58.
17. *Letters*, I, p. 434.
18. Rusk, *Life*, p. 228.
19. Ellen Tucker Emerson, *The Life of Lidian Jackson Emerson*, ed. Dolores Bird Carpenter (Boston: Twayne, 1980) p. 68.
20. *Letters*, I, pp. 440–1.
21. *Letters*, II, p. 264.
22. Pommer, pp. 93–5.
23. *Journals*, III, p. 299 (1831); and VI, p. 181 (1824–1836).
24. Rusk, *Life*, p. 260.
25. Harry R. Warfel, 'Margaret Fuller and Ralph Waldo Emerson', *PMLA*, L, no. 2 (June 1935), 576–8.
26. *Journals*, VII, p. 400. And Gay Wilson Allen, *Waldo Emerson* (New York: Viking, 1981) p. 355.
27. Warfel, p. 593.
28. *The Selected Writings of Ralph Waldo Emerson* (New York: Random House, 1950) p. 211. Parenthesised page references are to this volume.

4

'This Terrible, Irrepressible Yearning': Whitman's Poetics of Love

ROBERT J. SCHOLNICK

In the 1876 preface Whitman asserted that a major purpose of *Leaves of Grass* was to 'express . . . the eternal body composite, cumulative' and the 'natural character' of the poet. He then added a 'full confession' of his own emotional vulnerability and his excruciating need to be loved by the reader:

> I also sent out *Leaves of Grass* to arouse and set flowing in men's and women's hearts, young and old, endless streams of living pulsating love and friendship, directly from them to myself; now and ever. To this terrible, irrepressible yearning, (surely more or less down underneath in most human souls) – this never-satisfied appetite for sympathy, and this boundless offering of sympathy . . . I have given in that book, undisguisedly, declaredly, the openest expression.[1]

Poetry is a means to 'arouse' the reader erotically, but it is the artist who most needs love. Whitman, who in his great sequence of love poems 'Calamus' had identified himself as 'the tenderest lover' recognises that he is doomed never to be satisfied romantically.

In the 1855 preface Whitman also cast the poet in the role of lover but here we find no hint of unsatisfied love:

> The known universe has one complete lover and that is the greatest poet. He consumes an eternal passion and is indifferent which chance happens and which possible contingency of fortune or misfortune and persuades daily and hourly his delicious pay. What balks or breaks others is fuel for his burning progress to contact and amorous joy. Other proportions of the

reception of pleasure dwindle to nothing to his proportions. All expected from heaven or from the highest he is rapport with in the sight of the daybreak or a scene of the winter woods or the presence of children playing or with his arm around the neck of a man or a woman. His love above all love has leisure and expanse . . . he leaves room ahead of himself. He is no irresolute or suspicious lover . . . he is sure . . . he scorns intervals. His experience and the showers and thrills are not for nothing. Nothing can jar him . . . The sea is not surer of the shore or the shore of the sea than he is of the fruition of his love and of all perfection and beauty. (11–2)

Like the sun, the confident poet-lover radiates a passionate heat by converting into fuel for love the disappointments that 'balk or break others'.

Between the 1855 and 1876 prefaces Whitman's emotional landscape has totally changed. The erotic exuberance of 'Song of Myself' gives way to the later poetry's chastened acknowledgement of the implications for love of rejection and death. Thematically, this compelling body of love poetry grows in complexity. Whitman's implicit avowal of homosexuality in the 'Calamus' poems (1860) introduces a complicating dimension in the search for a satisfying love relationship. In 44 (later 'Here the Frailest Leaves of Me') he refuses to speak explicitly: 'I shade down and hide my thoughts – I do not expose them'. And yet, Whitman recognises that language does not lie; even indirectly, words reveal the deepest self one way or another. His 'Calamus' poems, he knew, 'expose me more than all my other poems' (1860, 377). Whitman implicitly directs the reader's attention to that which he himself does not name, what in 36 ('Earth, My Likeness') he calls that 'something fierce and terrible in me, eligible to burst forth, / I dare not tell it in words – not even in these songs' (1860, 374). Whitman's inability to go beyond the indirect confession of 'Here the Frailest Leaves of Me', marks the effective end of the powerful body of love poetry that he published in the editions of *Leaves of Grass* of 1855, 1856, and 1860.

In the poetry up until 'Calamus' (1860) love is expressed primarily in autoerotic terms. As extensive and wide-ranging as is the love-making in 'Song of Myself', never does it involve a particular human being, a recognisable lover. The poet's sexual partners – 'Winds whose soft-tickling genitals rub up against me, it shall be you, / Broad muscular fields, branches of liveoak, loving lounger in

my winding paths, it shall be you' – are drawn from the natural
world, which is to say that they are self-projections (51). Remarkably the adult poet calls to mind and explores an early stage of
development, which reminds us of Freud's description of that 'time
in the development of the individual at which he unifies his sexual
drives (which have hitherto been engaged in autoerotic activities)
in order to obtain a love-object; and he begins by taking his own
body as his love-object, and only subsequently proceeds from this
to the choice of some other person than himself'. As Bice Benvenuto
and Roger Kennedy have written in commenting on this passage,
'presumably, the ego in this scheme is formed at the stage of
narcissism, between the stage of auto-eroticism and object love,
while itself being taken as a love object. But it is not clear in Freud
what is this new psychical action that brings about ego formation,
though we are told that the ego first picks out objects by
identification and by incorporating objects into itself. Hence one is
dealing with fundamental dilemmas in analytic theory'.[2] Our job as
readers of Whitman's love poetry is not to worry about the niceties
of analytic theory, but rather to see that in these early poems
Whitman's loving attention to his own body (and his pervasive
identification with the external world, becoming what he sees and
caressing and incorporating everything into the self) has its source
in a recognisable stage of development. For Whitman then, the
imaginative reconstruction of an earlier stage serves as a vehicle for
a loving and simultaneous exploration of the poet's own body and
the external world.

In 'Calamus', however, the poet, having left behind this early
stage of self-involvement, searches for a love relationship with
another. He discovers that he must have 'a friend, a lover, near', as
he writes in 20 ('I Saw in Louisiana a Live-Oak Growing'):

I saw in Louisiana a live-oak growing,
All alone stood it, and the moss hung down from the branches,
Without any companion it grew there, uttering joyous leaves of
    dark green,
And its look, rude, unbending, lusty, made me think of myself,
But I wondered how it could utter joyous leaves standing alone
    there, without its friend, its lover near – for I knew I could not,
And I broke off a twig with a certain number of leaves upon it, and
    twined around it a little moss,

And brought it away – and I have placed it in sight in my room,
It is not needed to remind me as of my own dear friends,
For I believe lately I think of little else than of them,)
Yet it remains to me a curious token – it makes me think of manly
    love;
For all that, and though the live-oak glistens there in Louisiana,
    solitary, in a wide flat space,
Uttering joyous leaves all its life, without a friend, a lover, near,
    know very well I could not.

                                                    (1860, 364–5)

A symbol of the poet's former self, the tree is self-sufficient in its creativity, able to 'utter joyous leaves' without depending upon another. But through this leave-taking of his former self, Whitman confesses that he is no longer self-sufficient in love and in poetry. 'Calamus' explores the surpassing joys and crushing loss of romantic love. But it was primarily through the autoerotic poems before 'Calamus' that Whitman discovered his voice, a poetic language which could speak the language of love and desire.

                                    I

'Spontaneous Me' (1856) glories in autoeroticism, which Whitman implicitly links to poetic creativity. In the 1860 edition Whitman included the poem in the 'Children of Adam' sequence, which ostensibly celebrates heterosexual love, and the poet does boast of 'the oath of procreation I have sworn, my Adamic and fresh daughters, / The greed that eats me day and night with hungry gnaw, till I saturate what shall produce boys when I am through'. Yet no other person, male or female, figures significantly in the poem. The opening reference to a lover is merely a part of setting the scene. 'Spontaneous Me, Nature, / The loving day, the mounting sun, the friend I am happy with, / The arm of my friend hanging idly over my shoulder'. Shortly the 'friend' disappears as the poet engages in a 'spontaneous' masturbatory fantasy:

The curious roamer the hand roaming all over the body,
    the bashful withdrawing of flesh where the fingers soothingly
    pause and edge themselves,
The limpid liquid within the young man,

The vex'd corrosion so pensive and so painful,
The torment, the irritable tide that will not be at rest,
The like of the same I feel, the like of the same in others,
The young man that flushes and flushes, and the young woman that
    flushes and flushes,
The young man that wakes deep at night, the hot hand seeking to
    repress what would master him,
The mystic amorous night, the strange half-welcome pangs,
    visions, sweats,
The pulse bounding through palms and trembling encircling
    fingers, the young man all color'd red, ashamed, angry;
The souse upon me of my lover the sea, as I lie willing and naked.
                        .   .   .
The wholesome relief, repose, content,
And this bunch pluck'd at random from myself,
It has done its work – I toss it carelessly to fall where it may.
                                            (261–2)

At a time when onanism was considered immoral and self-
destructive, this daring poem is a risky act. Initially 'ashamed' and
'angry', the speaker allows his 'encircling fingers' to bring him
'wholesome relief, repose, content'. And with a play on words he
asserts that his masculine 'bunch' has brought him at once the
semen and the poem.

The 'spontaneous' expression of his sexuality opens to Whitman
a perception of the 'spontaneous' generativity of nature. 'Willing
and naked', he envisages a delicious world bound together by love:

Love thoughts, love-juice, love-odor, love-yielding, love-climbers,
    and the climbing sap,
Arms and hands of love, lips of love, phallic thumb of love, breasts
    of love, bellies press'd and glued together with love,
Earth of chaste love, life that is only life after love,
The body of my love, the body of the woman I love, the body of the
    man, the body of the earth,
Soft forenoon airs that blow from the south-west,
The hairy wild-bee that murmurs and hankers up and down, that
    gripes the full-grown lady-flower, curves upon her with amorous
    firm legs, takes his will of her, and holds himself tremulous and
    tight till he is satisfied.

At once erotic and innocent, sexual and yet protected, this is a world which has the 'mother never turning her vigilant eyes' from her twin babes that crawl over the grass' and where the 'great chastity of paternity' 'match[es] the great chastity of maternity'. Nothing compels the speaker to risk the rejection that a romantic encounter with another person might bring.

To possess this world requires a re-conceiving of poetry as itself a sexual act:

Beautiful dripping fragments, the negligent list of one after another
    as I happen to call them to me or think of them,
The real poems, (what we call poems being merely pictures,)
The poems of the privacy of the night, and of men like me,
This poem drooping shy and unseen that I always carry, and that
    all men carry . . .

(260–2)

Rejecting the sexless work of his contemporaries as 'merely pictures', Whitman insists that 'real poems' are phallic; only such a sexual poetry is capable of possessing in love the 'body of the world'. While 'Spontaneous Me' dramatises the most solitary of acts, Whitman succeeds in involving the reader, who joins imaginatively with the poet as he exuberantly fuses himself to the world's body. Through the act of reading he completes the poet's masturbatory fantasy, discovering in the process that creativity and love of the natural world begin with love of one's own body.

By writing a frankly erotic poem, by writing with the penis, Whitman overcomes the abstractions of conventional poetry and, by association, the repression of language itself. Elizabeth Wright has summarised the insight of the French psychoanalyst Jacques Lacan on this point: 'The structures of language are marked with societal imperatives – the Father's rules, laws and definitions, among which are those of "child" and "mother". Society's injunction that desire must wait, that it must formulate in the constricting word whatever demand it may speak, is what effects the split between conscious and unconscious, the repression that is the tax exacted by the use of language'.[3] In 'Spontaneous Me' Whitman explicitly rejects the imprisoning language of abstractions of his contemporaries in favour of a liberating speech written directly out of the 'spontaneous' sexual self.

As I have indicated above, autoeroticism figures prominently in

'Song of Myself', Whitman's great poem of self-transformation and liberation, a love poem to the entire universe. The reader finds none of the conventional features of love poetry: courtship, proposals, lovers' quarrels and reconciliations. Other human beings are not presented with any depth and yet, as Whitman's early readers recognised, the poem is powerfully erotic.

From this perspective the critic Leslie Fiedler has commented that while 'Song of Myself' can be read as 'a heroic poem intended to define the ethos of a nation', it is 'also a love poem: simultaneously a love song, a love affair (the poet's only successful one) and a love child (the only real offspring of his passion'). Yet, interpreting 'Song' as a poem of failed love, Fiedler asks, 'who is the poet's beloved, the Beatrice he could never leave off wooing, the Penelope to whom he could never return?' Fiedler concludes that Whitman's 'loneliness becomes a symbol of the alienation of the modern artist and of modern man in a godless universe. He lived, after all, at a moment when some thinkers were declaring the death of God, and wrote at a time when poets grew increasingly unsure of whom they were addressing'.[4]

But is Whitman's a 'godless universe' and is he 'a symbol of alienation'? In the 1855 preface he did assert that the 'work' of the priests 'is done'. But in the void left by the collapse of traditional religion he saw arising a 'new breed of poets' who would function 'as interpreters of men and women and of all events and things'. Finding 'their inspiration in real objects today, symptoms of the past and future', the new breed are poets of the body capable of using the language of desire (25). The universe of 'Song of Myself' is not, then, godless but rather reconstituted in a radically new way. Here the world of man with all his desires takes on a numinous quality: 'I do not despise you priests; / My faith is the greatest of faiths, and the least of faiths, / Enclosing all worship ancient and modern . . . Dancing yet through the streets in a phallic procession . . . rapt and austere in the woods, a gymnosophist . . .' (77). And in the stanzas that would become section 44, the phallic poet-prophet rewrites the creation story from the perspective of modern scientific theory and finds cause not for 'lamentation', but celebration: 'All forces have been steadily employed to complete and delight me, / Now I stand on this spot with my Soul' (80).[5]

Certainly, however, Fiedler is right in asserting that 'Song of Myself' is, paradoxically, a love poem which lacks a beloved. But the Whitman of 'Song of Myself' is devoted to demonstrating that love takes many forms. Even without a human beloved, 'Song of Myself' is a passionate, sexual poem, one whose rhythms are based on 'the procreant urge of the world'. The poet ecstatically joins the creative and generative powers of his own body with the analogous energies in the external world, the 'voluptuous and coolbreathed earth': 'Prodigal! you have given me love . . . therefore I to you give love! / O unspeakable passionate love!' (47). But where does this love come from and what is its object?

The poet's starting point is self-love. Before we can share our bodies with others, he implies, we must first learn to love them ourselves. In the passages he would label section 5, body and soul come together in a passionate act of love-making:

I believe in you my soul . . . the other I am must not abase itself to
    you,
And you must not be abased to the other.

Loafe with me on the grass . . . loose the stop from your throat,
Not words, not music or rhyme I want . . . not custom or lecture, not
    even the best,
Only the lull I like, the hum of your valved voice.

I mind how we lay in June, such a transparent summer morning;
You settled your head athwart my hips and gently turned over upon
    me,
And parted the shirt from my bosom-bone, and plunged your
    tongue to my barestript heart,
And reached till you felt my beard, and reached till you held my
    feet.

Swiftly arose and spread around me the peace and joy and
    knowledge that pass all the art and argument of the earth;
And I know that the hand of God is the elderhand of my own,
And I know that the spirit of God is the eldest brother of my own,
And that all the men ever born are also my brothers . . . and the
    women my sisters and lovers,
And that a kelson of the creation is love.

                                                    (30–1)

The consummation brought about through the 'marriage' of body and soul brings sexual fulfilment and the insight that 'a kelson of the creation is love'. In this ecstatic act of self-love Whitman turns the tables on the great Cartesian dualism, demonstrating that

knowledge of the other as love begins with the loving – and sexual –
exploration of one's own body, giving birth to a self capable of
responding to the entire cosmos in love.

The poet's courageous avowal of his own sexuality, of the penis,
also gives birth to a physical poetic speech. As in 'Spontaneous Me',
the new poetry demands an act of repudiation, but here Whitman
goes beyond repudiating the abstract 'pictures' of conventional
poets to disclaim language itself: 'Not words, not music or rhyme
. . . not custom or lecture, not even the best'. Paradoxically, then,
Whitman wishes to return to the very origin of speech as sound, the
point before the self has been restricted by language's repressive
categories: 'Only the lull I like, the hum of your valved voice'. The
palpable silence which is heard in the word 'lull' issues into a bare
'hum', a pre-verbal sound which in this context is 'pregnant' with
meaning. To be able to speak directly of desire, Whitman demonstrates, one first repudiates the conventional face of language, the
language of injunctions and prohibitions, so that he can return to
the infant's pre-verbal world and develop, through contact with the
unconscious, an authentic speech of the body. Such a speech
combines the unfiltered immediacy of the child's utterance with the
linguistic skill and awareness of the adult poet.

Through a series of rhetorical questions, Whitman makes similar
demands of the reader, that he imaginatively return to a point of
origin: 'Have you practised so long to learn to read? / Have you felt
so proud to get at the meaning of poems?' The customary forms of
interpretation, the poet suggests, must be put aside for a form of
reading which enables the reader, much as had the poet, to return to
a hypothetical starting point, of himself, of the cosmos and of
language itself to discover there his own self as if for the first time.
Through such a radically new form of reading, the poet promises,
'you shall possess the origin of all poems', 'no longer take things at
second or third hand . . . nor look through the eyes of the dead . . .
nor feed on the spectres in books, / You shall not look through my
eyes either, nor take things from me, / You shall listen to all sides
and filter them from yourself' (28).

It is only through such direct seeing that the reader too can
disclaim the conventional status of poetry as abstract symbols and
comprehend the poet's language in a way that allows him to
perceive the sexual energy of the world's body: 'There never was
any more inception than there is now, / Nor any more age than
there is now; / And will never be any more perfection than there is

now, / Nor any more heaven and hell than there is now'. Whitman, then, returns the reader to a point of origin, an original state where language can speak directly of desire, of 'inception' and 'Urge and urge and urge, / Always the procreant urge of the world' (28).

The reader becomes a partner with the poet in creating a poetry in which the world's body speaks a newly physical language: 'A child said, What is the grass? fetching it to me with full hands; / How could I answer the child? . . . I do not know what it is any more than he' (31). Though the speaker rejects any attempt in a conventional sense to name the external world, he absorbs all into him, becoming 'the caresser of life wherever moving . . . backwards as well as forward sluing' (37). Poetic meaning springs through and from the body: 'the press of my foot to the earth springs a hundred affections, / They scorn the best I can do to relate them' (38). The fact is, of course, that the 'best' the speaker can do to 'relate' those 'affections' of the natural world is quite effective, as he later confesses: 'My voice goes after what my eyes cannot reach, / With the twirl of my tongue I encompass worlds and volumes of worlds. / Speech is the twin of my vision . . . it is unequal to measure itself' (52–3). What that poetic voice, born in the loving acceptance of self in the ecstatic union of body and soul, 'goes after' is the entire cosmos, which it embraces in love.

So at one with this delicious natural world is the poet's body that to explore one is to explore the other and to find oneself brought to a sexual-verbal ejaculation:

If I worship any particular thing it shall be some of the spread of
    my body;
Translucent mould of me it shall be you,
Shaded ledges and rests, firm masculine coulter, it shall be you,
Whatever goes to the tilth of me it shall be you,
You my rich blood, your milky stream pale strippings of my life;
Breast that presses against other breasts it shall be you,
My brain it shall be your occult convolutions,
Root of washed sweet-flag, timorous pond-snipe, nest of guarded
    duplicate eggs, it shall be you
Mixed tussled hay of head and beard and brawn it shall be you,

                    .   .   .

Winds whose soft-tickling genitals rub against me it shall be you,
Broad muscular fields, branches of liveoak, loving lounger in
    my winding paths, it shall be you,

Something I cannot see puts upward libidinous prongs,
Seas of bright juice suffuse heaven.

                                                          (51–2)

The sexual climax also brings new vision: the 'bright juice' of his
ejaculation 'suffuse[s] heaven'. Sexual energy is the metaphoric
vehicle for the speaker's loving exploration of the universe.

The speaker develops a self of such extraordinary powers that he
is able to strengthen the weak and restore the ill. As Whitman had
rejected the conventional poetic language of 'pictures', so he rejects
all of the usual sources of aid to the unfortunates, good words and
good deeds. He gives instead the full measure of his love: 'What I
give I give out of myself'. He is thus empowered to elevate the
despised – 'To a drudge of the cottonfields or emptier of privies I
lean . . . on his right cheek I put the family kiss, / And in my soul I
swear I never will deny him' – and to restore the dying: 'I seize the
descending man . . . I raise him with resistless will' (72–3).

The reader is an active participant with the poet in his loving
exploration of the external world. Indeed, Whitman 'conceives' the
poem as a means of 'bestow[ing]' and 'infold[ing]' himself on the
reader. He does 'not give lectures or a little charity, / What I give I
give out of myself', he declares and commands the reader to receive
him: 'You there, impotent, loose in the knees, open your scarfed
chops till I blow grit within you, / Spread your palms and lift the
flaps of your pockets, / I am not to be denied . . . I compel . . . I have
stores plenty and to spare, / And anything I have I bestow'. The
athletic poet-lover does not even 'ask' the reader's identity: 'You
can do nothing and be nothing but what I will infold you' (72). The
reader has no choice but to accept the poet's compelling act of love.
Its promise is imaginative, if not physical, potency.

Perhaps the very fact that the poet's energies in 'Song of Myself'
are not absorbed by a romantic relationship enables him to explore
with such dazzling powers other forms of love. This is the case with
'The Sleepers', which also appeared in 1855. Whitman brilliantly
treats the hesitant growth of the adolescent's capacity to love,
focusing on his challenge of crossing the bridge between childhood
and adulthood.

Whitman begins with the tentativeness and gravity of the
adolescent, describing himself as 'Wandering and confused . . . lost
to myself . . . ill-assorted . . . contradictory'. His emotional state

reflects the difficulties of many of those he describes in the ensuing dream-vision, including the 'wretched features of the ennuyees, the white features of corpses, the livid faces of drunkards, the sick-gray faces of onanists'. Distressingly, these men are as 'ill-assorted' as himself. Yet, they have crossed the bridge, and under the cover of darkness and in their company, the speaker discovers the imaginative power of sympathy: 'I dream in my dream all the dreams of the other dreamers, / And I become the other dreamers'.

The darkness that enables him imaginatively to experience the sexuality of the sleepers stimulates him to discover his own. His 'clothes . . . stolen while I was abed', he is 'thrust forth' and has no place to find cover:

Pier out from the main, let me catch myself with you and stay . . . I
    will not chafe you:
I feel ashamed to go naked about the world,
And am curious to know where my feet stand . . . and what is this
    flooding me, childhood or manhood . . . and the hunger that
    crosses the bridge between.

The cloth laps a first sweet eating and drinking,
Laps life-swelling yolks . . . laps ear of rose-corn, milky and just
    ripened:
The white teeth stay, and the boss-tooth advances in darkness,
And liquor is spilled on lips and bosoms by touching glasses, and
    the best liquor afterward.

The boy intuitively understands that the night, which brings him the sexual release that enables him to envisage adulthood, has the power to restore the other sleepers as well. Now he can envisage adulthood confidently.

The speaker's passage enables him to affirm that 'the myth of heaven indicates peace and night' and that 'the myth of heaven indicates the soul'. His vision of a world transformed through love is an analogue to the boy's state of sexual innocence. Coming from 'its embowered garden', his soul makes 'perfect and clean the genitals previously jetting, and perfect and clean the womb cohering'. The speaker rediscovers the peace of childhood while retaining the phallic excitement of his newly awakened sexuality.

This unique perspective enables the speaker to envisage a world restored through love: 'The sleepers are very beautiful as they lie unclothed, / They flow hand in hand over the whole earth from east to west as they lie unclothed; / The Asiatic and African are hand in hand . . . the European and American are hand in hand, / Learned and unlearned are hand in hand . . . and male and female are hand in hand; / The bare arm of the girl crosses the bare breast of her lover . . . they press close without lust . . . his lips press her neck, / The father holds his grown or ungrown son in his arms with measureless love . . . and the son holds the father in his arms with measureless love'. In a world where such love reigns, every division and source of suffering is overcome: all 'pass the invigoration of the night and the chemistry of the night and awake'. The final image is of the night as a nurturing, loving, god-like mother, presiding over a world where there is no suffering or loss and where the awakening adolescent can be confident that he will become an adult lover (107–17).

II

But in the great ode 'Out of the Cradle Endlessly Rocking' (published in 1859 as 'A Child's Reminiscence') the poet faces a world where love, for all its magic, is unable to restore loss. Recalling a childhood experience, the poet becomes the boy on the Long Island shore who witnesses the arrival of two birds from Alabama and vicariously experiences first their great love and happiness as they create their nest and then the surpassing pain of the male bird with the disappearance of his mate. Calling in vain for his mate to return, the he-bird knows loss and death:

> *O past! O happy life! O songs of joy!*
> *In the air, in the woods, over fields,*
> *Loved! loved! loved! loved! loved!*
> *But my mate no more, no more with me!*
> *We two together no more.*

Powerless to summon back his lover, the he-bird knows a grief which is the more intense because it erupts suddenly and in a world everywhere inflamed with love. He cannot, as had Whitman's ideal poet of the 1855 preface, be 'indifferent which chance happens and which possible contingency of fortune or misfortune'. The he-bird's 'songs of joy' are transformed into songs of loss. The cries of this 'singer solitary' awaken in the boy 'a thousand songs, clearer, louder and more sorrowful than' those of the bird, as he realises that a major poetic challenge will be to find a way to reconcile himself to 'the low and delicious word death'. The boy's sudden insight into the tragic impermanence of love and life, then, awakens him to an understanding of his poetic vocation: 'O you singer solitary, singing by yourself, projecting me, / O solitary me listening, never more shall I cease perpetuating you, / Never more shall I escape, never more the reverberations, / Never more the cries of unsatisfied love be absent from me, / Never again leave me to be the peaceful child I was before. . .' His understanding of life completed by his insight into death, the poet accepts a new 'destiny' as the singer of 'unsatisfied love' (388–94).

Whereas 'Out of the Cradle Endlessly Rocking' treats the loss of love through death, the 'Calamus' sequence confronts areas of loss within romantic love itself. The delicious abandonment of romantic love is threateningly countered by the irresistible demand of such love that the individual change his identity. How can one know what self will emerge from merging with another? The uncertainty of romantic love intensifies the uncertainty of personal and sexual identity. To love as Whitman does in these poems is to leave oneself vulnerable both to painful self-knowledge and rejection. Yet it is no longer possible to turn around and re-cross the bridge to childhood, to return to the satisfying autoeroticism of the earlier work. Only by accepting the risk of change, of exploring 'In Paths Untrodden', can one hope to discover the liberation of romantic love, which demands that one be prepared to free himself from his former, socially conditioned identity, 'From all the standards hitherto published – from the pleasures, profits, conformities, / Which too long I was offering to feed my Soul' (1860, 341).

In 'Calamus' Whitman speaks of his need for love and his need to express that unstandard, unconventional love which he came to recognise was his: 'I proceed, for all who are, or have been, young men, / To tell the secret of my nights and days, / To celebrate the need for comrades' (1860, 342). While for the most part Whitman glories in the love experience, there is also evidence that he did not fully accept and openly avow a homosexual identity. He writes passionately of his love for a man or several men, and the poems seem to promise biographical revelation. Yet they remain, he admitted in 44 ('Here the Frailest Leaves of Me') 'baffling':

Here my last words, and the most baffling,
Here the frailest leaves of me, and yet my strongest lasting,
Here I shade down and hide my thoughts – I do not expose them,
And yet they expose me more than all my poems.

                                        (1860, 377).

Whitman later removed the first line; its reference to 'last words'
implies that he had decided to give up poetry, so threatening was
the exposure of his emotions. If as Geoffrey Hartman, drawing on
Lacan, has written, 'psychic development is therefore a balance
between the hope of immortality and the continuous fear of mortal
exposure', Whitman has reached the limit of what he can reveal.[6]
And yet these 'frailest leaves', which call attention to that which the
poet ostensibly wishes to conceal, are a moving exploration, from
multiple points of view, of love. These are poems of love desired
and love achieved, of celebration of love's joy and grief over its loss.

The core of the 'Calamus' sequence is a group of twelve poems
which, we know from manuscript evidence, Whitman wrote first
and grouped under the heading 'Live Oak with Moss'. According to
Fredson Bowers, these poems 'appear to be highly unified and to
make up an artistically complete story of attachment, crisis, and
renunciation'.[7] These twelve poems were not published in their
original order in the 1860 'Calamus', as Whitman devised a new
ordering scheme for the entire body. But the original sequence, as
Gay Wilson Allen has observed, 'tells such a story as might have
been found in an Elizabethan sonnet sequence, which was perhaps
its archetype'.[8] We might say of this extraordinary sequence what
W. H. Auden observed of Shakespeare's sonnets, many of which
are addressed to a young man: 'That we are confronted in the
sonnets by a mystery rather than an aberration is evidenced for me
by the fact that men and women whose sexual tastes are perfectly
normal but who enjoy and understand poetry, have always been
able to read them as expressions of what they understand by the
word *love*, without finding the masculine pronoun an obstacle'.[9] In
these intense twelve poems Whitman recounts a love of such
passion that the lover is rendered powerless before its consuming
power.

In the first, 14 ('Not Heat Flames Up and Consumes'), not even
the most powerful of natural forces, heat, sea-waves, or wind is
more powerful than the 'flames of me, consuming, burning for his
love whom I love!' So intense is this love that the soul of the poet,

like the 'high rain-emitting clouds' and 'the white down-balls of myriads of seeds' is 'borne through the open air . . . Wafted in all directions, O love, for friendship, for you' (1860, 360). Love takes the lover where it will. The next, 20 ('I Saw in Louisiana a Live-Oak Growing'), defines the consequences of such love. Now the speaker is unable to exist, as does the tree, without his lover.

Love is so inherently satisfying that all other rewards, including those of the public realm, pale beside its possession. Despite the poet's success in 11 ('When I Heard at the Close of Day') in winning 'plaudits in the capitol' and accomplishing all his 'plans', still he is 'not happy' because his lover is absent. Only when he learns that his 'dear friend, my lover, was on his way coming, O then I was happy'. With his arrival,

I heard the rustle of the liquid and sands as directed to me,
    whispering, to congratulate me,
For the one I love most lay sleeping by me under the same cover in
    the cool night,
In the stillness, in the autumn moonbeams, his face was inclined
    toward me,
And his arm lay lightly around my breast – and that night I was
    happy.

So intensely passionate is the poem that even the trite word 'happy', which Whitman uses four times, comes to assume fresh meaning. Indeed, the poem might be said to be an exercise in the definition of 'happiness', which appears in the first line and is the last word in the poem. Happiness is possible only when 'the one I love most [lies] sleeping by me under the same cover in the cool night' (1860, 357–8).

If the possession of love alone brings such happiness, why not devote oneself exclusively to it? In 8 ('Long I Thought that Knowledge Alone Would Suffice Me'), a poem later removed from *Leaves of Grass*, Whitman explicitly renounces his former goals: knowledge, patriotism, 'songs of the New World', and even a 'life . . . spent in singing'. 'Indifferent to my own songs', the lover devotes himself entirely to 'him I love, / It is enough for us that we are together – We never separate again' (354–5). Such is the transforming power of love that it threatens all other pursuits, even that of art. But 32 ('What Think You I Take Pen in Hand to Record') takes something back. If he is to be a poet, Whitman will not write about conventional subjects, but only of love, which he captures in the concluding image of 'two simple men I saw to-day . . . parting the parting of dear friends, / The one to remain hung on the other's neck, and passionately kissed him, / While the one to depart, tightly prest the one to remain in his arms' (1860, 372–3).

In the 1855 preface Whitman had asserted that as poet he was the most powerful and potent lover, implying that love is a vehicle for art. But here the connection between love and art is put into question. Now Whitman prefers to be known not as poet, but as 'the tenderest lover', as he writes in 10 ('Recorders Ages Hence'). He requests that future poets remember him as one 'who was not proud of his songs, but of the measureless ocean of love within him – and freely poured it forth', a man whose happiest days were with his lover. He wishes us to 'hang up my picture as that of the tenderest lover, / The friend, the lover's portrait, of whom his friend, his lover, was fondest' (1860, 356–7).

But this is a story of unrequited love, and in 9 ('Hours Continuing Long'), Whitman presents the reversal at exactly the right moment, after the lover, moved by love's transforming happiness, has renounced all his former goals. His lover is now lost to him, and he knows 'hours discouraged, hours distracted – for the one I cannot content myself without, soon I saw him content himself without me'. The man who had identified himself as 'the tenderest lover' now must ask, 'Is there even one other like me – distracted – his friend, his lover, lost to him?' In the anguish of rejection, Whitman confronts a new, disturbing identity: 'Sullen and suffering hours! (I am ashamed – but it is useless – I am what I am;)'. As Gay Wilson Allen has written, this poem carries unusual conviction, being 'neither imaginary nor symbolical, but written out of shame and remorse'.[10] Not only has he been rejected by one he had loved unconditionally, but Whitman also must accept a sexual identity that brings him shame. But it is 'useless', he courageously admits, to attempt to change what one fundamentally is: 'I am what I am' (1860, 356–7).

The final four poems search for a means to resolve the pain. One way, recounted in 34 ('I Dreamed in a Dream'), is to imagine a 'new City of Friends' where nothing is more prized 'than the quality of robust love – it led the rest' (1860, 373). However satisfying such a wish may be, still love is of the body. In 43 ('O You Whom I Often and Silently Come'), addressing his secret beloved, he confesses that he knows the constant pain of unsatisfied sexual desire, 'the subtle electric fire that for your sake is playing within me' (1860, p. 377). Yet, for all the power of his desire, Whitman cannot directly avow his love; paradoxically, the only outlet for such physical desire is art.

And yet, Whitman uses the idea that art has its limits as a way of emphasising the power of a love that exceeds all limits. In 36 ('Earth! My Likeness!') he does not 'dare . . . tell . . . in words – not even in these songs', that something 'fierce and terrible in me, eligible to burst forth', the attraction he feels for the 'athlete . . . enamoured of me'. Whatever the resolution of his love affair, sexuality, now more intense even than the 'subtle electric fire' of the previous poem, remains a part of his being. The poem, by identifying the sexual power which it claims cannot be spoken, suggests its power. And so in 42 ('To a Western Boy'), the final poem of the initial group, Whitman, addressing the young man wishing to 'become eleve of mine', affirms a legacy of love: 'If you be not silently selected by lovers, and do not silently select lovers', it will be useless for him to be his pupil. Although Whitman implicitly reconciles himself to a life without a romantic love relationship in this world, he concludes by affirming its value.

In this regard the poem points toward the works that Whitman would add to 'Calamus'. In the 1876 preface he claimed that 'important as [the poems] are . . . as emotional expressions of humanity, the special meaning of the 'Calamus' cluster of *Leaves of Grass* . . . mainly resides in its political significance', which he described as 'this old, eternal, yet ever-new interchange of ad-hesiveness, so fitly emblematic of America' (1011). ('Adhesive-ness' is a term borrowed from phrenology.) Some of the 'Calamus' poems, such as 24 ('I Hear It Was Charged Against Me'), where Whitman speaks of 'the dear love of comrades' as forming a new institution in American life, do reflect such a purpose. But the essential concern of the best of the 'Calamus' poems is to under-stand the mystery which is romantic love.

'Calamus' 7 ('Of the Terrible Doubt of Appearances') describes the doubt that we all face in philosophical questions, the 'uncer-tainties after all / That may-be reliance and hope are but specula-tions'. The question of how we know what we know is complex, as this reference to our perceptions dramatises: 'May-be they only seem to me what they are, (as doubtlessly they indeed but seem,) as from my present point of view – And might prove, (as of course they would,) naught of what they appear, or naught any how, from entirely changed points of view'. But in a world where there is love, why should such metaphysical questions concern us? 'I walk or sit indifferent – I am satisfied, / He ahold of my hand has completely satisfied me' (1860, 362–3).

The possession of love makes us conscious of its loss, and, as Whitman revealed in 'Out of the Cradle Endlessly Rocking', we are led to confront death itself. This is the theme of the mysterious 2 ('Scented Herbage of My Breast'). Addressing the 'Tomb-leaves, body-leaves, growing up above me, above death', Whitman admits that he does not understand their meaning – except that they suggest the unfathomable connection between love and death:

Death is beautiful from you – (what indeed is beautiful, except
    Death and Love?)
O I think it is not for life I am chanting here my chant of lovers – I
    think it must be for Death,
For how calm, how solemn it grows, to ascend to the atmosphere of
    lovers,
Death or life I am then indifferent – my Soul declines to prefer,
I am not sure but the high Soul of lovers welcomes death most.

Death is a presence behind the 'mask of materials' waiting 'patiently' to 'take control of all, / That you will perhaps dissipate this entire show of appearance, / That may be you are what it is all for – but it does not last so very long, / But you will last very long' (1860, 342–4). Paradoxically, it is through that most intense presence which is love that the absence that is death becomes a palpable presence in our imaginations.

And yet the major symbol of these poems is not the 'tomb-leaves' but the calamus root, which symbolises the persistence of love, as Whitman reveals in 4 ('These I, Singing in Spring'). Through love the poet becomes a godlike presence, traversing 'the garden, the world' and then 'pass[ing] the gates' to the next, to 'collect for lovers' a procession of individuals. Passing out such potent flowers as the lilac, live-oak, pinks and laurel leaves, the god-lover leads the awakened spirits to the pond-side, where his followers exchange the calamus root. 'Compassed around by a thick cloud of spirits', Whitman concludes by bestowing his transforming gift, 'but only to them that love, as I myself am capable of loving' (1860, 347–8). The visionary, hopeful quality of this springtime poem carries a numinous meaning; love overcomes death and rejection.

Yet Whitman was unable to find a way to unify the many diverse, sometimes contradictory themes of 'Calamus'. In 44 ('Here My Last Words'), as we have seen, he came to the point where he could reveal no more. But that meant that he could no longer write what in 'Spontaneous Me' he called 'real poems, (what we call poems being merely pictures,) / The poems of the privacy of the night, and of men like me / This poem drooping shy and unseen that I always carry, and that all men carry . . .'. Not willing to explore his 'frailest leaves', Whitman now lacked access to that potent and true language of desire that had propelled his art.

In 'Of the Terrible Doubt of Appearances' Whitman recognised the complexity of the interpretive act, that what one sees depends upon his point of view and things may prove 'naught of what they appear, or naught anyhow, from entirely changed points of view'. It is wise to keep these cautionary words in mind in trying to reach a comprehensive interpretation of the 'Calamus' sequence itself. With their shifting intentions and multiple concerns, these poems are responsive to many readings, depending upon the reader's starting point, his point of view. But as poetry expressing the surpassing joy of love and crushing despair at its loss and love's mysterious connection with death, 'Calamus' takes its place as perhaps the greatest poetic treatment of love in American literature.

In the opening poem of the 1860 edition, 'Proto-Leaf' (later 'Starting from Paumanok'), he signifies his desire to escape the pain of love by celebrating instead religion: 'It is a painful thing to love a man or woman to excess, and yet it satisfies, it is great, / But there is something else very great, it makes the whole coincide, / It, magnificent, beyond materials, with continuous hands sweeps and provides for all' (181). That 'something else' is 'the greatness of Religion'. But to the extent that Whitman elevated love to the level of such abstractions as religion and democracy, then physical passion, 'the subtle electric fire' of 'Calamus' 43, would be lacking from his poetry. Whitman may have found a way to transcend the suffering of love through turning his attention instead to democracy and religion, but the artistic price that he paid was severe. The power of his writing, his access to the power of the unconscious, which Lacan asserted is structured like a language, had been made possible by his rejection of the language of abstractions. But now, in subsuming this powerful language of desire under the abstraction of religion, Whitman emasculated it. Romantically, the only place he had to go was the confession in the 1876 preface of a 'terrible, irrepressible yearning ... this never satisfied appetite for sympathy'.

In the concluding poem of 'Calamus', 45 ('Full of Life Now'), Whitman addresses his 'yet unborn reader' whom he envisions 'seeking me, / Fancying how happy you were, if I could be with you, and become your lover; / Be it as if I were with you. Be not too certain but I am now with you' (1860, p. 378). In his intimate, intensely physical approach to the reader, Whitman found a relationship that did not fail him. And it was finally for the reader, whom he thought of as his responsive lover, that he gave the best of himself in a poetry that was also an act of love. In 'Crossing Brooklyn Ferry' ('Sun-down Poem' in the 1856 edition), after recalling that 'I too had receiv'd identity by my body, / That I was I knew was of my body, and what I should be I knew I should be of my body', Whitman infuses his meaning, which is inherently sexual, into the reader, whom he approaches in an act of love:

What Gods can exceed these that clasp me by the hand, and
    with voices I love call me promptly and loudly by my nighest
    name as I approach?
What is more subtle than this which ties me to the woman or
    man that looks in my face?
Which fuses me into you now, and pours my meaning into you?

We understand then do we not?
What I promis'd without mentioning it, have you not accepted?
What the study could not teach – what the preaching could not
    accomplish is accomplish'd, is it not?

                                                        (307–13)

Notes

1.   Walt Whitman, *Complete Poetry and Collected Prose*, ed. Justin Kaplan (New York: Library of America, 1982) pp. 1010–11. With the exception of 'Calamus' all quotations from Whitman's poetry and prose will be taken from this edition and given in the text. Quotations from 'Calamus' are from the facsimile edition of the 1860. *Leaves of Grass* edited by Roy Harvey Pearce (Ithaca: Cornell University Press, 1961). Page references will be given in the text as follows: (1860, p.   ).
2.   Bice Benvenuto and Roger Kennedy, *The Works of Jacques Lacan: An Introduction* (New York: St. Martin's Press, 1986) p. 50. The passage

from Freud appears in Volume 12 of the *Standard Edition* (London: Hogarth Press, 1954) pp. 60–1.

3.   Elizabeth Wright, *Psychoanalytic Criticism* (London: Methuen, 1984) p. 109.

4.   Leslie Fiedler, *No! in Thunder* (Boston: Beacon Press, 1960) p. 70.

5.   For a full analysis of this passage in the context of Whitman's knowledge of contemporary science, see my ' "The Password Primeval": Whitman's Use of Science in "Song of Myself" ', in *Studies in the American Renaissance: 1986*, Joel Myerson (ed.), (Charlottesville: University Press of Virginia, 1986) pp. 385–425.

6.   Geoffrey H. Hartman, 'Psychoanalysis: The French Connection' in Hartman (ed.), *Psychoanalysis and the Question of the Text* (Baltimore: Johns Hopkins University Press, 1978) p. 86.

7.   Fredson Bowers (ed.), *Whitman's Manuscripts: Leaves of Grass (1860)* (Chicago: University of Chicago Press, 1955) p. lxvi.

8.   Gay Wilson Allen, *The Solitary Singer* (New York University Press, 1967) p. 222.

9.   W. H. Auden, 'Shakespeare's Sonnets' in *Forewords and Afterwords* (New York: Random House, 1973) pp. 99–100.

10.   Allen, p. 300.

5

Varieties of Love: Henry James's Treatment of the 'Great Relation'

ELSA NETTELS

Early in James's first novel *Watch and Ward* the protagonist Roger Lawrence falls asleep while his young ward Nora, whom he is educating to become his wife, reads to him from *The Heir of Redclyffe*. When he awakens, he excuses himself by declaring: 'all novels seem to me stupid. They are nothing to what I can fancy: I have in my heart a prettier romance than any of them.' When Nora begs to hear it, he replies, 'My denouement is not yet written . . . Wait till the story is finished; then you shall hear the whole'.[1]

Although rudimentary in execution, this scene prefigures James's mature novels in several ways. In Roger Lawrence, James introduced the first of many characters who desire to create their own stories, sometimes inspired by fiction they have read. In Nora, James created the first of a succession of characters, always young, usually women, whom others try to mould for their own uses.[2] Through Roger Lawrence, James expressed his own dissatisfaction with the fiction of his day. He also identified a famous example of the popular romances which provided him with motifs, plot devices and character types that he transformed in such works as *The American, Washington Square* and *The Portrait of a Lady*.

Had James written 'love' instead of 'romance' in Roger Lawrence's speech, he would have named the main preoccupation of his characters and the primary subject of his fiction. Each of the twenty novels that follow *Watch and Ward* centres on love relationships in which different elements – sexual desire, adoration, infatuation, sympathy, frustration, jealousy – may commingle. Romantic love, which in the traditional novels leads to happy marriage, or in its adulterous form threatens or destroys marriage,

has its place in most of James's novels. But other kinds of love –
homoerotic, filial, paternal, incestuous, vicarious, necrophilic –
may evoke feelings as powerful as those generated by socially
sanctioned heterosexual love. To establish the central importance of
love in James's fiction, to analyse his conception of love in some of
its varieties, and to show how he transformed traditional motifs
and types through the formal properties of his art is to recognise
James as the American novelist who not only represented more
different kinds of love than any American writer before him, but
was also the first to define artistic principles to inform its portrayal.

I

How James thought fiction should treat of love is revealed in his
criticism of English and continental novelists. From his first
reviews in the 1860s to his last critical essays in *Notes and Novelists*
(1914), his views were consistent. The great deficiency of Anglo-
Saxon fiction, he repeatedly asserted, was its failure to deal in more
than a guarded way with what he called 'the great relation between
men and women, the constant world-renewal'.[3] The male writers
had established their characters' relations 'with the pistol, the
pirate, the police, the wild and tame beast' but not 'man's relation
with himself, that is with women'.[4] Dickens and Scott, for instance,
were unimaginable *'without* the "love-making" left . . . out' (*FN*, 39).
The greater and lesser female novelists of the nineteenth century
had not filled the gap; in 1900 James was still observing the
'immense omission in our fiction' (*FN*, 39).

Much continental fiction seemed to James unsatisfactory for the
opposite reason, in its concentration on sexual appetite to the
exclusion of other impulses and interests. He complained of the
characters of the Italian novelist, Matilde Serao, that we know them
'by nothing but their convulsions and spasms' (*NN*, 310). He noted
in the fiction of Pierre Loti 'that oddest of all French literary
characteristics', the divorcing of love from affection, the depiction
of sexual intimacy 'as unaccompanied with any moral feeling, any
impulse of reflection or reaction'.[5] He objected to the businesslike
way George Sand catalogued the mysteries of 'the divine passion'
(*Theory*, 133). In ruling supreme in 'the empire of the sexual sense'
Maupassant seemed to him to remain blind to 'the moral nature of
man'.[6]

As a subject for fiction, sexual passion was to James very much like the supernatural. Just as ghostly presences in themselves lack intrinsic values and keep their force only 'by looming through some other history – the indispensable history of somebody's *normal* relation to something',[7] so passion gains dignity and importance only as it is treated in relation to the whole texture of civilised life. If the essential requirement of a novel is that it be interesting, as James held in 'The Art of Fiction', then the novelist was ill-advised to divorce passion from the 'common humanities and sociabilities', for passion in itself is not interesting; it is only the characters, 'with the ground they stand on and the objects enclosing them, who give interest to their passion' (*NN*, 310–1). To James, the intensity with which D'Annunzio dwelt on sexual passion as '*only* the act of a moment' debased it. 'Shut out from the rest of life, shut out from all fruition and assimilation, it has no more dignity than – to use a homely image – the boots and shoes that we see, in the corridors of promiscuous hotels, standing, often in double pairs, at the doors of rooms' (*NN*, 292).

When James wrote his essays on Serao and D'Annunzio he had long since moved beyond the social realism of 'Daisy Miller' and *Washington Square*. But he never repudiated his idea of the novel as 'a direct impression of life' or ceased to ask that fiction create 'an immense and exquisite correspondence with life' (*PP*, 402). *Truth*, *verisimilitude* and *representation* remained key words in his critical vocabulary. He could insist to H. G. Wells, that 'it is art that *makes* life, makes interest, makes importance',[8] but he also insisted upon the mimetic function of the novel, of all literary forms to be valued as 'the most immediate . . . picture of actual manners . . . a reflection of our social changes and chances' (*FN*, 38). Serao's characters who were illumined by the 'exclusively sexual light' he judged artistic failures because their love 'is simply unaccompanied with any interplay of our usual conditions' (*NN*, 310). Passion given its 'whole place', quickly pre-empts the entire space, shuts out all but itself and thus 'greatly modif[ies] the truth of things' by locating passion 'in a strange false perspective, a denuded desert which experience surely fails ever to give us the like of' (*NN*, 309).

James's dissatisfaction with the novels of his contemporaries moved him to treat love in a different way, to write. novels that would unite the virtues and correct the deficiencies of English and continental fiction. Without making the entrails of his characters the stage of the action, he would give 'the great relation between men and women' the central place. In novel after novel, he made love the primary force in the lives of his main characters – not the history of consummated passion though, but the growth of a passion that is never fulfilled. And when love is portrayed as a process, a development unfolding in time, it is of necessity more than, or other than, sexual hunger. In its highest form, James asserted, love cannot exist without affection, which by definition is constancy, '*is* durability' (*NN*, 209). But more than this, love in James's fiction is an animating force, 'an inner fire of the imagination that is fed more by unsatisfied desire than by emotional fulfilment'.[9]

That love is the vital force in James's world is indicated by the repeated association of the verbs 'live' and 'love'. When Roger Lawrence adopts the twelve-year-old Nora after his proposal of marriage to Isabel Morton is rejected, he asks himself: 'was he to believe then, that he could not live without love, and that he must take it where he found it?' (*WW*, 34). It is immediately after Strether, in *The Ambassadors*, first sees Madame de Vionnet with Chad, about whose 'virtuous attachment' he has speculated, that he exhorts Little Bilham to 'live all you can; it's a mistake not to'.[10] For some characters, loving another is a lifelong occupation that ends only when hope is crushed or passion consumed; Morris Townsend's betrayal of Catherine Sloper does not prevent her memory of him from sustaining in her for twenty years the sense of having lived: 'She had lived on something that was connected with *him*, and she had consumed it in doing so'.[11] If John Marcher in 'The Beast in the Jungle' feeds on the sympathy and interest of May Bartram, she in turn lives by her hope of awakening in him the power to love. The 'disorder of the blood' offered as the cause of her death identifies him as the vampire who learns at the end that in draining her life's blood he has destroyed himself: 'The escape would have been to love her; then, *then* he would have lived. *She* had lived – who could say now with what passion? – since she had loved him for himself' (xvii, 126)

This symbolic fable dramatises most starkly the inseparability of disease and love in James's fiction. Physical maladies are usually the symbol or the result of emotional starvation; the will to live revives or declines as love is offered or denied. Roger Lawrence when about to die of typhus is saved by Nora's professions of love, but more often James shows the powerful effects of love by portraying the fate of the rejected and deprived. Ferdinand Mason, the stricken Civil War veteran convalescing in 'A Most Extra-ordinary Case' (1868), seems to gain strength until the woman he secretly loves announces her engagement to his doctor. Then, 'the shattered fragments of his long-resisting will floated down its shallow current into dissolution'.[12] Daisy Miller's cry to Winterbourne, 'I don't care . . . whether I have the Roman fever or not' (xviii, 89) suggests that his rejection of her is one cause of her death. (In James's play, *Daisy Miller*, the heroine recovers when Winterbourne kneels at her bedside and declares his love.) The 'imagination of loving' sustains Ralph Touchett in his mortal illness until the sterility of Isabel's marriage to Osmond is fully revealed, when Ralph dies. Morgan Moreen, in 'The Pupil', dies of heart failure when his parents propose to foist him off on his tutor, who doesn't want him either.

Love, or the hope of being loved, may sustain the will to live in the person seemingly doomed, but the animating force may itself be a disease that kills. In writing of the entanglements of George Sand and her circle at Nohant, James dwells on the 'ravaging' effects of the 'malady' of passion (*NN*, 203). He represented sexual passion as a predatory bird with beak and talons fixed in the flesh of its victim. In the person of May Server, whom the narrator of *The Sacred Fount* posits as the source of mental energy upon which another male guest feeds, the narrator sees 'as never . . . before what consuming passion can make of the marked mortal on whom, with fixed beak and claws, it has settled as on a prey'.[13] Strether has a similar vision when he sees Madame de Vionnet as the abject victim of 'the strange strength of her passion' and marvels 'that a creature so fine, could be, by mysterious forces, a creature so exploited' (xxii, 284). Enthralled by James's most fatal woman, Christina Light, the sculptor, Roderick Hudson, loses his creative power and dies. In *The Wings of the Dove*, Merton Densher, frus-trated in his passion for Kate Croy, feels the force of 'an impatience that, prolonged, made a man ill'.[14] Sexual passion alone, however, cannot sustain a relationship, as is shown by the disintegrating liaisons of Chad and Madame de Vionnet and of Prince Amerigo and Charlotte Stant. James would have endorsed the words of Lawrence's Ursula in *The Rainbow*: 'Passion is only part of love. And it seems so much because it can't last. That is why passion is never happy'.[15] James's characters who are incapable of love are spiri-tually dead; deprived of love they may die, but passion satisfied may vitiate desire, if the nature of their love or of those they love does not preclude fulfilment altogether.

James's frequent images of experience as a cup to be drained, love as money to be hoarded or spent, the loved one as a source or fount imply that one's store of energy is limited; unless one receives in exchange for what one gives one eventually dies. The fear of loss fans the 'spark of conflict, ever latent in the depths of passion' (*Wings of the Dove*, Bk.2, 6). James's characters thus may find their best account in the contemplation of passion while it is still safe in the cage of the imagination, as Fleda Vetch in *The Spoils of Poynton* cherishes her secret understanding with Owen Gereth as she might protect 'some dangerous lovely living thing that she had caught and could keep – keep vivid and helpless in the cage of her own passion and look at and talk to all day long" (x, 108–9). The impulse to protect and appropriate is rather like that which moved James, on learning of the death of his beloved cousin, Minny Temple, to feel that in his loss of the living woman he had gained the ultimate value, her image unthreatened by change.[16]

In certain ways, love in James's fiction is not differentiated along gender lines. His habitual depiction of bonds between characters who are in some way opposites represent his view that love in both men and women reflects the longing to complete the self through union with another. For instance, the 'deep harmony' which initially binds Kate Croy and Merton Densher in *The Wings of the Dove* arises from the awareness of each of the 'precious unlikeness' of the other, the sense of each 'of being poor where the other was rich' (Bk.1, 56–7). Both men and women are capable of constancy; the gift of the 'undiverted heart' which Catherine Sloper brings to Morris Townsend is not the exclusive possession of women: it is offered to Isabel Archer by Ralph Touchett, to Mary Garland by Rowland Mallett, to the Princess Casamassima by Hyacinth Robinson.

Conversely, women no less than men are capable of that coercion and manipulation which violates what Hawthorne called 'the sanctity of the human heart'. Both men and women deny the integrity and identity of others by perceiving them as objects or images or icons (e.g. Milly Theale as 'the dove', 'the princess'; Prince Amerigo as 'a pure and perfect crystal' and 'a great Palladian church'). But in James's world, women almost always are the chief victims in passionate encounters. The suffering of Daisy Miller, Catherine Sloper, Isabel Archer, and Madame de Vionnet is greater than that of the men who exploit or betray them. Even James's 'dark heroines' who inflict suffering on others more often than not make other women their chief victims and are in the end thwarted or overmastered by men: Madame Merle by Osmond, the Princess Casamassima by Paul Muniment, Charlotte Stant by both her lover, Prince Amerigo, and her husband, Adam Verver. As seen by Maggie Verver, Charlotte is a magnificent animal, the 'splendid shining supple creature' who breaks out of her cage but then is 'led to her doom' by her husband, as if he holds a 'silken halter looped round her beautiful neck' (xxiv, 287).[17]

The artist figure seems to be the exception to the rule that women are more often the victims of men than men are the victims of women. The sculptor Roderick Hudson is destroyed by his passion for Christina Light, but no woman artist in James's fiction loses her creative power when her affections are engaged. The actress, Miriam Rooth, in *The Tragic Muse*, marries her manager without apparent sacrifice of her artistic power. Women writers are usually too commonplace, too much servants of the marketplace, to be injured ('Greville Fane', 'The Next Time', 'The Velvet Glove'.) Most of the dedicated male artists, such as Nick Dormer in *The Tragic Muse* and Paul Overt in 'The Lesson of the Master', remain celibates who renounce love for their art. In 'The Middle Years', the writer Dencombe finds his personal bond in the devotion of a young male disciple, as did James himself. Through such pictures of male characters whose art requires their sacrifice of romantic attachments and the sublimation of sexual energies, James created a myth of the artist that justified his own choice of the celibate's life.

In his late years, James wrote letters of ardent tenderness and longing to young artists like Hugh Walpole and Henrik Anderson, whose affection he cultivated. But in his fiction, his portrayal of the bonds of friendship or discipleship that unite men rarely if ever carries homosexual overtones. No question of erotic attachment touches the friendship of Newman and Valentin in *The American*, or Bernard Longueville and Gordon Wright in *Confidence*, or Nick Dormer and Gabriel Nash in *The Tragic Muse*. Hyacinth Robinson looks to Muniment as a mentor and a comrade, not as a lover. The friendship of Nick Dormer and Peter Sherringham rests not on love but on a deep foundation of sociability.

The case is different in James's portrayal of a woman's love for another woman in *The Bostonians*. The difference is evident if one compares that novel with *Roderick Hudson*, in which Rowland Mallett's relation to Roderick is analogous to Olive Chancellor's relation to the artist figure and public performer, Verena Tarrant. Both Rowland and Olive, well-endowed financially but feeling

themselves incomplete and unfulfilled, in a sense buy companionship by sponsoring gifted persons of their own sex, whose physical
beauty and artistic gifts represent what the sponsors lack and
whose friendship becomes the principal interest in their lives. Loss
of the beloved protegé subjects the patron to anguish as keen as that
suffered by any partner in a heterosexual relationship. Rowland,
watching in the Alps by Roderick's dead body, 'fallen from a great
height', understands 'how up to the brim, for two years, his
personal world had been filled. It looked to him at present as void
and blank and sinister as a theatre bankrupt and closed' (I, 526).
(The image of the empty theatre replaces the allusion to Othello in
the first edition: 'his occupation was gone'.) Olive is not the
detached spectator of an empty theatre but suffering incarnate as
she wanders alone along the shore after losing Verena to Ransom,
making 'long stations' by the rocks and shedding 'slow still tears'
that fail to quench the pain that 'burned within her like a fire'.[18]

These passages in themselves suggest the essential difference
between the two relationships. In Rowland's thoughts and in his
scenes with Roderick there is little hint of erotic passion. The case is
very different with Olive, whose possessive fears, gusts of adoration and compulsive embraces of Verena betray a sexual hunger
from which James exempts Rowland. Until Roderick degenerates,
Rowland feels their relation as a 'comradeship', which at its best
attains to a 'high, rare communion' (I, 91). More fervidly, Olive
craves 'a friend of her own sex with whom she might have a union
of soul'; she holds Verena in a grasp that Verena feels 'too clinching,
too terrible' to break (325).

In *Roderick Hudson*, it is Roderick, the protegé, who has qualities
of the opposite sex; (his voice is 'soft and not altogether masculine'
I, 21). In *The Bostonians* it is Olive who has qualities of the opposite
sex; ('manly things were . . . what she understood best' 102), while
Verena is pure femininity. The implication that Rowland is
'normal' while Olive is not is reinforced by physical description.
Rowland is a 'fresh-coloured yellow-bearded man' of 'a manly
stoutness' (I, 13). Olive, with her fits of nervous shyness, her limp
cold hands, her shapeless figure, and her glittering green eyes, is
'visibly morbid' (8). James provides Rowland with a woman to love,
Mary Garland, and Rowland is friend and confidant to every
woman in the novel. Olive, who tells Verena her great fault is that
'you don't dislike men as a class!' (243), yearns for the last particle of
expiation 'from the brutal, bloodstained, ravening race' (30).

Given the conventions of his time, the difference in James's treatment of same sex relationships was to be expected. As Lillian Faderman[19] has shown, romantic friendships between women, unlike those between men, were accepted as normal by English and American societies in the nineteenth century. Thus the expression of passionate love between women in fiction did not necessarily brand them as perverse or depraved. James's description of *The Bostonians* as 'a study of one of those friendships between women which are so common in New England'[20] indicates his awareness of writing within a tradition, already well established by such writers as Longfellow, Oliver Wendell Holmes, Charles Brockden Brown, and Louisa May Alcott. Had James sought precedents for representation of perverse eroticism displayed by one woman towards another he could have found them in Balzac's *The Girl with the Golden Eyes* (1835), Gautier's *Mlle. de Maupin* (1835), Hardy's *Desperate Remedies* (1871), and Swinburne's *Lesbia Brandon* (1877).

No such array of literary examples could be summoned to sanction the portrayal of erotic attachments between men. As James was aware, the amorous relationship of male characters was not a legitimate subject of fiction in a society that condemned homosexuality as a criminal offence. James's never failing care for his reputation and his position in Victorian society would have forbidden the portrayal of male counterparts of Olive and Verena had he desired to create them. He reserved his guarded expressions of interest and sympathy in the fates of Oscar Wilde and John Addington Symonds for his letters to friends and fellow writers such as Gosse, Daudet, Bourget, and William James.

James did not hesitate to portray other kinds of perversity in male characters, however, and to reserve for them certain kinds of obsessions. It is only men in James's fiction who worship the dead or images of them as in 'Maud-Evelyn', 'The Altar of the Dead' and *The Wings of the Dove*; or who find more satisfaction in an exhumed statue than in a living person ('The Last of the Valerii'); or who become obsessed with their buried (i.e. libidinous) selves ('The Beast in the Jungle' and 'The Jolly Corner'). Only male characters, notably the narrators of 'The Aspern Papers' and *The Sacred Fount*, devote themselves to speculating about the sexual relations of others, for whom they have no personal care, in the quest for secret knowledge. (Such knowledge in James is never attained in this fashion but comes suddenly, unbidden, often in the impression of a moment, as when Strether sees Chad and Madame de Vionnet in a boat on the river and knows them to be lovers.)

At worst, female characters are ravaged and broken. At worst, male characters evade the perils of intimacy through fantasy and speculation which rewards them ultimately with the humiliation of failure and the vision of a wasted life. At best, James's characters are granted the prospect of a happy marriage but their number is few: Gertrude Wentworth and Felix in *The Europeans*, Henrietta Stackpole and Mr Bantling in *The Portrait of a Lady*, Biddy Dormer and Peter Sherringham in *The Tragic Muse*. But each of these pairs is set off by a relation that fails: the Baroness and Robert Acton, Isabel and Osmond, Julia Dallow and Nick Dormer. In James's fiction, renunciation, betrayal, and loss are the common doom. And yet, it is in apparent failure that virtue in James's world most fully realises itself – in the capacity of characters to love and to remain faithful in their love without hope of return, to grow through suffering as do Strether and Isabel, Maisie and Hyacinth, Maggie Verver and many more.

In his portrayal of love James unites diverse strains in American literature. Like Emerson, he embraced the principle of compensation, convinced that 'personal cost' was the price of authentic experience, that suffering was the 'downright consecration of knowledge, that is of perception and, essentially, of exploration, always dangerous and treacherous'.[21] Like Thoreau and Emily Dickinson, celibates as he was, he celebrated the paradoxes of an economy which locates wealth in poverty, teaches water by thirst and success by failure, and discovers

> That Spices fly
> In the Receipt – It was the Distance –
> Was Savory – [22]

James also shared Poe's preoccupation with the creation of intense effects and studied the means of producing certain shades and tones. Like Poe, he found his strongest dramatic effects in the portrayal of love frustrated, obsessive, or otherwise diverted from the realistic paths of middle class courtship and marriage. What Flannery O'Connor has written of the function of violence in modern fiction could be applied to James's portrayal of love in its darker manifestations: 'It is the extreme situation that best reveals what we are essentially . . . the man in the violent situation reveals those qualities least dispensable in his personality, those qualities which are all he will have to take into eternity with him'.[23]

II

The reader may ask at this point, what is new in James's fictions about love? How has he realised the ambition introduced in *Watch and Ward*? Are not unrequited love, the ravages of passion, the death of the betrayed, the conquests of the temptress and the sacrifices of the angelic among the most common subjects of nineteenth century fiction?

James would have answered that it is not the subject in itself that creates new values and meaning but the treatment of the subject. 'So long as there is a subject to be treated, so long will it depend wholly on the treatment to rekindle the fire' (*FN*, 42). For James, 'treatment' embraced two concerns: the formal requirements of fiction, which dictated certain narrative methods, and the obligation to secure the interest of the reader. In his prefaces to the volumes of the New York Edition, he dwelt upon such devices as foreshortening and the alternation of 'scene' and 'picture' because he saw form as the essence of the subject. Form creates meaning in giving shape to life, which by itself 'has no direct sense whatever for the subject and is capable . . . of nothing but splendid waste' (*AN*, 120). He deplored 'all the loose and thin material that keeps reappearing in forms once ready-made and sadly the worse for wear' (*FN*, 40). He prized *Madame Bovary* for its 'unsurpassable form' which was 'as much of the essence of the subject as the idea, and yet so close is its fit and so inseparable its life that we catch it at no moment on any errand of its own' (*NN*, 80).

James's care for form was inseparable from his care for the response of the reader, for the end of form is to create and sustain the reader's interest. No other American writer has written so fully on the methods by which the writer produces the desired effects upon his readers. James's prefaces contain scores of references to the reader, whose probable needs, tastes and judgements James has ever in mind. He gauges the merit of techniques by their likely effect upon the reader. He constructs dialogues with an imaginary reader, who poses questions and raises objections, to which James responds. As Daniel Schwarz observes: 'Frequently, James thinks of himself as a surrogate for the reader. When he speaks of 'we' and 'us' he is making common cause with the community of readers he as an artist seeks'.[24]

James's most important, most innovative, way of securing the interest of the reader and achieving formal unity was to place at the centre of his narrative the consciousness of a character who participates in the action and also reflects it to the reader. In the preface to *The Princess Casamassima* he noted in novel after novel 'that provision for interest which consists in placing advantageously, placing right in the middle of the light, the most polished of possible mirrors of the subject' (*AN*, 70). In such novels as *The Ambassadors*, *The Wings of the Dove*, and *The Golden Bowl*, impressions and perceptions are crucial events, and action becomes a 'process of vision' (*AN*, 309). Through the creation of the central consciousness James created the two indispensables: a compositional centre and a central action, which he compared to a chain upon which 'the pearls of narrative' are strung.

By shifting the reader's attention from events to the characters' perception of events, to 'the reflected field of life, the realm not of application, but of appreciation' (*AN*, 65), James asserted the moral and artistic values of perception over mere sensation, the values of Strether's 'wonderful impressions' over Chad's sexual adventures, of Fleda's discriminations over Mona Brigstock's animal spirits, of Hyacinth Robinson's mental life over the sexual energies of the Princess Casamassima and Muniment. By centring novels in the consciousness of observers like Strether, Fleda, and Hyacinth, James not only proposed to engage the sympathy of readers who instinctively lend themselves to the character whose view they share; James's method also expresses the superiority of the characters whose consciousnesses are most fully represented. James's complaint that Emma Bovary was 'too small an affair' to serve as an adequate centre (*NN*, 81) indicates his conviction that characters must earn their prominence, so to speak, by their powers of insight and feeling and by their capacity for moral and spiritual growth.

The means by which James transformed the traditional novel about love can be studied in many of his works. In our limited space we may consider one novel, *The Wings of the Dove*, which most fully dramatises his favourite subject, unrequited love, and creates, in the experience of Merton Densher, James's history of frustrated passion. Additionally, *The Wings of the Dove* exemplifies most strikingly the ways the form of James's fiction engages the imagination of the reader in the creation of the text.

Summary of the plot of *The Wings of the Dove* shows how far apart are story and discourse in this novel. Let us recall the main elements: the fatally stricken heroine (Milly Theale), in love with an impoverished journalist (Merton Densher), who is secretly engaged to another woman (Kate Croy); the plot of the lovers to effect the marriage of Densher to Milly in the expectation that she will soon die, leaving her fortune to Densher; the revelation to Milly by a rejected suitor (Lord Mark) of the secret engagement, which destroys her will to live; her final act, bequeathal of her fortune to Densher despite his betrayal of her – these elements would appear to be the stuff of which fictions of sensation and sentiment are made. But no novel by James is further removed from the cheap romance of the newspaper serial than is *The Wings of the Dove*, which weaves dense webs of consciousness as the narrative expands through the minds of the three main characters and, with its references to Wagner and Maeterlinck, Bronzino and Veronese, evokes the worlds of French Symbolist drama, Arthurian legend, and Renaissance art.[25] So richly caparisoned, the novel seems the expression of Densher's wish to escape 'reading the romance of his existence in a cheap edition' (2, 193). In his comparison of Kate to 'a "new book", an uncut volume of the highest, the rarest quality,' which never fails him of 'the thrill of turning the page' (2, 243) we may read James's desire to create in *The Wings of the Dove* not the shopworn tale of intrigue, but a new book, likewise of the highest rarest quality.

The world of the novel, imaged as a text the characters read and a stage upon which they act, is crowded with objects and images. The main settings – Lancaster Gate, the Victorian mansion where Kate's Aunt Maud presides; the country house, Matcham, where Milly sees herself transfixed in the Bronzino portrait; and the rented Venetian palace where she dies, are like museums filled with the spoils of conquest. In no other novel by James are women's costumes of more symbolic importance: Kate in light colours, Milly in the black of habitual mourning, until her last scene when she appears in white, Kate in black. Filling the minds of the characters is a profusion of imagery – of animals, ships, islands, water, money, gold, jewels, soldiers, weapons and silken webs.

No less present to the consciousness are silences, voids, and mysteries left unexplained. *The Wings of the Dove* is a novel about love in which what is not represented is as crucial to the action and vital to the effect as what is. What James deliberately leaves out of the novel are exactly those episodes which traditional novelists would turn into their 'big' scenes: Lord Mark's revelation to Milly that Densher and Kate are secretly engaged; Densher's and Kate's consummation of their love in Venice, Milly's last interview with

Densher, by which he feels that he has been 'forgiven, dedicated, blessed' (2, 372). Indeed, more encounters and interviews are presented retrospectively, as the characters' memory of them, than are dramatised in the fictional present.

In leaving to the imagination of the reader certain pivotal scenes, James applied the principle he set forth later, in the preface to 'The Turn of the Screw', in which he concludes that he can best evoke the sense of the ghosts' unutterable evil by declining to specify any particular act. By so doing, he stimulates the reader's imagination to create a reality that lies beyond the power of specification. 'Only make the reader's general vision of evil intense enough . . . and his own experience, his own imagination, his own sympathy . . . and horror . . . will supply him quite sufficiently with all the particulars. Make him *think* the evil, make him think it for himself, and you are released from weak specifications' (*AN*, 176).

James's decision not to dramatise the scene where Kate comes to Densher in his rooms was perhaps also dictated by the sense he imputes to Densher that 'in love, the names of things, the verbal terms of intercourse, were, compared with love itself, vulgar' (2,7). In any case, it is not the act itself that is of first importance but its effect upon Densher. Thus James represents not the scene but Densher's memory of it:

> What had come to pass within his walls lingered there as an obsession importunate to all his senses; it lived again, as a cluster of pleasant memories, at every hour and in every object; it made everything but itself irrelevant and tasteless . . . It played for him – certainly in this prime afterglow – the part of a treasure kept, at home, in safety and sanctity, something he was sure of finding in its place when, with each return, he worked his heavy old key in the lock. The door had but to open for him to be with it again and for it to be all there; so intensely there that, as we say, no other act was possible to him than the renewed act, almost the hallucination, of intimacy. (2, 257–9)

The working of the key in the lock suggests Densher's access to a private world of the imagination in which the memory of physical gratification is as potent as the experience itself. Again James's conception suggests his affinity to Emily Dickinson, in the capacity of his characters to know 'That polar privacy / A soul admitted to itself — / Finite Infinity' (Dickinson, III, 1149).

The imagery of lock and key also represents the characters' sense of their power or powerlessness in relation to others. Milly in London feels that 'not she but the current acted, and that somebody else, always, was the keeper of the lock or the dam' (1, 299). After his return to London, Densher recalls his saying more than once to Kate: 'You keep the key of the cupboard, and I foresee that when we're married you'll dole me out my sugar by lumps' (2, 18). After Kate's surrender it is Densher who keeps the key and works the lock. The act by which he regains possession of his rooms and the memory they contain reflects his new found sense of mastery and marks the beginning of the shift in the control of their relationship from Kate to him.

Reasons as compelling determined James to omit the climactic last interview between Densher and Milly, what John Auchard calls another of the 'major structural silences of the novel'. Since this interview is instrumental in effecting the shift of Densher's allegiance from Kate to Milly, and since its essence is 'ineffable', 'beyond words', James would have run a risk in portraying it, in exposing himself to the reader's judgement of whether in fact it was overwhelming enough to cause the change attributed to it. Instead, James depended upon absence to move the reader's imagination to evoke whatever the reader deemed necessary to effect the conversion of Densher. Auchard argues, persuasively, that the silences and voids in the narrative of *The Wings of the Dove* 'place a tense emotional vacuum at the center of the novel's formal complexity'.[26] The reader's imagination, like nature, abhors a vacuum and enters to fill it. As Gary Lindberg observes, 'the gaps between a novelist's scenes have a curious power to implicate us, for somehow we must tacitly account for the lapsed time, and to this degree we participate in constructing the narrative movement itself'.[27]

Like Kate's surrender to Densher, Milly's last conversation with him is presented through his memory of it, appropriately so, since its importance lies in its effect upon him, and through him, upon Kate. Like his memory of Kate, his memory of Milly is represented as contained within his room – the chamber of the mind being James's favourite metaphor of consciousness – to which Densher retreats to gain possession of the past. His imagination of the feeling expressed in Milly's letter to him which Kate burns unopened is, like his memory of Kate, a 'treasure kept in safety and sanctity' which he can reveal to no one.

He kept it back like a favourite pang; left it behind him, so to say, when he went out, but came home again the sooner for the certainty of finding it there. Then he took it out of its sacred corner and its soft wrappings; he undid them one by one, handling them, handing *it*, as a father, baffled and tender, might handle a maimed child.' (2, 429)

The image of the maimed child, the most powerful expression of Densher's sense of what he has done to Milly, suggests also what his union with Kate has produced. When juxtaposed to the key which unlocks the door of his memory with Kate, the maimed child, and the father's tenderness for it, convey the unique quality of Densher's love for Milly. Because he has not possessed her as he has possessed Kate, Milly, like the figure on Keat's Urn, can be 'forever fair', although it was always Kate, never Milly, who roused in him the 'breathing human passion' from which Milly's sacrificial gift of her fortune has released him.

As the voids and gaps in James's novel invite the reader to invest blank space with spiritual force, so Kate's destruction of Milly's letter creates a void for Densher to fill, forcing him to imagine in what terms Milly would have willed him her fortune, allowing him to conceive 'possibilities that, somehow, by wondering about them, his imagination had extraordinarily filled out and refined' (2, 430). In other words, Milly's gift requires the imagination of Densher to be fully realised by the reader as an act of transcendent love. The wings of the dove become then the symbol of the creative power of the imagination – the imagination of the novelist, of the reader and of the characters, which infuses the void, as Milton's holy spirit 'with mighty wings outspread / Dove-like satst brooding on the vast Abyss / And mad'st it pregnant'.

Whether Densher is shown to be spiritually transformed, whether Milly's love is realised as a power that can illumine what is dark and raise and support what is low is open to question. Most readers accept Milly's gift of her fortune to Densher as the 'act of passionate beneficence' that James described in his Notebook (172) – J. A. Ward writes of a 'sublime gesture of forgiveness',[28] Ruth Yeazell of 'an act of supreme self-sacrifice, an affirmative gesture of grace and love'.[29] But Densher has been seen as selfish and vacillating, 'divided to the end', according to Daniel Schneider, and eternally passive in his desire 'to escape everything' by forcing upon Kate the burden of choice.[30] In Sallie Sears's reading, Densher is sanctimonious and priggish, without charity for Kate, almost cruel in his setting of 'little tests and traps' for her, incapable of the spiritual growth that James intended him to represent.[31]

The novel does not enforce any one reading of Densher in the final chapters. One may interpret his refusal to deny his engagement to Kate when he last sees Milly as foolish inconsistency or as evidence of his sense of honour and fidelity to Kate. When at the end he does not give his 'word of honour' to Kate that he is not in love with Milly's memory, one can see him as acknowledging the truth of Kate's statement: 'her memory's your love. You *want* no other' (2, 435): or as wishing to spare Kate's feelings; or as uncertain of his own feelings; or as unwilling to make himself the cause of their final rupture. When shortly before Milly's death, he speaks to Maud Lowder of his last hour with Milly as 'his supreme personal impression' (2, 369), its effect as 'something [that] had happened to him too beautiful and too sacred to describe' (2, 373), he may be playing the part of the desolate lover that he knows both Kate and her aunt wish him to play. But the statement: 'He had been, to his recovered sense, forgiven, dedicated, blessed' (2, 372) carries the weight of the narrator's authority. Densher's refusal to accept Milly's bequest may be read as a sign of spiritual regeneration or simply as an act dictated by shame, by his need to expiate his guilt in lending himself to the 'dreadful game' he accuses himself and Kate of having played.

Because the text yields multiple readings of Densher it is difficult to say whether or not James intended to represent him as spiritually redeemed by Milly's death. What the novel does make clear is that Milly's generosity, moved by no hope of earthly reward, works more powerfully on Densher than Kate's celebrated 'talent for life', which under the pressures of circumstances and the needs of all three characters, degenerates to the point that she uses sexuality – her own, Densher's and Milly's – as an instrument of manipulation.

Milly's spirit is more powerful in death than in life, but the novel is not a celebration of death over life. The image of Milly facing death is not of one yearning to escape the pain of life but of one resisting to the last, clinging 'with passion to her dream of a future', torn from it, 'not shrieking indeed, but grimly, awfully silent, as one might imagine some noble young victim of the scaffold, in the French Revolution, separated, in the prison-cell, from some object clutched for resistance' (2, 370). Thus *The Wings of the Dove*, James's supreme tribute to the power of love in death, reaffirms, through

Milly's impassioned resistance, the words Ralph Touchett speaks to Isabel on his deathbed: 'life is better; for in life there's love. Death is good – but there's no love' (IV, 414).

III

A year after *The Wings of the Dove* appeared, James published 'The Story in It' (1903), a short tale set in an English country house where three characters – Mrs Dyott; her lover, Colonel Voyt; and her guest, Maud Blessingbourne – debate the question James had pondered for forty years: how love should be portrayed in fiction. Are the French novelists justly to be criticised, as Maude argues, because they harp on the same string, because they 'give us only again and again, for ever and ever, the same couple'? Or is Colonel Voyt right when he contends that there *is* only one kind of passion, one kind of adventure, one kind of relation; that a 'drama of virtue' is impossible because one must choose between passion and innocence? James presents Maud as the living refutation of the Colonel's view, for in her belief that she has hidden her love for him she finds her 'attachment', her 'passion', her 'little drama'.

No doubt there will always be readers to side with Colonel Voyt, to find James wanting because he held 'the shy romance' of the finer spirit superior in interest to the lovers' intimacy; readers who will sympathise with Forster's complaint that James makes his characters exquisite but sexless deformities whose clothes do not come off; readers who find in James's novels evidence to support Leslie Fiedler's claim that American writers have failed to portray mature heterosexual love. It is true that mutually fulfilling love is not the central subject in most of James's novels. From the early story, 'DeGrey: A Romance', to *The Sacred Fount* and *The Ambassadors* he was fascinated by the dynamics of relationships which force the sacrifice of one partner's vitality to sustain the other's. Likewise, James's novelistic sense of the dramatic effects inherent in acts of exploitation and renunciation dictated his choice of subjects. But the very fact that so many of James's characters yearn for the mutually sustaining love that circumstances deny them, that they seek to live in the imagination of such a love, attests to the power of the ideal, to the desire that remains to the end the animating force in the world of James's fiction.

Notes

1. Henry James, *Watch and Ward* (London: Rupert Hart-Davis, 1960) p. 70. Henceforth abbreviated in text as *WW*.
2. This group of characters includes, in addition to Nora, Pansy Osmond in *The Portrait of a Lady*, Verena Tarrant in *The Bostonians*, Maisie in *What Maisie Knew*, Nanda Brookenham in *The Awkward Age* and Chad Newsome in *The Ambassadors*.
3. James, *The Future of the Novel: Essays on the Art of Fiction*, ed. with an Introduction by Leon Edel (New York: Vintage Books, 1956) p. 39. Henceforth *FN*.
4. James, *Notes on Novelists* (New York: Charles Scribner's Sons, 1914) p. 300. Henceforth *NN*.
5. James, *The Theory of Fiction*, ed. James E. Miller, Jr., (Lincoln: University of Nebraska Press, 1970) p. 137. Henceforth *Theory*.
6. James, *Partial Portraits*, with an Introduction by Leon Edel (Ann Arbor: University of Michigan Press, 1970) pp. 254, 258. Henceforth *PP*.
7. James, *The Art of the Novel*, with an Introduction by Richard P. Blackmur (New York: Charles Scribner's Sons, 1934) p. 256. Henceforth *AN*.
8. *Henry James and H. G. Wells: A Record of their Friendship, their Debate on the Art of Fiction, and their Quarrel*, ed. with an Introduction by Leon Edel and Gordon N. Ray (London: Rupert Hart-Davis, 1958) p. 267.
9. Philip Sicker, *Love and the Quest for Identity in the Fiction of Henry James* (Princeton University Press, 1980) p. 19.
10. *The Novels and Tales of Henry James*. 26 vols. (New York: Charles Scribner's Sons, 1907–17), xxi, p. 217. Citations by volume and page number are to this edition.
11. James, *Washington Square* (New York: Harper, 1901) p. 260.
12. *The Complete Tales of Henry James*, ed. with an Introduction by Leon Edel (Philadelphia: Lippincott, 1961), i, p. 365.
13. James, *The Sacred Fount* (New York: Grove Press), i, pp. 135–6.
14. James, *The Wings of the Dove* (New York: The Modern Library, 1946) Book 2, p. 7. Henceforth references in textual parentheses.
15. D. H. Lawrence, *The Rainbow* (New York: The Modern Library, 1943) p. 389. Sicker, op. cit., pp. 140–4, compares James's and Lawrence's treatment of love.
16. Leon Edel, *Henry James: A Life* (New York: Harper & Row, 1985) pp. 108–12.
17. Joseph A. Boone, 'Modernist Maneuverings in the Marriage Plot: Breaking Ideologies of Gender and Genre in James's *The Golden Bowl*', *PMLA* (May 1968) pp. 374–88, offers a fine analysis of the way both Maggie and Charlotte are trapped by the conventions of the Victorian marriage. The analysis applies to most of James's women.
18. James, *The Bostonians* (New York: Dial Press, 1945) pp. 343, 345. Henceforth references in textual parentheses.
19. Lillian Faderman, *Surpassing the Love of Men; Romantic Friendship and Love Between Women from the Renaissance to the Present* (New York: William Morrow, 1981) pp. 167–77.

20. *The Notebooks of Henry James*, eds F. O. Matthiessen and Kenneth B. Murdock (New York: Oxford University Press, 1947) p. 47.
21. *Henry James: Autobiography*, ed. Frederick W. Dupee (New York: Criterion Books, 1956) pp. 560–1.
22. *The Poems of Emily Dickinson*, 3 vols, ed. Thomas H. Johnson (Cambridge Mass: Harvard University Press 1955), I, p. 339.
23. Flannery O'Connor, *Mystery and Manners*, eds Sally and Robert Fitzgerald (New York: Farrar, Strauss & Giroux, 1957) pp. 113–4.
24. Daniel R. Schwarz, *The Humanistic Heritage: Critical Theories of the English Novel from James to Hillis Miller* (Philadelphia: University of Pennsylvania Press, 1986) p. 25.
25. Parallels between Densher and the priest Caponsacchi in Browning's *The Ring and the Book* are noted by Ross Posnock in 'The Novel in *The Ring and the Book*: Henry James's Energetic "Appropriation" of Browning', *The Centennial Review*, 25 (Summer, 1981) pp. 277–93. Oscar Cargill, *The Novels of Henry James* (New York: Macmillan, 1981) pp. 338–43, contrasts James's recreation of the Tristan story with Wagner's 'Tristan and Isolde', Tennyson's 'The Last Tournament', and Swinburne's 'Tristram of Lyonesse'.
26. John Auchard, *Silence in Henry James: The Heritage of Symbolism and Decadence* (University Park: Pennsylvania State University Press, 1986) pp. 85, 89.
27. Gary H. Lindberg, *Edith Wharton and the Novel of Manners* (Charlottesville: University Press of Virginia, 1975) p. 47. The effects of voids and silences are also discussed by J. A. Ward, *The Search for Form: Studies in the Structure of James's Fiction* (Chapel Hill: University of North Carolina Press, 1968), p. 172 ff., and by Nicola Bradbury in her deconstructive reading, '"Nothing that is not there and the nothing that is": The Celebration of Absence in *The Wings of the Dove*,' in *Henry James: Fiction as History*, ed. Ian F. A. Bell (London: Vision Press, 1984) pp. 82–97.
28. Ward, op. cit., p. 181.
29. Ruth Yeazell, *Language and Knowledge in the Late Novels of Henry James* (University of Chicago Press, 1976) p. 56.
30. Daniel Schneider, *The Crystal Cage: Adventures of the Imagination in the Fiction of Henry James* (Lawrence: Regents Press of Kansas, 1978) p. 63.
31. Sallie Sears, *The Negative Imagination: Form and Perspective in the Novels of Henry James* (Ithaca: Cornell University Press, 1963) pp. 93–4.

6

Narcissa Benbow's Strange Love/s: William Faulkner

T. DANIEL YOUNG

Narcissa Benbow is a central character in three of Faulkner's works: two novels – *Flags in the Dust* (published in 1974, but written in 1927) and *Sanctuary* (1931) – and a short story, 'There Was a Queen', (1933). The history of Narcissa Benbow begins in overt serenity and moves through passion, fulfilment and frustration to perversity. The tragedy of Narcissa Benbow lies in her increasingly narrow and ultimately twisted sense of what it is to love.

The reader gets his first glimpse of her at a party in the home of Belle Mitchell, another resident of the town of Jefferson, Mississippi. Narcissa is sitting quietly at a card table watching her companions play out a bridge hand. She 'wore gray and her eyes were violet, and in her face was that serene repose of lilies'.[1] She is twenty-six and beautiful and Miss Jenny, Old Bayard Sartoris's eighty-year-old aunt asks her curiously, admonishingly, why she does not marry 'and let that baby' – Narcissa's thirty-six-year old brother, Horace – 'look after himself for a while' (33). She responds with composure that she had promised her mother she would look after him.

The time is 1919 and the Sartoris family is awaiting the return of Bayard, the grandson of old Bayard (president of the local bank), from World War I. During the war Bayard's wife and child have died and his twin brother John, a flier, has been killed in combat. That the returning Bayard is deeply disturbed is quickly evident from his behaviour. Before the train bringing him back to Jefferson from the war reaches the depot, he slips off it and goes to the graveyard to visit John's grave. His appearance in town is noted and reported to Old Bayard and Miss Jenny, and they are sitting on

88

the front porch when at about eight o'clock, he walks up. Before they can do more than greet him, he proclaims hysterically, 'I tried to keep him from going up there on that goddam little popgun . . . He was drunk . . . Or a fool. I tried to keep him from going up there on that damn Camel . . . I couldn't keep him from it. He shot at me' (44–6). When his grandfather and great-aunt can get Bayard calm enough to tell a coherent story, it becomes obvious that John has virtually (and seeming intentionally) committed suicide by attacking with inferior equipment an entire German squadron led by one of their ace pilots, a flier who had destroyed almost two dozen American planes. Bayard had taken off in attempt to aid John, but there was nothing he could do. After he has told his story, he goes to bed (in the bed in which his wife and son had died), but he has nightmares and yells so loud that he keeps Old Bayard and his Aunt Jenny awake.

Narcissa had become infatuated with the daring John Sartoris at first sight. On that occasion she had gone downtown to see a travelling show, which had as its main attraction a balloon ride. When she reached the show, however, she discovered that the man who was to go up in the balloon had been taken ill and the event had been cancelled. The disappointment of the crowd was so evident – an unbelievable feat they had travelled forty miles by wagon or horseback to witness for the first time was cancelled! – that John, after brief instructions from the carnival man said, 'I'll take her up', although he had never seen a balloon before, either. Narcissa watched him slowly ascend, 'feeling her breath going out faster than she could draw it in' (73). After it was up and floating away, she 'found herself clinging to Horace [her brother] behind the shelter of a wagon, trying to get her breath' (73–4).

The next time John and Narcissa met, 'his face was merry and wild and his unruly hair was hatless. . . . She gazed at him with wide, *hopeless* eyes' [my italics] (74). She's never been so consumed by feeling and by someone else; she's never felt the threatening lack of self-control until now. But this is only the first of many occasions when she is torn between adventure and security, sexuality and self-containment, brother and lover, conformity and self-expression. Now she is simply mystified. Before she can properly identify the complex of feeling, John is away at the war and is soon dead.

John's violence was spontaneous and merry, while the connotations of Bayard's, she would decide later, were appropriately cold and ruthless. Bayard would swing off a water tower on a rope and calculatingly drop into a swimming pool as he passed over it. She was glad her brother Horace was different. She thought of him as having a 'fine and electric delicacy' and she remembered 'to thank her gods he was not as they' (the Sartoris boys) (77).

In Faulkner's portrayal of the relationship between Narcissa and her brother Horace there is no overt statement of incestuous love between the two. However, Faulkner's description of their behaviour towards each other suggests that the relationship is very close indeed; unhealthily close. When he returns from the post he has held with the Red Cross (young Bayard has only scorn for these non-combatants), Horace is initially involved in getting the glass-blowing equipment he has brought from Europe off the train. (There are some resonances of inflation and enlargement here; it is a – disembodied? – sexuality to set beside the potent ballooning imagery associated with John Sartoris). He is so completely absorbed in his task that he is unaware of what is happening around him. Then he hears Narcissa's voice: 'He turned at her voice and came completely from out of his distraction and swept her up in his arms until her feet were off the ground, and kissed her on the mouth' (170). After a moment he exclaims 'Dear old Narcy', and kisses her again and begins stroking her face. He keeps repeating 'Dear old Narcy . . . gazing at her as though he were drinking that constant serenity of hers through his eyes' (171). A little later, after they have reached home, Horace asks if the Sartoris boys have returned home. Narcissa answers his questions and tells him that the young Bayard has bought a car which he drives recklessly around the countryside, almost frightening to death Old Bayard, who rides with him occasionally. 'Dear old Narcy', Horace says, dismissing what he has just heard, 'Well, it's their trouble'. Narcissa responds, 'I *am* glad you're home again' (177).

To add a further complication to her personal life, she has a secret admirer who is sending her anonymous love letters. She shows one of these to Miss Jenny, who makes Narcissa promise to burn it. But she does not. Many other letters follow this one; each one more personal until the writer is describing explicitly and lustfully what he would like to do to Narcissa. Each time she receives one of the mysterious letters she carefully hides it among her most intimate and personal possessions, her undergarments. She confesses to Miss Jenny that she showed the first letter to her because she 'wouldn't feel so filthy after I had shown it to someone else'. Miss

Jenny is suspicious. 'How can this thing make you feel filthy', she asks. Intuitive of Narcissa's secret reaction, Miss Jenny adds, 'Any young woman is liable to get an anonymous letter. And a lot of 'em like it. We are all convinced that men feel that way about us, and we can't help but admire one that's got courage to tell us about it' (70). Although Narcissa is forbidden by what is known as respectable behaviour in Mississippi in 1919 to admit even to herself that some man has imaginatively possessed her, the fact that she keeps the letters – and hides them where she does – suggests her true feelings. She is as guilty of sexual fantasies as her admirer; by showing her letter to Aunt Jenny she is indulging her eroticism as indirectly as her communicative yet evasive admirer. Narcissa harbours a sexuality that needs an outlet, a port. Neither her brother, whom she adores, nor Bayard, whom she declares she detests, nor her anonymous admirer, whose letters diagnose her while expressing him, seem to meet her needs.

The patterns of behaviour already established for the principal characters continue, and in a sequence of scenes Faulkner underscores the mixture of violence and sentimentality in both Bayard and Narcissa, and prefigures the history of the relationship. In an unmistakable attempt to destroy himself and anyone else who happens to be riding with him, Bayard drives at eighty miles an hour on what then passed for roads in Mississippi. One day he stops at the café in town, where he meets Rafe MacCallum, one of six brothers who live on a farm eighteen miles from Jefferson. Before the war John and young Bayard had hunted on the MacCallum place and nostalgically he and Rafe go into the backroom of the café, where they drink a bottle of moonshine. Almost drunk, young Bayard then goes with Rafe to look at a horse he is interested in buying. The horse is so wild that not even his owner can touch him. Suddenly Bayard leaps over the fence, grabs the rope tied to the horse's halter and after almost literally manhandling him gets close enough to spring on his back. The horse leaps over the fence and hurls himself down the street, running down and leaping over everything in his path.

> Bayard crouched on its shoulders and . . . swept past the motor car, remarking for a flashing second a woman's face [Narcissa's] and a mouth partly open and two eyes round with a serene astonishment. . . . Someone screamed from a neighboring

veranda and the group of children broke, shrieking; a small
figure in a white shirt and diminutive pale blue pants darted
from the curb into the street, and Bayard leaned forward and
dragged at the rope, swerving the beast toward the opposite
sidewalk. . . . The small figure came on, flashed safely behind . . .
and for Bayard a red shock, then blackness. (140–1)

Bayard, in shock, but having recognised 'the Benbow girl', is
taken to Dr. Loosh Peabody, the Sartoris family doctor for fifty
years, and seems, momentarily, to be in the bosom of the
community. Peabody bandages Bayard's head while he is still
unconscious; then when he comes to, gives him a stiff drink and
threatens to call Miss Jenny if he doesn't go straight home. Rafe
MacCallum promises to see that he does as the doctor ordered and
engages V. K. Sauratt (in later stories called V. K. Ratcliff) to take
him home in his Ford car that he has converted into a small van in
which he delivers the sewing machines he has sold to housewives
all over Yoknapatawpha County. But the whiskey Dr. Peabody has
given Bayard merely makes him want more to ease his aching head,
so Sauratt picks up a youth named Hub, who takes them out to the
barn on his farm where he has a gallon of moonshine hidden. Two
or three hearty turns at the jug make Bayard oblivious to his pain, so
he suggests that the three of them go to the nearby university and
serenade the ladies, which they do after going back to Jefferson
where they pick up another young man, the freight agent, and a
three-piece Negro band. At each of the residence halls, the band
unload from the back of the car and set up their instruments – a bass
fiddle, a guitar and a clarinet – and play a medley of old tunes, some
of which 'were sophisticated tunes and formally intricate, but in the
rendition this was lost and all of them were imbued instead with a
plaintive similarity, a slurred and rhythmic simplicity, and they
drifted in rich plaintive chords upon the silver air, fading, dying in
minor reiterations among the treacherous vistas of moon and
shadow' (155). After a while they play 'Home, Sweet Home', and
sing 'Goodnight, Ladies', by which time the girls have gathered on
the lawn in front of the building. They then drive over to the next
women's dormitory and repeat the same procedure. Finally they
visit Narcissa's house.

For Narcissa to register and to confront the volatile and over-
whelmingly physical Bayard is to admit her own complex nature,
and she is fighting against his presence, his significance, his

attraction, against the very thought of him. It is a classic psychological and sexual battle, a textbook case history.

> All of her instincts were antipathetic toward him, toward his violence and his brutally obtuse disregard of all the qualities which composed her being. His idea was like a trampling of heavy feet in those cool corridors of hers, in that grave serenity in which her days accomplished themselves; at the very syllables of his name her instincts brought her upstanding and under arms against him, thus increasing, doubling the sense of violation by the act of repulsing him and by the necessity for it. And yet, despite her armed sentinels, he still crashed with that hot violence of his through the bastions and thundered at the very inmost citadel of her being . . . [like] that mad flaming beast he rode almost over her car (158–9).[2]

But then she remembers that in utter disregard for his own safety he had thrown the animal onto the wet sidewalk to keep from killing or seriously injuring a frightened child, and that at the time Bayard had looked like a fine piece of Roman statuary. Recollection of the scene makes it impossible to eat her supper; and acting on an impulse she doesn't care to analyse, she gets up from the supper table and rings Miss Jenny to ask about Bayard. Miss Jenny responds that she has not seen him, that Dr. Peabody had telephoned at four o'clock and told her he was sending him home 'with a broken head', but she had not believed a word of it and doubted that she would ever see him again.

At this juncture in the story, to emphasise the variety of Narcissa Benbow and her range of options as a woman, Faulkner introduces two of the other men in her life. The uncontroversial, reassuring, placid Dr. Alford, another physician in town who has been trying for months to establish a formal courtship with Narcissa, calls on her, but her mind is so preoccupied with Bayard she has trouble keeping her part of the conversation alive. He represents a norm that is not, at this time, for her. Next she has another 'caller', the person from whom she has been getting the secret notes. Although each of them has become more and more evocative and personal, she has continued adding each letter to the packet in her underwear-drawer. 'He' is out on the roof outside the bedroom window so he sees Dr. Alford leave, watches her undress for bed, and observes Bayard and the three-piece band arranging their

instruments on the front lawn. Soon the singing begins and
Narcissa goes to the front window and listens while the Negroes
complete their repertoire. She recognises Bayard standing beside
the car and telephones Miss Jenny who cannot believe that Bayard
is serenading. Bluntly Miss Jenny asks why Narcissa is so concerned about him. After the recent, almost irrational tirade Narcissa
has levelled against him, the reader might well ask the same
question.

Narcissa and Horace try to settle in to the youthful pre-war
routine in which the two of them composed a completely self-
sufficient unit. 'I hate Bayard', she says more than once; 'I hate all
men. . . . I'm glad I have you rather than one of those Sartorises,
Horry'. His response seems the same. 'Dear old Narcy' (176–7). But
is it? Is Horace any more reliable than Bayard? He is spending much
time with Belle Mitchell, a married woman who lives next door.
When Narcissa learns they are having an affair, she lets her feelings
be known: 'You've got the smell of her all over you. Oh, Horry, she's
dirty'. When she tells Miss Jenny of Horace's indiscretion and of
complications between Horace and Belle, she sobs, 'I wouldn't have
treated Horace that way' (223, 227). She behaves like a rejected wife.

For the past several months the anonymous letters have come
regularly, and one day she tells Miss Jenny, surely only half in jest,
'I'm saving them until I get enough for a book, then I'll bring them
all out for you to read' (225). There seems little doubt that this chaste
woman with submerged unacknowledged incestuous designs on
her own brother is pleased that some man whom she does not know
thinks of her, as Miss Jenny would put it, 'in that way'. Faulkner
emphasises the almost inextricable mixture of self-knowledge and
self-deception in this sometimes satisfied, sometimes frustrated
woman. What is certain is that she still lacks the male focus she
seeks in order to define her role, her identity as a woman. Is she to
be mother? sister? whore? mistress? wife?

When Bayard wrecks his car in a ditch and is pinned under it
until he is rescued by a man and his son who just happened to be
passing in a wagon, he is critically injured and is confronted with a
period of convalescence in which he must lie in bed in a cast that
covers almost his entire body. Miss Jenny reports the details of the
accident and its devastating results to Narcissa who believes she
finds and to some degree genuinely does find the entire affair
revolting and repulsive. There are so many differences between a
controlled, civilised life – such as the one to which she has been

accustomed in the person of her brother Horace – and the raw, impulsive desire for violence and disorder that dictates the whole of Bayard's existence – that she can regard him only as some creature less than human. She is as relieved as she is appalled to think of him impotently confined in a plaster cast. Miss Jenny looks in amazement at Narcissa's expression when she invites Narcissa up to his bedroom, 'What's the matter?' Miss Jenny asks, 'You look worse than he does. You're as white as a sheet'.

> "Nothing," Narcissa answered, "I—, she stared at Miss Jenny for a moment, clenching her hands at her sides. "I must go," she said . . ."It's late and Horace . . ."
>
> "You can come in and speak to him, cant you?" Miss Jenny asked, watching the other curiously. "There's not any blood if that's what you are afraid of."
>
> "It isn't that," Narcissa answered. "I'm not afraid." But she was rigid with repressed trembling; Miss Jenny could see her teeth clenched upon her lower lip.
>
> "Why, all right," Miss Jenny agreed kindly, "if you had rather not. I just thought perhaps you'd like to see he is all right, as long as you are here. But dont, if you dont feel like it."
>
> "Yes, yes. I feel like it. I want to . . ."
>
> "What's the matter?" Miss Jenny demanded, still watching the other. "What happened to you? Have you fallen in love with him?" (242).

For once Miss Jenny's astuteness has led her slightly astray. She is anticipating the action of the novel. Narcissa proceeds up the stairs cautiously, aware of the rising odor of ether, and as she enters the room she views a Bayard she had not expected to see. His head lay on a pillow, 'pallid and calm, like a chiselled mask brushed lightly over with the power of his spent violence'. (The face she remembers and the one she expects to see is dominated by uncontrolled violence – the one swinging from the tower with his hands attached firmly to the end of the long rope, or the one with teeth bared trying to control the run-away horse, or the one filled with excitement as he swings his car in and out of a ditch attempting to avoid colliding with the wagon he is overtaking without having to decrease his speed.) 'You beast, you beast', she says thinly, 'Why must you always do these things where I've got to see you?' (243). The uncontrolled sense of self which he engenders and which, narcissistically, she resents (*she* wants to reflect her image; she doesn't want to know herself through him), threatens. For Narcissa, at this moment, hate outweighs love.

But her attitude soon changes, and she is reading to him – always keeping far enough from him so that he cannot touch her – and he is passing in and out of sleep because he cares nothing for books, has never read one voluntarily. She is usually careful to come out to Sartoris only when Miss Jenny or Old Bayard will be there, but one day she comes prepared to spend the day and finds they have both gone to Memphis. Bayard sees the look of concern on her face and asks, 'Why do you come when you don't want to?' 'Why are you afraid to talk to me?' As he lies helplessly in the bed she reads to him. When he closes his eyes and appears to be asleep, she quits reading, but he opens his eyes and says, 'Not yet'. So she begins reading again, a passage she has already read, and soon he is asleep again and has a nightmare. She is so frightened that she turns to run away, but he calls for her to bring him a cigarette. As she lights it for him, staring at him 'with ebbing terror and dread', he grabs her wrist and talks of his brother 'brutally', a story of useless violence and 'at times profane and grim'. She watches him with 'terrified fascination' and weeps 'with *hopeless* [italics mine] and dreadful hysteria' (280). His sexual presence, her sparking, supportive role and his dominance are now undeniable.

Once the crisis of admission is past, Narcissa moves into a new state of being. Fatalistic hopelessness is replaced not by hope but by certainty. In this affirmative, romantic section of the novel, Faulkner charts the growth of a full and mature relationship which involves mutual supply and demand, emotional give and take, increasing self and other awareness. Bayard feels the magic of the moment: 'Far above him now the peak among the black and savage stars, and about him the valleys of tranquillity and peace' (282). Narcissa confidently asks Bayard not to drive his car so fast again. For all that it proves ephemeral, his promise is given in earnest. When he breaks that promise, with Narcissa in the car, the violent side of her nature is positively aroused. 'Her crazed hands were on his face and she was sobbing wildly against his mouth' (292).

The marriage seems to work, then. Bayard begins to settle down and is content to supervise the farming on Old Bayard's place. Dutifully, pleasurably, successfully, Narcissa participates in Bayard's activities. After the crops are laid-by and the harvest is completed, she visits a cane-mill with him and watches the making of syrup. Leaving him to complete his business she goes back to the car.

> Then he would return and get in beside her, and she would touch his rough clothing but so lightly that he was not conscious of it, and they could drive back along the faint road, beside the flaunting woods, and soon, above turning oaks and locusts, the white house simple and huge and steadfast, and the orange disc of the harvest moon beyond the trees, halved like a cheese by the ultimate hills (315).

But the idyll is short. Narcissa can see Bayard's restlessness. Despite the fact that she is pregnant he drives the car with consistent and increasing recklessness. (Faulkner does not suggest this is because of the baby. Bayard is Bayard because of the loss of his twin and his first wife and their baby; because of the hopelessness revealed in man's inhumanity to men in war and because of the deathly, daring violence which seems to him less pointless and more enviable than anything else. Because he – and all men, all people – are, in Faulkner's motif word, doomed.) As he seems to relax, at the end of an opossum hunt on which she had accompanied him Narcissa discovers her own doom.

> Bayard was leaning against the tree . . . she moved closer against him. But he did not respond, and she slid her hand into his. But it too was unresponsive and again he had left her for the bleak and lonely nights of his frozen despair. . . . She took his face between her hands and drew it down, but his lips were cold and upon them she tasted fatality and doom (323–4).

She can't keep him in that peaceful and tranquil valley that she'd brought him to after his nightmare, and the echoes of that scene (278–82), are cruel for her. In bed there is an abeyance of 'the despair and isolation of that doom he could not escape' but it is temporary. Gradually she comes to realise that 'he doesn't love anybody. He won't even love the baby' (324, 331).

Narcissa's rationalisation of the failure of love to prevail – she subscribes to Bayard's nihilism – insulates her in an accentuated hopelessness that renders her tragic to the reader. When Miss Jenny asks her if she wishes she'd not married a man who was incapable of sustained love, Narcissa denies regretting it; she'd do it over again. Faulkner seems to approve, but with such dark resonances that this is a nadir in the novel's emotional statement, not an apogee. 'Without words they [Miss Jenny and Narcissa] sealed their hopeless pact with that fine and passive courage of women throughout the world's history' (331–2).

But if Narcissa is fatalistic she is also, for a time, nostalgic. After this conversation with Miss Jenny she goes into town and visits Horace. Briefly they re-enact their life together. On this rainy day he sweeps Narcy into his wet arms; and like a wife who has deserted him and repented, 'she clung to him again, wet clothes and all, as though she would never let him go. "Oh Horry," she said, "I've been a beast to you".' But they can't repeat the past; and for the time being rest in Horace's sombre vision of love: '"Clotting for no reason, breaking apart for no reason still. Chemicals. No need to pity a chemical."' (336–7).

Narcissa has also gone to town to re-enact her other strange love affair. She remembers those letters 'fretfully and with a little brooding alarm, deprecating anew her carelessness in not destroying them . . . and so entered again into the closed circle of her first fear and bewilderment' (333). She is relieved but distraught not to find the letters in their hiding place among her underwear. What if the letters had somehow fallen into the hands of some stranger? The prospect scares and titillates. Wildness privately expressed within the confines of marriage to the socially élite Sartoris seems to her to be irreproachable; but for the wildness that welcomed and kept and savoured such explicit and obscene letters to be exposed would be a public violation of the serenity that she cherishes as public surface and which is part of her substance, too.

Soon after Narcissa's visit to Horace, Bayard is racing with Old Bayard in the car with him when he sees a wagon directly in front of him; he swerves to miss it, and overturns. Old Bayard's ailing heart stops beating. Having effectively killed his grandfather, Bayard does not even go home. After a few days at the MacCallum's, he leaves Mississippi and except for occasional postcards, which are usually requests for money from Miss Jenny, he is not heard of again. Finally, he is killed as violently as he had lived, testing a plane so unreliable that no professional test pilot would test it. Narcissa has her baby – whom Aunt Jenny is already calling John, a family name for generations among the Sartorises, but Narcissa names him Benbow, the surname of her family. It is her name and (Horace's); not Bayard's; and in *Sanctuary* (1931) Faulkner indicates that Narcissa Benbow, who had sought to know and fulfil herself through a strange spectrum of lovers, increasingly refers only to herself and becomes narrow and warped in that unloving process.

The action of *Sanctuary* occurs about ten years after that of *Flags in the Dust*. As the story opens Horace is seen drinking from a spring on the Old Frenchman's place, now occupied by a bootlegger named Goodwin, his common-law wife Ruby, a half-wit named Tommy, and a senile old man who is blind and apparently dumb. As Horace drinks he is watched by Popeye, 'a man of under size, his hands in his coat pockets, a cigarette slanted from his chin. . . . His face had a queer, bloodless colour, as though seen by electric light . . . he had that vicious depthless quality of stamped tin'.[3] Popeye thinks a book in Horace's pocket is a gun, but Horace assures him that it is not, that he is merely a harmless lawyer trying to make his way from Kingston to Jefferson. Popeye allows Horace to ride into Jefferson on the truck loaded with moonshine whiskey he is transporting to Memphis.

When he arrives at Sartoris the next afternoon, Horace presents himself to Miss Jenny, and they watch his sister who is walking in the garden. They see a Narcissa who is physically changed since Bayard's death. Now she is 'a big woman' and her face is not so much serene as 'broad and stupid' (22). They are to discover a Narcissa who is emotionally crippled. She has been living, Faulkner writes, 'a life of serene vegetation like perpetual corn or wheat in a sheltered garden instead of a field' and during Horace's two days with her she 'went about the house with an air of tranquil and faintly ludicrous tragic disapproval' (85). Horace has left his wife. For selfish, passionate, unconventional reasons Narcissa had disapproved of his marriage to Belle Mitchell; she now disapproves for selfish, conventional, social reasons. Since he has broken up Belle's marriage to Harry Mitchell and taken Harry's daughter from him, too, Horace has certainly not acted the gentleman by leaving Belle after a mere ten years. And the only reason Horace can give for the separation is that he cannot face the prospect of having to transport a bucket of Belle's favourite shrimp from the railroad station to their home for the rest of his life. A reason worthy of the Narcissa of *Flags in the Dust*; a sign of the degree to which Horace has come to embody the wildness which once existed in Narcissa and which she now denies, with obsessive vigour, in Horace as well as herself. There is too much of the unloving and rejecting Bayard in Horace for her taste now.

Horace goes into Jefferson to live in his childhood home which he and Narcissa still own. When Miss Jenny asks why he is leaving Sartoris, he responds: 'It wasn't Narcissa I was running to. I haven't quit one woman to run to the skirts of another.' Now he speaks of 'Narcissa', not of 'Dear old Narcy'. Narcissa insists that Horace has walked out on Belle 'like a nigger' and mixed himself up 'with moonshiners and streetwalkers' (86, 104). This statement shows not only Narcissa's cavalier unfamiliarity with the facts (Horace has merely hitched a ride into town), but it foreshadows her future, perverting actions.

After he has been living again in Jefferson less than a week, Horace goes downtown and observes a crowd of people looking at the body of Tommy, the half-wit from the Old Frenchman's place, which had just been brought into the funeral parlour. Goodwin, the bootlegger, is accused of the crime and brought to jail. Although he is innocent, he will not admit he did not kill Tommy because he is terrified of Popeye, who had killed Tommy and then raped the student Temple Drake. When Narcissa hears that Horace has taken Goodwin's case, her reaction is immediate and certain and pitiless.

> "You're just meddling," his sister said, her serene face, her voice, furious. "When you took another man's wife and child away from him I thought it was dreadful, but I said, At least he will not have the face to ever come back here again. And when you just walked out of the house like a nigger and left her I thought that was dreadful too, but I would not let myself believe you meant to leave her for good. And then when you insisted without any reason at all on leaving here and opening the house, scrubbing it yourself and all the town looking on and living there like a tramp, refusing to stay here where everybody would expect you to stay and think it funny when you wouldn't; and now to deliberately mix yourself up with a woman you said was a streetwalker and a murderer's woman". (93)

Narcissa's enviable serenity has turned into a specious kind of moralising and her psychic wildness now merely reinforces her defences against real, full life. The positive if unconscious feeling of incest she had for her brother has given way to a fear of the way the community will regard his actions. She will have to share any disgrace he brings on the Benbows, and Benbow is her son's Christian name. Her concern, finally, is not really for her brother, but for the way in which her brother's actions will reflect upon her position in the community. Narcissa has become conventional.

The increasingly unconventional Horace insists that he must help Ruby Goodwin because she has no one else to turn to. Narcissa demands to know where she is staying: 'Did you take that woman in to my house?' Horace reminds her that it's his house, too. But Narcissa is unrepentently egotistical. 'The house where my father and mother and your father and mother, the house where I . . . I won't have it!' (94). (Though Narcissa has lived with a 'murderer' – Bayard, and has 'defiled' the house with her horde of sexually explicit letters.) Horace promises Narcissa that he will take Ruby to the hotel tomorrow. Miss Jenny believes he'd better because the opposition will think that the woman is paying in sexual favours for the assistance her common-law husband is receiving. Clearly that will not advance Horace's effectiveness as Goodwin's lawyer. Narcissa wants him to go back to Kingston, where Belle lives. As so often in this novel, Miss Jenny, Narcissa's constant companion, is used by Faulkner to diagnose and state Narcissa's feeling with a bluntness Narcissa avoids. 'Do you think Narcissa'd want anybody to know that any of her folks could know people that would do anything as natural as make love or rob or steal?' (95).

Horace goes back to town. He takes Ruby Goodwin to a hotel in the Sartoris coach and registers mother and baby. Then Isom, Narcissa's black coach driver, starts to drive Horace back to Sartoris. 'Miss Narcissa say to bring you back out home.' Horace gets out. He has acted on Miss Jenny's good advice, not because of Narcissa's provincial prejudices. The distance between brother and sister can barely be represented by the distance between Sartoris and Jefferson. Horace wants to be his own man; Narcissa, society's woman. And to an extreme degree. As Miss Jenny says, 'It is a good thing Narcissa ain't going to be on that jury'. Later she agrees that Narcissa 'has no heart. She cannot be satisfied with less than insult' (99, 102, 132). Indeed she can't. She activates the ladies of the Baptist church to get the hotel keeper to evict the 'disreputable' Ruby; she visits the District Attorney and casts effective doubt on Horace's professional propriety; she helps marshal 'evidence' against the innocent Goodwin. Horace's defence is demolished, Goodwin is lynched, and Horace himself seriously threatened. He crumbles under his sister's multiple assault, and returns to his life with Belle in Kingston.

The decline of Narcissa Benbow is completed in 'There Was a

Queen' (1933). The decline is not explained, exactly; as with so
much in Faulkner, it just is. Certainly Narcissa becomes increasingly repressed and overtly sexless, and the denial of life in herself
seems to generate a generally life-denying stance. She's worn white
ever since the first anonymous letter arrived; then she needed to
preserve and present the fiction of purity. Now she wears white
with what Faulkner calls 'the stupid impregnability of heroic
statuary' (*Sanctuary*, 85). Her decline has surely to do with this
tendency toward role-playing, too. She goes through some formal
flirtatious manoeuvres with Gowan Stevens, a lawyer; but like her
voice she is 'unbending' toward him. The failure of her love to
prevail and of Bayard's to survive, the losses that she believes
ensued from being the whole natural self she'd finally identified,
come to dominate her. She goes into reverse, as it were; denying her
abandoned love for Bayard and her almost abandoned feeling for
Horace. And in 'There Was a Queen' she also achieves a perversely
satisfying denial of her anonymous lover.

She has already guessed who had written to her; she admits that
the letters disappeared from her drawer the day she announced her
engagement to Bayard Sartoris, and that later in the day Byron
Stopes, the bank clerk, had run off with money stolen from the
Sartoris bank. And with her letters. She 'went crazy' for a while, she
tells Miss Jenny, 'I thought of people, men, reading them, seeing not
only my name on them but the marks of my eyes where I had read
them again and again . . .' Even 'when Bayard and I were on our
honeymoon I was wild. I couldn't even think of him alone'.[4] Clearly
the multiple violation is an act of her imagination and as willed and
desired as it is resented and feared.

Now a Federal Agent who is on the trail of the criminal Snopes
has come across the letters and visits Narcissa, ostensibly to see if
she can help him locate the writer. But it transpires that the agent
has had the letters for twelve years. *He* has hidden them and has
read them again and again. Now he'll send them to Washington
unless Narcissa, whom he's come to view as lustfully as Byron did,
buys them from him. And as she tells Miss Jenny 'I knew I couldn't
buy them from him with money.' So she says. So she meets him in
Memphis and sleeps with him. For the sake of the Sartoris name. So
she says. The reader detects another motive. Narcissa submits to, or
seeks, a multiple violation by another (a stranger, a Yankee and a
Jew, and a version of Byron) to cancel out what she perceived as
essentially a violation of herself by herself.

Narcissa recounts the scenes in Memphis to Miss Jenny with a frightening serenity. Securely, she can now call all men 'all the same' and 'fools' (221). And in a curious, silent scene she takes her son Benbow down to the creek in which they sit fully clothed for half a day. It is a perverse cleansing, and as much a burial as a baptism. Later she makes him promise with her 'never to leave one another' (222). She has transferred what strange love she still has to a boy whom she refuses to admit will ever be a man. She calls the last of her strange loves, her son, by the nickname Bory: a strange name, which suggests neither age nor sex.

Before Narcissa had decided to marry Bayard she had asked Miss Jenny's advice. It was characteristically blunt:

> I wouldn't advise anybody to marry. You wont be happy but women haven't got civilized enough yet to be happy unmarried, so you might as well try it. (*Flags*, 287).

Faulkner does not attempt to counter Miss Jenny's dry, negative, realistic advice; but his depiction of Narcissa Benbow is compassionate as well as clinical, and suggests that he finds it difficult to reconcile himself to the inevitable failures of women and men and love.

Notes

1. William Faulkner, *Put Out More Flags* (New York: Vintage Books, 1974) p. 31. Parenthesised page numbers are from this edition.
2. Perhaps Faulkner also endowed Narcissa with that clichéd feminine intuition here, for Bayard at this stage can be seen as a ritualistically wild young Southerner.
3. Faulkner, *Sanctuary* (Harmondsworth: Penguin Books, 1972). Parenthesised page numbers are from this edition.
4. Faulkner, 'There Was a Queen', in *Dr. Martino and Other Stories* (London: Chatto & Windus, 1958) pp. 219–20. Parenthesised page numbers are from this edition.

7

Ernest Hemingway: Men With, or Without, Women

BRIAN HARDING

'There are, however, no *women* in his books!' wrote Leslie Fiedler in *Love and Death in the American Novel* (1960). The 'however' was central to Fiedler's argument. Hemingway, he believed, was much addicted to describing the sexual act in his fictions – it is the 'symbolic center of his work'[1] – but since he did not succeed in making his females human, the sexual encounters described in his writings are either ridiculous or horrible; the 'women' are fantasy figures whose function is to gratify the men's desires, and the act is nothing more than a wish-fulfilment or, in Fiedler's brutally frank words, a wet dream. Since the strategy here, as throughout *Love and Death*, is to foreground the theme of male companionship in American literature, Fiedler's verdict on the women in Hemingway's fiction is hyperbolic, but that, perhaps, is a price worth paying for the perception that 'the West' in Hemingway is not limited to the geographical West of the United States but is a 'world of male companionship and sport, an anti-civilization' whether in the mountains of Spain or the hills of Africa. No reader who has shared Fiedler's embarrassment with the 'inarticulate sentimentality' of the dialogue between Jake Barnes and his arch-buddy 'Good old Bill' at Burguete can fail to be grateful for this perspective on the 'earthly paradise for men'. However, such a reader may well become suspicious when he is told that Hemingway is 'only really comfortable' when dealing with men without women and that the world of male companionship is 'simple and joyous'.

Leaving aside the possibility that the creator of Jake Barnes, of old buddy Bill and of good old Harris might have found them – at least

104

partly – ridiculous, we have to face the fact that Fiedler's thesis involves a misreading of an important story in the 1925 *In Our Time* volume: 'Cross-Country Snow'. To fit the schema, this must become a tale in which fatherhood is perceived as an irritating accident 'which forces a man to leave his buddies behind at the moment of greatest pleasure'.[2] Since 'Cross-Country Snow' has been almost routinely misread as a sad farewell to the 'simple and joyous' pleasures of bachelorhood in the Swiss mountains of 'the West', it is worth insisting that simple (male) joy is placed in a very complex human context in the story. Philip Young pointed out, long ago, that the Nick Adams of the story approves the idea of the baby, even though he does not want to return to the United States, but even Young – surely the most perceptive commentator on the *éducation sentimentale* of the young Adams – could find no more meaning in the tale than its opposition between 'the fellowship and freedom of the slopes, and the mixed blessings of the United States and parenthood'.[3] To be sure, the story does begin with a wonderfully vivid account of the exhilaration of skiing and the intense feeling of freedom in the mountains. What is more, when the two young men talk together in the inn after their run down the mountain, Nick begins by saying 'There's nothing really can touch skiing, is there?' Since he also states quite clearly that he does not want to leave Europe, his acceptance of the idea of becoming a father may be reluctant, or even grudging. Nick, presumably, is not happy about the restrictions adulthood will impose on the freedom not to give a damn about anything, yet when George says 'It's hell, isn't it?' and plainly expects his friend to concur in this expression of boyish resentment, he gets the reply 'No. Not exactly.'[4] Nick cannot say why he feels as he does, but his response obviously relates to his reply to an earlier question. Asked if he is glad about becoming a father, he replied 'Yes. Now.' The comments are terse and Nick is barely articulate, but the implication must be that he has begun to grow out of his boyish enthusiasms and fixations. That he is already more than a callow devotee of the simple life (and that he is anything but the obtuse extrovert) is clear from his earlier comments on the Swiss waitress. Both young men noticed that she was somewhat unfriendly, but Nick was the one to observe that she was unmarried as well as pregnant, and to deduce that she might well have been 'touchy' because of her awkward situation. There is no suggestion that George is a stupid or cruel young man, but there is an implied contrast in maturity and in sensitivity between the two friends. However, it is the near-silence of Nick's response to conventional male attitudes that indicates his capacity to respond to – and sympathise with – the woman with whom he is involved.

'Cross-Country Snow' is an important story because it skilfully evokes the world of male companionship, convincingly suggests the 'simple and joyous' life of the young man who loves sport, and at the same time offers hints and clues to a more complex and emotionally mature side of one young man's character. My purpose is not merely to reiterate the point – made effectively by Philip Young – that Nick Adams is portrayed as a highly sensitive and vulnerable boy and young man, totally unlike the caricature of the Hemingway male offered by Wyndham Lewis, but also to call attention to a distinctive feature of Hemingway's art in the early short stories. Repeatedly, in those stories, crass conceptions of masculinity and sexist attitudes to gender roles are expressed in the dialogue, while the silence, or near-silence, of Nick Adams implies his (and Hemingway's) dissent. The significance of what is said in the dialogue is determined by what is *not* said, by the implications of silences that indicate refusal to accept the confidently stated prejudices. This technique is not used only in the Nick Adams stories; it is a staple of Hemingway's art at this stage of his career. Its effect is to endorse – without any direct authorial intrusion – values and qualities such as sensitivity, emotional generosity and capacity for suffering that do not belong to the 'masculine' in any crude system of gender differentiation. The implication is not that Nick and the other sensitive males in Hemingway's fictions are 'feminine' but that the cultural code that identifies the manly with the hard-boiled is itself inadequate.

In the stories based on incidents in Nick's childhood, youth and young manhood, we watch him encounter or observe difficulties and anguish in heterosexual relationships. Two of the Michigan stories which deal with Nick's life before he leaves for Europe and the war are concerned with the breakdown of a love affair that might have led to marriage. 'The End of Something' tells of his rejection of Marjorie, a girl with whom (as we later learn) he has been sufficiently involved to talk of taking her to Italy. Nick has evidently planned to break with Marjorie while they are fishing together at Hortons Bay. He has talked over his plan with his friend Bill, who – once he knows that Marjorie has left – comes to ask whether she went without making a scene. There is something callous and even gloating in Bill's questions, as if he is glad to have Marjorie out of the way, but the episode has shown that the young woman is controlled and dignified, not at all the clinging female, and Nick's reaction to his friend's questions is to ask him to go away for a while and leave him alone. Clearly, Nick is not enjoying a sense of freedom or of triumph over his former girl-friend. The implication is that he feels wretched and far from elated. In the sequel – 'The Three-Day Blow' – when the two young men get drunk together, Bill congratulates Nick on escaping from a possible marriage with Marjorie and goes on to expound his young bachelor's philosophy: 'Once a man's married he's absolutely bitched. . . . He hasn't got anything more. Nothing. Not a damn thing. He's done for. You've seen the guys that get married'.[5] In this tale, the drunken bravado of the two young friends is treated with gentle humour by the narrator, but it is significant that Nick, who responds eagerly to the opportunities to talk about sport (baseball and fishing) does not endorse his friend Bill's remarks on marriage, even though he is obviously appalled at the possibility that Marge might turn out to be like her mother. In response to Bill's confident assertions, 'Nick said nothing'. The phrase is repeated more than once before Nick feels cheered by the thought that his break with Marjorie may not, after all, be irreparable. Though Bill suspects nothing, Nick clearly does not share his friend's confident (or brash) masculine code of independence from heterosexual entanglements. The possibility of picking up the relationship with Marjorie again does not horrify him; rather it gives him a sense of relief.

The two stories that deal with Nick's relationship with Marjorie show just how delicately Hemingway could treat love affairs in his fictions. The tone is assured in both tales and the ironies are mild. In both episodes the dominating voice is that of a relatively insensitive and dogmatic speaker whose lack of sensibility constrasts with all that is implied about Nick Adams by his silences. Because Hemingway has been celebrated as a writer who excelled at evoking scenes and capturing violent action in his prose, the skill with which he suggested intensity and complexity of feeling by a counterpoint of speech and silence has hardly been noticed. Consequently, some of his most intriguing tales concerning the relationships between men and woman have been interpreted without regard for their narrative structure. A further consequence has been that attitudes to love and marriage expressed within the frames of the stories are sometimes attributed to the author, with no recognition of the aesthetic distancing provided by the tale.

In Our Time is patently not a celebration of the simple joys of heterosexual love. Insofar as it is the fragmented story of one man's life, it selects those moments in his life when he learns that emotional commitment can be dangerous and destructive. The first lesson Nick Adams learns is that a man can be physically destroyed by his wife's suffering. It is not necessary to suppose that the Indian husband has been betrayed by his wife (in a liaison with the Uncle George of the story)[6] to account for his self-destruction in 'Indian Camp'. The horror of his situation is sufficiently explained by his helplessness throughout the protracted agony of the woman. But if marriage involves disaster from a biological cause here, in 'The Doctor and the Doctor's Wife', the next story in the sequence, emotional difficulties are seen to be almost as destructive. Dr Adams, it is clear, is being bullied by his Christian Scientist wife more subtly than he is bullied by the tough Indian named Dick Boulton, but the long-term effects of Mrs Adams' browbeating must surely prove more harmful. Nick's role is peripheral to the story's action but central to its meaning. His decision to go off with his father, though he knows that his mother wants him, clearly indicates where his sympathies lie. But neither parent emerges with credit from the episode. If Mrs Adams is infuriatingly smug in her piety, Dr Adams is dishonest both practically (the logs he intends to appropriate are clearly marked with their owner's stamp) and emotionally (he talks tough to the Indian, but he plainly does not want to risk a fight). In this painful encounter, the characteristic pattern of the early fiction can be seen: the dominant voices are those of the confidently insensitive characters (Mrs Adams, Dick Boulton), while the vulnerable and easily damaged characters either choose the wrong words (Dr Adams) or hardly speak at all (Nick).

Ad Francis, the former prize-fighter in 'The Battler', is a more obvious candidate for the role of the Hemingway 'tough-guy' than the weak and harassed Dr Adams, but Nick's encounter with the battler quickly teaches him that there are more ways than one in which a man can be maimed. Bugs explains that the beatings his disfigured and punch-drunk friend took in the ring merely made him simple; Ad Francis went crazy when his wife, who was an 'awfully good-looking woman' went off and left him. Ad's physical toughness and his ability to take physical punishment left him psychologically damaged.

Here, as in the earlier stories in *In Our Time*, the cruelty and the
brutality of life are registered by the painfully responsive Nick
Adams, who feels sick when he sees Ad's mangled face. We are not
told explicitly how he feels when he hears the story of the boxer's
life, but when he walks off into the darkness, Nick is too numbed
even to notice that he is carrying a sandwich in his hand.
Everything, it seems, conspires to warn Nick of the emotional
hazards ahead, and to teach him that love is dangerous and even
deadly, so the tough and bitter tone of 'A Very Short Story' might
seem like an inevitable climax of a consistently hostile view of
women. Yet the two stories in which we observe young married
couples – 'Out of Season' and 'Cat in the Rain' – focus on incidents
that show the men to be either insensitive and indifferent or
awkward and somewhat foolish. In both stories, though more
obviously in 'Cat in the Rain', the narrator is closer to the woman
than to the man and seems to feel with her rather than with her
partner. It may be, as has been argued, that the young wife who
feels neglected and frustrated in 'Cat' speaks rather petulantly and
whiningly,[7] but the narrator knows how she feels inside, whereas
her husband is seen from a detached point of view as an oafish,
brutish creature. The conclusion must surely be that the tales resist
any attempt to find sexual chauvinism in them.

The title of Hemingway's second volume of Stories, *Men Without
Women* (1927), could be taken to indicate that the young writer had
capitulated to conventional pressures, particularly when we know
that in his own gloss on that title he stated that the 'softening
feminine influence' was absent from his stories due to 'training,
discipline, death, or other causes'.[8] Clearly, that was how Cyril
Connolly took it when he reviewed the volume in the *New Statesman*
on 26 November 1927, for he asserted that the title was intended to
'strike the note of ferocious virility which characterizes the book'.[9]
Connolly made no attempt to justify his assertion, but it must surely
have been based on the assumption that such tales as 'Fifty Grand',
'The Undefeated' and 'The Killers' should be read as endorsements
for the code of physical courage necessary for the professional
fighter. To be sure, Hemingway's professionals do show courage,
but in each story the professionalism is undermined by corruption
and falsehood.[10] Brennan the boxer is himself corrupt. Garcia the
bullfighter is destroyed by the cynical commercialism of the
bullfighting business. Andreson is doomed to die because he is
double-crossed by the gangsters who control the ring. In none of
these tales can the virility of the fighter he abstracted from the

complexity of motive or mood attributed to him; nor is anything a
simple as 'toughness' the theme of these complex human situ
ations. Moreover, far from celebrating the sturdy independence o
the man who lives without women, the stories suggest the misery o
living without the sympathy and support of a woman.

The boxer in 'Fifty Grand' is obviously one of the 'Men Witho
Women' in the sense that he is separated from his wife while i
training for his big fight, but he makes no secret of the fact that h
hates to be away from his wife and family. Obviously strong an
brave, he is also a family man who gives no sign of enjoying th
possible camaraderie of the camp. On the contrary, Brennan
meanness with money (if we can believe our possibly unreliab
narrator)[11] may be the result of his lack of sympathy with the me
who work for him. In 'The Undefeated', Manuel Garcia seems to b
totally without wife and family – he is seen as a man very muc
alone in a harsh world of bullfighting as business – but even in th
story there are 'softening' if not 'feminine' influences, for th
picador Zurito shows a genuine concern for his old friend.[12] In 'Th
Killers' the cruelty and inhumanity of the adult world is registere
by the apparently marginal figure of Nick Adams. Nick's bri
attempt at heroics once he is untied – ' "Say, . . . What the hell?" H
was trying to swagger it off' – does not obscure the implications o
the conclusion: his sensitivity is such that he cannot bear even t
stay in a town where something as awful as Andreson's murder i
planned. In Connolly's scheme of values, Hemingway's ferociou
virility contains a latent sentimentality that is 'strong and silent
The formulation, like the judgement, is perverse but, if we reje
the question-begging 'sentimentality' and focus on the cruci
silences[13] in the stories, we may begin to approach their distinctiv
qualities.

In contrast to the stories so far discussed from the *Men Witho*
Women collection, 'A Canary for One' has nothing to do wit
boxing, bullfighting, or gangsterism. Instead, it is 'about' a
American lady who is travelling with a canary she has bought fo
her daughter. Thoroughly banal and inconsequential in its surfac
meaning, it may prove to be the keynote story in the volume whe
we examine the relationship between the narrative method of th
tale and the experience it conveys. The unidentified voice tha
begins to give an account of a train journey through souther
France could be that of a third-person omniscient narrator wh
is mainly concerned with the actions and the feelings of 'th

American lady' who is travelling with a canary she has bought in Palermo. The opening pages of the story contain a detailed catalogue of her trivial actions. She buys a half-bottle of Evian water and a copy of the *Daily Mail* in the station at Marseilles, but she stays near the steps of the carriage because she almost missed the train when it left without warning at Cannes. The narrator seems to observe the landscape from within the compartment of the train, but it is only after he has reported the American lady's fears of the speed of the *rapide* in the night and her cheery comments about the canary in the morning that he uses the first person and identifies himself as a fellow-traveller who is accompanied on the journey by his wife. Though his wife explains that she and her husband are both Americans, the narrator continues to refer to 'the American lady' when he reports her conversation, or rather her monologue, since she is 'a little deaf'. Later, he decides that she is 'quite deaf' for the narrator obviously perceives that the lady's inability to hear what is said to her indicates something more serious than a physical defect. He reports her words and opinions in what at first seems a natural tone, but the meticulous account of her banalities quickly builds an impression of a trivial and complacent woman who has an untroubled assurance that everthing connected with her life is worth mention. She has bought her clothes from the same *maison de couture* in the Rue Saint Honoré for twenty years now. The *vendeuse* there knows her taste and can select dresses for her and send them to America. This is the most important item of information about herself that 'the American lady' supplies, except that she broke off her daughter's relationship with a Swiss engineer two years previously and is taking the canary to console the young woman, who – as she says – was madly in love with her foreigner and who no longer takes an interest in anything. As dogmatic as she is trite, the American mother couldn't have her daughter marrying a foreigner because, as she repeatedly says, 'American men make the best husbands'.

In a very useful article on Hemingway's technique of omission, Julian Smith treats 'A Canary for One' as an example of the author's lack of faith in his own technique of leaving things out. The true ending of the tale, in Smith's view, is the bleak factual statement 'We followed the porter with the truck down the long cement platform beside the train. At the end was a gate and a man took tickets'. The sentence that actually concludes the story – 'We were returning to Paris to set up separate residences' – seems to Smith to be a concession to the kind of WOW ending that Hemingway explicitly rejected in *Death in the Afternoon* (1932).[14] But it may be that Hemingway included information that he might have left out in a different story because in 'A Canary for One' the text resonates with unstated ironies and makes the reader acutely conscious of *characters* who have been left out: the young Swiss lover who is, necessarily, the man without a woman and the desolate American daughter who is the 'one' for whom the canary is intended. The apparent displacement of interest onto the insensitive 'American lady' is this story's most striking characteristic. Without doubt the conclusion suggests a sense of loss and emptiness, whether or not the final sentence is effective, yet the bulk of the story is concerned with the platitudinous American mother; Nick is silent about his own emotional crisis until the last sentence. If the sole purpose of this narrative strategy is ironic deflation of the mother's fatuous opinion about American husbands, then the story is laboured and factitious. Possibly, however, the full significance of the structure is to be found in the characteristic contrast between verbal assertiveness and silence. The implication here, as elsewhere in the early stories, would then be that intensity of feeling and emotional vulnerability are present in inverse ratio to readiness to offer conventional wisdom about love and marriage.

'In Another Country', which was published in *Scribner's* in April 1927, is one of the most powerful of the Hemingway stories on the theme of love, though it begins as if it were concerned primarily with the physical courage of the military hero. The story is atypical in that its narrator (identifiable as Nick Adams from his wound and his recuperation in Milan) starts by using the first person plural. He tells us that 'we did not go to it [the war] any more. . . . We were all at the hospital every afternoon'. The sense of solidarity with the other wounded soldiers expressed by this plural does not last long, however, for the narrator admits that he was not a hero like the three young Italians with whom he walked through Milan from the hospital. They are hunting hawks, but he seems to feel for (or even associate himself with) the slaughtered game that he sees hanging outside the shop fronts in the town. Having been wounded almost by accident rather than as a result of an heroic action, the narrator of the story admits that he is 'very much afraid to die', and often spends sleepless nights wondering about his possible courage when he returns to the front. He feels most drawn to another wounded Italian who has not had a chance to prove his heroism and

ould probably turn out to be no more a hunter than the young
merican.

In this story, the confident voices are those of the doctors who
landly assure the injured soldiers that the therapeutic machines
ill totally restore shattered or withered limbs. The central dialogue
; that in which Nick and a wounded Italian major engage. The
najor, who has been a great fencer before a wound mangled his
and, has no confidence in the machines and does not believe in
ravery. His response to the professional optimism of the doctor
ho promises him full recovery is clipped and cynical. He amuses
imself by improving Nick Adam's command of Italian and insists
unctiliously on correct grammar. Military in bearing and ironi-
ally terse in speech, the major loses control when Nick tells him
hat he hopes to be married when he returns to the States. His
utburst, and his bitterness about marriage are explained when we
earn that the major's young wife, whom he married only after
eing invalided and thus safe from death in battle, has just died
rom pneumonia. The major's denunciation of marriage contains
he bitterness of a man who has been passionately in love. To 'lose
hat' means to lose the wife who, in the major's almost incoherent
utburst, is plainly 'everything'. Consequently, the effect of the
peech is to affirm exactly what it purports to deny: married love is
he supreme value for the man who experiences it. Its loss is
herefore devastating. The major's tears do not, of course, prove that
ne is unmanly; other details in the story establish his character as
oldierly enough to satisfy any code. His emotional outburst rather
hows that manliness is compatible with qualities of sensitivity
nd passionate love. Nick's response to the major's revelation is to
eel sick *for* him. Obviously the incident must increase Nick's
anxiety about his own emotional commitments, but it has also been
 lesson in the strength of love as well as its dangers.

'Now I Lay Me', the companion piece to 'In Another Country' (it
vas first intended as part two of the same story), shows Nick
Adams listening to another Italian who has decided opinions on the
ubject of marriage. Nick's orderly John is an American-Italian from
Chicago who has been conscripted while visiting Italy and has no
lesire to be a hero. John has a wife and three daughters in Chicago
and, though he wants a son, has suffered no tragic loss. His wife is
naking money for the family back home and John is absolutely
convinced that the wounded young Tenente Adams ought to marry
 rich Italian girl. Any Italian girl will make him a good wife says

John, ironically reversing the American mother's national prejudic
about marriage, because they are brought up that way. Nick i
unable to sleep without a light because the trauma of his woundin
has left him convinced that he will die if he sleeps in the dark. Th
sublime confidence of his orderly – 'You ought to get marriec
Signor Tenente. Then you wouldn't worry' – makes little impres
sion on Nick, who finds that his fantasies about trout streams ar
more interesting than his fantasies about the women he has knowr
His closing remarks are portentous. From an unspecified futur
point Nick looks back and states that he has never married, thoug
at his last meeting with John, the latter 'was very certain abou
marriage and knew it would fix up everything'.

The antithetical comments on marriage provided by the tw
Italian stories are none of them Nick Adams' own. He observes an
listens. In doing so, he vicariously experiences tragic loss an
complacent possession. He also learns to distinguish between th
sort of manliness represented by the three Italian war heroes (th
'hunters' of other men) and that of the major, whose physicz
bravery is not at issue but whose emotional commitment to
woman has made him vulnerable and has made him a comple
human being. Because of his tears, rather than in spite of them, th
Italian major is one of the most interesting presences ('characters
would not be the appropriate word) in Hemingway's short fiction

In both the early collections of short stories the theme of failure i
love relationships dominates to such an extent that it seems to giv
these volumes their coherence. Yet – paradoxically – the stories tha
deal with emotional frustration and the loss of love repeatedl
suggest the value of what has been corrupted or lost. Many of th
tales reveal the insensitivity of the male protagonist and clearl
indicate that the collapse of the relationship is due to his weaknes
or obtuseness, but my contention is not that Hemingway was a
secret champion of women who disguised his better nature under
mask of *machismo*; rather it is that he was, in the early stories at leas
a wonderfully acute observer of human interactions and a remark
ably responsive listener who devised an aesthetic that allowed him
to suggest emotions and states of mind ignored or despised by
complacent believers in sexual stereotypes.

According to Scott Fitzgerald, in the stories that preceded /

arewell to Arms (1929) Hemingway had been 'really listening to
women'. In that novel, in contrast, Hemingway was only listening
to himself.[15] Fitzgerald's attempt to account for what he obviously
considered unsatisfactory in the presentation of Catherine Barkley
may not be convincing now that we know that Hemingway actually
borrowed from Pauline Pfeiffer's love letters to him when he
created Catherine's self-abnegatory speeches,[16] but the older
novelist's response may yet have shown insight. The striking fact is
that in the text Catherine Barkley's voice is subordinated to Frederic
Henry's to such an extent that she is hardly a character, though she
appears in a novel that is constructed on conventions of character-
isation. The argument that she is a 'very real woman'[17] whose
apparent weakness can be explained by her troubled state of mind
(she is just clinging to sanity at the beginning of the novel) does not
account for the emptiness of Catherine's character. She exists, in the
text, only to be 'a good girl'; that is, to serve Frederic sexually.
Hemingway's reluctance to work in what he considered – in 1925 –
the 'awfully artificial and worked out form'[18] of the novel may have
been due to a sense that the method of implication through minimal
statement that he had developed in the short story would not work
to the same effect in a medium that, as he understood it, demanded
the creation of characters. Hemingway's difficulty may then have
been formal rather than personal. He solved it in *The Sun Also Rises*
(1926) through the exotic figure of Brett Ashley, whose British
idiom gives her a forceful, if not a subtle, presence in that novel.
With Catherine Barkley, the use of English idiom produces little but
rapidity.

The difference between the brilliantly resonant and suggestive
dialogue of 'Hills Like White Elephants' (1927) and the embarrassing exchanges between Catherine and Frederic cannot be explained in terms of a loss of sensitivity on the part of the author because
some of the stories in his third collection, *Winner Take Nothing* (1933)
are among his most successful in their use of a significant counter-
pointing of speech and silence. 'A Clean, Well-Lighted Place' works
effectively, through the contrast between the brash, uncompre-
hending speech of the younger waiter – whose 'confidence' makes
him impatient and unsympathetic – and the more hesitant comments of the older waiter, whose lack of confidence makes him less
ready to pronounce judgement on the old man. In this story, the
total silence of the old man who has lost his wife and lives on in a
soundless world without love is as resonant with implication as any

of the silences in the earlier tales. Another of the stories in thi
collection, 'The Sea Change', shows Hemingway at his mos
assured in the management of point of view. In it, the shock an
outrage of the young man at his wife's (or lover's) lesbianism i
experienced with immediacy in the dialogue, yet both youn
people are also observed as if from the detached angle of vision c
the barman, or even the other casual visitors to the bar, with th
effect that the moral righteousness of the man is no more endorse
than the self-pity of the male figures in 'Homage to Switzerland'

Winner Take Nothing has less coherence and is a less consistentl
powerful volume than either of its predecessors, but its best storie
show no slackening in artistic achievement. However, 'After th
Storm', which was to have been the title story of the volume, doe
show a significant change in the way in which the woman i
presented. The narrator, a simple, tough male who uses an idiom
that anticipates that of Harry Morgan in *To Have and Have Not* (1937
discovers a sunken liner off the Florida coast and is excited at th
prospect of the immense wealth that lies waiting to be picked up
from the ship. The liner is describes in conventionally feminin
terms: 'There I was looking down through the glass at that line
with everything in her and I was the first one to her and I couldn'
get into her. She must have five million dollars worth in her'. I
expressing his desperate longing to get 'into her' the man describe
his frantic efforts in terms that suggest sexual paroxysm and bring
the gender of the ship to grotesque life. He risks his own life i
trying to break through one of the portholes that he can se
tantalizingly deep in the water. Through the glass he can see a
woman 'with her hair floating all out' and he tries furiously to break
through to her. He lusts for money, of course, but the woman's body
clearly becomes an icon of desire.

In *For Whom the Bell Tolls* (1940) a shift from listening to women to
looking at them has obviously occurred, for Maria is there to be
looked at and desired. Robert Jordan tells himself to 'look at' her
When he does look it is to note that she is lovely and that she walks
as a colt moves. To Robert, Maria is a beautiful animal rather than a
complex human being: she is a colt, a kitten or a rabbit. When he
wants to take his mind off the task of blowing up the bridge, Jordan
tells himself to think about something else. That 'something' is
Maria's body, about which he fantasises. Before they sleep togethe
he imagines how 'smooth it would be, all of her body smooth'. He
has indulged in fantasies about many women before meeting

Maria. When Garbo came to his bed, in one of those erotic fantasies, it was to be fondled, to be 'just lovely to hold' and to be, of course, 'kind and lovely'. With remarkable self-awareness, Jordan admits that the women who have come to his sleeping bag have come 'when he was asleep and they were all much nicer than they ever had been in life'. Only Maria will be as nice in life as in his dreams, because she will act out his fantasy of the woman who exists only to be sexually gratifying. The war, and her rape at the hands of the fascists, have (in terms of her 'character') released her from the moral prohibitions that must have been part of the upbringing of a Spanish girl of her class; they have also released her into the world of male wish-fulfilment.

Maria's speech, when it is recorded in the text, is 'translated' into a stilted and unidiomatic English that inevitably suggests inferiority to the fluent, inflected language used by Robert Jordan. Perhaps Hemingway intends her to be charming when she says 'If I am to be thy woman I should please thee in all ways', but it is the charm of the naive and the childlike; the language robs her of adulthood. Renata, the beautiful woman of *Across the River and into the Trees* (1950), hardly has a voice at all. In the dialogue she either protests her love for Colonel Cantwell or attempts to please him by using American idioms of the sort he uses. In this novel, the emphasis on looking – on the male protagonist's gaze at the desirable female – reaches its climax in Colonel Cantwell's address to the *portrait* of Renata. The portrait, we are told, made no reply when Cantwell said 'I love you'. Renata's own replies contribute little or nothing to her relationship with the colonel, since she is there to be admired and desired. On her first appearance, Cantwell's opening remark is 'Hullo, my great beauty'. She has come into the room 'shining in her youth and tall striding beauty' which – we are told – 'could break your, or anyone else's heart'. So 'the girl' Renata exists in the text as an object to be looked at and even to be touched, for to Cantwell she 'looks as lovely as a good horse, or as a racing shell'. Her body is 'wonderful, long, young, lithe and properly built'. The arrogance and bad taste of Cantwell's 'properly' almost pass unnoticed in the constant tendency of the language to reify the woman.

The belief that Hemingway was always hostile to the woman in his fictions has been challenged over the past twenty-five years by a number of scholars who have pointed out that in the early stories at least some of the female characters are presented with sympathy and even admiration. As long ago as 1963, Alan Holder called attention to Hemingway's ability to empathise with the women in his stories of marital unhappiness, though he conceded that the dominant tendency in the writings was to look at women through the eyes of a man.[19] Holder also admitted that in his view Hemingway often displayed a deep hostility towards women. More recently, Linda Wagner has argued that the women in the early stories often behave admirably. Noting the qualities of dignity and self-control shown by Marjorie in 'The End of Something' and by Liz in 'Up in Michigan', Wagner claims that the short stories in *In Our Time* and *Men Without Women* show us men who need initiation and who either learn from women or fail to learn from anyone.[20] The women, in this view, display a semi-stoic self-awareness that anticipates the code behaviour of the later male Hemingway hero. Implicitly contradicting Fiedler, Wagner notes that Hemingway made few changes in the manuscripts of these stories; clearly then, he was most comfortable in these portrayals of women who command respect. Broadening the issue, Charles J. Nolan, Jr, states that there is a strong sympathy with the plight of women in Hemingway's work up to the late 1930s.[21] According to Nolan, the obvious sympathy shown by the narrator of 'Up in Michigan' with Liz Coates, who is casually seduced by an indifferent and loutish Jim Gilmore, is echoed in 'The Snows of Kilimanjaro', where Helen – the 'rich bitch' of the Hemingway legend – is presented as a good woman who has been harshly treated by life and by her men (including Harry) and who therefore has a just claim on our sympathies. Similarly, Brett Ashley is treated 'compassionately' in *The Sun Also Rises*, while in *To Have and Have Not*, Helen Gordon's diatribe against the male idea of love can be taken as evidence of Hemingway's understanding of the woman's (even the feminist) notion of sexual exploitation. At greater length, Roger Whitlow has offered a novel-by-novel defence of the fictional Hemingway women, arguing that they represent values (love and devotion) that are clearly superior to those endorsed by the men who follow codes of heroism or public duty.[22] In the short stories, Whitlow believes, the women – including the much-abused Helen in 'The Snows of Kilimanjaro' – are treated with sympathy by the writer.

Most recently, Kenneth Lynn has confirmed earlier critics' claims about Hemingway's sympathetic treatment of the women in his stories and, more importantly, has directed attention to the author's uncertainty about his own sexual identity.[23] Claiming that Hemingway has been misunderstood by those who have seen in his writings the values of the supermasculine man's man, Lynn has argued that the apparently unequal love relationships in which the man dominates the woman should be read as stories in which the leading characters are halves of androgynous wholes. Thus Maria and Robert, in *For Whom the Bell Tolls*, like Catherine and Frederic in *A Farewell to Arms*, are lookalikes and 'siblings' whose sexual identities merge to express Hemingway's most significant fantasy.

The notion that Hemingway was an uncomplicated purveyor of a simple cult of masculine toughness in his fictions surely cannot survive Lynn's penetrating comments on *The Garden of Eden*,[24] yet – for all its merits – Lynn's study has the unfortunate effect of treating the writings as symptoms of their author's psychological difficulties; it allows for little, if any, creative imagination or aesthetic distance. In 'The End of Something' and 'The Three-Day Blow', we are told, Hemingway was looking for a way out of his marriage with Hadley. In 'Cat in the Rain' he voiced his own unhappiness in marriage, using a female mask. 'In Another Country' was written because Hemingway had decided that marriage was the cause of all his own misery. If, as I believe, Hemingway's art in the short stories was subtle and resourceful enough to triumph over sexual stereotypes and devise forms capable of expressing his keenest insights into human relationships, he deserves credit for his remarkable ability to distance himself from his own personal prejudices and problems in these stories.

Notes

1. Leslie Fiedler, *Love and Death in the American Novel* (New York, 1960), reprinted in Robert P. Weeks (ed.), *Hemingway: A Collection of Critical Essays* (Englewood Cliffs, NJ: Prentice-Hall, 1962) pp. 86–92, as 'Men Without Women'.
2. Ibid., p. 87.
3. Philip Young, *Ernest Hemingway* (New York: Rinehart, 1952), reprinted in Weeks (ed.), *Hemingway: A Collection of Critical Essays* as 'Adventures of Nick Adams'. See especially p. 103.
4. *The Short Stories of Ernest Hemingway* (New York: Charles Scribner's Sons, 1952) p. 187.

5.   Ibid., p. 122.
6.   For the theory that the presence of Uncle George at the birth of the Indian woman's child can be explained only if he is the father of the baby, see Gerry Brenner, *Concealments in Hemingway's Works* (Columbus, Ohio: Ohio State University Press, 1983) p. 11 and p. 239.
7.   Gertrude M. White, 'We Are All "Cats in the Rain"', *Fitzgerald – Hemingway Annual* (1978) pp. 241–5, writes of the childish petulance of the wife's speech in this story.
8.   *Ernest Hemingway: Selected Letters, 1917–1961*, ed. Carlos Baker (London: Granada, 1981) p. 245.
9.   Connolly's review is reprinted in *Hemingway: The Critical Heritage*, ed Jeffrey Meyers (London: Routledge & Kegan Paul, 1982).
10. Edmund Wilson, 'Hemingway: Gauge of Morale', *The Wound and the Bow* (Cambridge, Mass.: Houghton, Mifflin, 1941) p. 220, nevertheless writes of the 'code' which supplies moral backbone in the *Men Without Women* stories. He argues that the drama usually hinges on 'some principle of sportsmanship in its largest human sense'.
11. Sheldon Grebstein, *Hemingway's Craft* (Carbondale: Southern Illinois University Press, 1973), argues that Jerry Doyle is an 'almost-reliable' narrator who is biased in favour of his friend Brennan. The relevant passages are reprinted as 'The Reliable and Unreliable Narrator in Hemingway's Stories', in Jackson J. Benson (ed.), *The Short Stories of Ernest Hemingway: Critical Essays* (Durham, North Carolina: Duke University Press, 1975) pp. 113–31.
12. Brenner, *Concealments in Hemingway's Works*, p. 22, takes Zurito to be a father figure and regards Manuel Garcia's attitude to the picador as a projection of Hemingway's wish to obtain the affection and approval of his own father.
13. Erik Nakjavani, 'The Aesthetic of Silence: Hemingway's "The Art of The Short Story"', *The Hemingway Review*, III, no. 2 (Spring 1984), pp. 38–42, writes interestingly on the importance of silence in the stories, but his discussion is entirely in general terms.
14. Julian Smith, 'Hemingway and the Thing Left Out', in *The Short Stories of Ernest Hemingway*, ed. Benson, pp. 135–47, reprinted from *Journal of Modern Literature*, I (1970–71) pp. 169–72.
15. Fitzgerald's comment was made in a letter to Hemingway which is quoted in Linda W. Wagner's '"Proud and Friendly and Gently": Women in Hemingway's Early Fiction', in *Ernest Hemingway. The Papers of a Writer*, ed. Bernard Oldsey (New York and London: Garland, 1981) p. 63.
16. Bernice Kert, *The Hemingway Women* (New York and London: W. W. Norton, 1983) p. 219, quotes passages from Pauline's letters which talk of merging her personality with Hemingway's so that they will become one person. In Kert's opinion, Catherine's expressions of her love have an 'identical ring' of Pauline's letters in 1926.
17. This is Roger Whitlow's thesis, in his *Cassandra's Daughters: The Women in Hemingway* (Westport, Conn.: Greenwood, 1984) p. 18.
18. Hemingway, *Selected Letters*, p. 156.

19. Alan Holder, 'The Other Hemingway', *Twentieth-Century Literature*, 9 (1963) pp. 153–7.
20. Wagner, op. cit., pp. 63–8.
21. Charles J. Nolan Jr, 'Hemingway's Women's Movement', *The Hemingway Review*, III, no. 2 (Spring 1984), pp. 14–22.
22. Whitlow, *Cassandra's Daughters*. See particularly, chapters 2 and 4.
23. Kenneth S. Lynn, *Hemingway* (New York: Simon & Schuster 1987), pp. 9–10, 388–9, 487–8.
24. Written 1946–58; posthumously published in 1986.

8

Some Kind of Love Story: Arthur Miller

ANN MASSA

Arthur Miller's theatre essays seem to suggest that relationships are at the centre of his oeuvre. 'The fish is in the sea and the sea inside the fish',[1] he writes. Man and society are inextricable and man can only be seen as part of a social unit: a community, a family, a marriage, a fraternity, a friendship. But Miller's practice seems to run counter to his theory. The most striking scenes tend to be those which poignantly isolate the individual; the characteristic conclusion that of *Death of a Salesman* (1949) when Linda Loman demonstrates that she's never understood her husband and Willy's sons perceive their father in diametrically opposed ways and where the most understanding figure is a fatalistic and helpless friend who sees Willy in quintessentially American terms as a loner and a never-satisfied entrepreneur. 'Nobody dast blame this man', says Charley. 'You [the family] don't understand: Willy was a salesman. . . . A salesman is got to dream, boy. It comes with the territory.[2] Dreams came, self-reliance was attempted; generations of actual wanderers and literary isolatos walked the American continent. The play focuses not on society but on an American Everyman figure. For, to paraphrase Melville, who ain't a salesman? Willy's all-American funeral is a parodic social act, in which the mourners signally fail to comply with social tradition. They do not suspend their differences to eulogise the dead man.

Many of the nostrums of Miller's theory would be difficult to predict from his practice. Which of the plays communicates the problem of 'How may a man make of the outside world a home?'[3] Which can, when the homes exist so minimally, so paradoxically. *All My Sons* (1947) perhaps argues for the extension of familial morals into society at large, though equally the play implies that the extended family in turn would derive its strengths from feelings of protectiveness, assertion and ambition. The plays don't encourage the concept of a global family, either. If *Death of a Salesman* is a play that works in England, Spain, Norway and Beijing, it does so because it has somehow allowed itself to be read in a bewildering variety of ways. What is universal in the Miller oeuvre is articulated in the sombre statement of *Incident at Vichy*: 'Each man has his Jew; it is the other'.[4] Miller's society is a jungle, and the dignity of the common man about which Miller writes so eloquently in the essays is markedly absent from the plays. It isn't dignity that Joe Keller or Willy Loman or John Proctor or Eddie Carbone or Victor Franz need or want; it's a view of things that gives them self respect.

D.H. Lawrence of course would argue that the best American artists are duplicitous. To make money, to be published and read, to be popular and profitable they have to tell the acceptably optimistic American tale. They have to subscribe what Edward Albee calls the peachy-keenness of American life. With the subtexts of their art, however, they tell another tale; of man's inhumanity to man, of a great experiment gone wrong. The ambiguous endings of Miller's plays would allow for Lawrence's reasoning. Is Willy Loman's suicide a triumph or a tragedy? Has Joe Keller properly atoned for selling faulty and lethal aeroplane components or is his death useless because by killing himself he's left a legacy of guilt to his accusing son Chris? Has John Proctor died for the sake of his image rather than for the sake of his soul?

If Miller's theory rarely seems to square with his practice, it is none the less an important body of writing about the theatre, provocative, ardent and thoughtful. It is, as Robert A. Martin says, because Miller is convinced that theatre should be a 'serious business'[5] that he's written about it so much. And in Miller's words, his theory (and his practice) is based on the assumption or belief 'that life has meaning'.[6] His theatre and his theatre writings seek to answer such questions as 'why a man does what he does;'[7] the wonder of how people got to be what they are; the search for cause and effect. With the human race for cast, albeit selectively, and the human condition for subject matter and with a stated preoccupation with 'The Family in Modern Drama' and 'Social Plays' it is surprising that Miller's plays reduce half of the human race, women, to such subordinate roles. When we discover that the real life story which sparked the idea for *All My Sons* was how a girl turned her father over to the authorities on discovering that he had been selling faulty machinery to the army, the feminist critique seems set. 'During an *idle* chat in my living room, a *pious* lady from the Middle West' [italics mine] told that tale to Miller. 'By the time she had finished the tale I had transformed the daughter into a son.'[8] Why? Perhaps because it seems to Miller that women don't understand. Kate Keller is made to believe in astrology and confronts the real world with disastrous maladroitness. Linda Loman rests determinedly and blindly in her perception of Willy as a man whose problems reside in material lacks and which can be solved by material things. Willy is made to turn to men only for help, and Miller insists that no woman could have helped him.

QUESTION: In *Death of a Salesman*, how much would you say that Linda was responsible for the destruction of Willy and Happy and Biff?

MILLER: I don't see her that way. If they had had another kind of mother and wife – well, it is already impossible because she is the kind of woman that Willy had to marry. It's inevitable that she be as she is. But I can't imagine that another woman would have made all that much difference to him.

QUESTION: You don't think she contributed to Willy's destruction?

MILLER When somebody is destroyed, everybody finally contributes to it. She would have contributed, yes, but I would have to add that I don't see what she could have done about it finally. She would have done different things maybe, but I'm quite convinced that it would have come out substantially the same anyway.[9]

Even Esther Franz of *The Price* (1968), a play from Miller's later and unstereotypical period is put down – or, rather, is seen to put down her own belief that if two estranged brothers can only talk things out 'some crazy kind of forgiveness will come and lift everyone up. When do you stop being so . . . foolish?'[10] Hers is a moving speech, and she's a more complex character than Linda Loman. She is cruelly analytical of herself – '*I want money*'. She knows she is restless and in need of variety: 'I can't go to the same place day after day.'[11] She's reckless enough to drink to excess and imaginative enough to see beauty in her solid, middle-aged husband in his policeman's uniform as he lunges incongruously with his fencing foil. But she is ultimately typecast as the sacrificial, subservient woman who puts the empty Victor first. Men prevail in this play, men like Solomon the wise, who forget the existence of daughters, who divorce wives, who can't remember how many wives they've had. Miller's ambiguous stage directions after Esther's last speech – 'she walks out with her life'[12] – suggests some sympathy for her, or perhaps an attempt to present her sacrifice as life-enhancing. However, hers is presented as the lesser sacrifice when compared with Victor's. He sacrifices not because of typical weakness or natural protectiveness but because of his love for starving humanity exemplified in his father. 'The icebox was empty and the man was sitting there with his mouth open.'[13] And because he wanted to prove to his father that if Mrs Franz responds to news of the Depression bankruptcy by vomiting all over her husband's arms and hands there is still a loving response – Victor's. The male embarrassment at emotional talk Victor justifies giving up medical school to support his father in grandiose terms which the play as a whole reinforces.

> You're brought up to believe in one another, you're filled full of that crap – you can't help trying to keep it going, that's all. I thought if I stuck with him, if he could see that somebody was still . . . I can't explain it; I wanted to . . . stop it from falling apart.[14]

Miller often seems to have made the decision to have neither women nor heterosexual relationships at centre stage. 'In its earlier versions [*All My Sons*] the mother, Kate Keller, was in a dominating position'.[15] Even given that the play in its final state centres on her husband it is curious that Miller reduces her to the status of caricatured mother and unconvincing star-gazing crank. The origins of *The Crucible* (1953) too lay in Miller's response to a woman's story. When he was researching the Salem witch hunt he noted that with uncharacteristic fastidiousness one Abigail Williams refused to include John Proctor in her swingeing indictments, though she'd worked in his house as a servant. Miller's interest in the odd version of the triangular relationship is preserved in the play; and indeed, he argues in an essay that the structure centres on John, Elizabeth and Abigail. But the shift has been from love story to 'the interior psychological question, which was the question of that guilt residing in Salem'.[16]

Nevertheless, the play offers some insights into Miller's view of the relationship between the sexes. He seems to be arguing the need for both art and creativity in love; the need for seasoning, for

skill in presenting the natural product. (John Proctor has surrep-
titiously to add salt to his wife's bland cooking). The play speaks
with puzzled compassion of the situation in which two women
each fairly feel they have a claim on the same man. Abigail because
'John Proctor . . . put knowledge in my heart' and because of the
importance she rightfully attaches to the 'promise made in any
bed'. Elizabeth Proctor wants to explain away John's adultery –
he's good but 'bewildered' and it takes 'a cold wife to prompt
lechery' and yet understandably insists she's 'your only wife or no
wife at all'.[17] There is a darkly realistic background of hetero-
sexuality; but it is Proctor's fixation with his honour, his need to
feel he is honest in ways which satisfy him that transcends any
exploration of sexual inevitabilities or a consideration of sexual
morals.

What begins to look like a tendency to avoid placing adult
heterosexual love or a woman at the centre of a play is evident again
in *A View From the Bridge* (1955), where the figure of Alfieri, the
lawyer, who introduces the action and comments on it, is used to
transcend or to deny issues raised by a man who denies his wife his
body (when it comes to the bed he does 'what I feel like doin' or
what I don't feel like doin' '), who tries to own his niece and who
insists crudely on the gratification of his impulses and his ego.
Morality is what he feels good after. He can accuse Rodolpho, his
wife's cousin and his niece's fiancé, of homosexuality; he can
inform the police that Rodolpho and his brother Marco are illegal
immigrants and he can then self-righteously demand that they
rescind their public identification of himself as informer in order to
restore his local image. But the edge is taken off the study of
individual, familial and social perversion by Alfieri, who talks of
fate, of disaster, of the inability of advice, legal or commonsense, to
temper 'a passion that moved into his [Eddie's] body'. Alfieri
diminishes the responsibility of Eddie's feelings, and denies
Eddie's culpability. It is simply a question of too much 'parental'
love. Correct the imbalance by shifting it to marital love. A study of
perverse machismo is thus presented as a tragedy of temperament
and forces, and the eminently indictable Eddie is given heroic
status as he dies in his wife's arms. His last words to her are '*My* B'
[italics mine]. Alfieri claims that 'something perversely pure calls to
me from his memory', though he hastens to add 'not purely good,
but himself purely, for he allowed himself to be wholly known':[18] a
sizeable caveat.

A sense of Miller's uncertain and evasive handling of sex and of gender, of familial and heterosexual relationships arises, then, from the plays themselves. This interior imbalance is in part explained by the theory that so often seems at odds with the practice. Miller's perspective is so broadly and deeply and ambitiously philosophical and metaphysical that at times it becomes depersonalising. He is concerned with abstractions. He writes of his interest in 'sheer process', of 'how *things* connected' and of 'the *geometry* of relationships',[19] [italics mine]. It is less this imaginary man and that imaginary woman and their unique relationship that concerns him; it is Man. For all his ability to make characters live, these characters are for Miller the embodiments of issues; they stand for aspects of the human condition or parts of the social structure. When he writes in his essays of 'man' and when he creates plays which focus on fathers, sons and brothers, he is writing of figures and relationships which are emblematic of the whole human race. If the means and the vocabulary seem chauvinistic, the ends are probably not.

However, since the mid 1960s there has been a shift in the Miller oeuvre to heterosexual concerns. (The exception to the new rule is *Incident at Vichy*, 1964, a play in which women are as appropriately off stage as in *Moby Dick* – the humiliating criterion of life and death being the circumcised or uncircumcised penis.) Maya, in *The Archbishop's Ceiling* (1977), has been mistress to all three male characters and is at very least an equal member of the quartet. Thornton Wilder, Clifford Odets and *42nd Street* inform *The American Clock* (1982), a slice of depression life which arguably lacks a hero and has Rose, if anyone, at its centre. The two-hander form of four recent short plays demonstrates that Miller has moved from the exemplification of issue to the study of character and relationship. In *Elegy for a Lady* (1980), an ageing man enters a boutique to buy something for his dying mistress; the proprietress of the boutique may or may not be that mistress. In *Some Kind of Love Story* (1983), a detective sustains a complex love-hate relationship with a woman he hopes will give him a lead in a significant unsolved crime. *I Can't Remember Anymore* (1986), is a sad and funny minuet performed by an elderly man and woman who once knew each other well, and perhaps still do; and in *Clara* (1986), we have, at last, a father-daughter relationship.

The two plays of this later period which most remarkably break the Miller mould are *After the Fall* (1964) and *The Creation of the World and Other Business* (1972). It is difficult to read the latter except as a startlingly imaginative and subversive account of the primacy of sex. Even in God – who though an almost human figure in his irritation and pettiness and capriciousness and greed (he's never tasted better lamb than the one Abel sacrifices) can't manage arousal himself and wants his surrogate to do it for him. He sighs as Adam kisses the trees as well as Eve. If Adam does touch Eve with his penis, mourns God, it's in the wrong place. Lucifer suggests reconstructing creation. 'Reroute everything, so wherever he goes in it connects to the egg.' Indecisive, incompetent, contradictory – this impotent God encourages Lucifer to bring about the Fall. That achieved, Eve, the only woman in the cast – though she is all women, too – renders all the men sexual, together with Lucifer and the archangels. A voyeuristic God watches Cain and Eve copulate ('Abel trying to hold out till Cain is done').[20] But in this play Eve is not the accursed universal temptress; the sexuality of the species seems to be rendered both pagan and divine. The issue of the fall into good and evil is only sketchily addressed, and sin is treated perfunctorily. The fall is into potency; the question is what to do with that power.

But it is *After the Fall* which is at the heart of the second half of Miller's oeuvre. For all his disclaimers about the degree to which the play is autobiographical and for all the need to respect the privacy of Miller's relationship with Marilyn Monroe she, perhaps, is the catalyst in his work. She has caused the shift in the Miller oeuvre from studies of relatedness to the exploration of relationships. They were married from 1956 until 1960. She died in 1962, when Miller was already two thirds of the way through writing *After the Fall*.

Reminiscent of Saul Bellow's fictional attempt to reconcile the culture of the schoolroom and the poolroom, Miller's real-life marriage to Monroe offered the image of an homogeneous America and a paradigmatic marriage: the reconciliation of mind and body, intellectual impulses and sexual ones, private personalities and public roles. Norman Mailer wrote in *Marilyn* (1973) of a marriage between the Great American Brain and the Great American Body. Perhaps a more accurate and less dramatic rendering of the marriage was that it asserted an intellectual dimension in Monroe and suggested that Arthur Miller's powerful plays were matched by his personal presence. Indisputably it was a dramatic link, dramatically forged. And it is hard to imagine that Miller's life and work – that anyone's life and work – would not significantly reflect a relationship with the extraordinary Marilyn: the sad,· funny, beautiful child-woman in search of herself and of a relationship in which the whole self would be permanently and uncritically loved.

With defensive reticence Miller's theory continues to assert that in *After the Fall* as elsewhere he is writing of characters whose gender is irrelevant. In 'With Respect for Her Agony but with Love' he refers to Maggie/Marilyn in terms that almost deny she is a woman.

> Maggie is a character in a play about the human animal's unwillingness or inability to discover in himself the seeds of his own destruction. Maggie is in this play because she most perfectly exemplifies the self-destructiveness which finally comes when one views oneself as pure victim. And she most perfectly exemplifies this view because she comes so close to being a pure victim – of parents, of a Puritanical sexual code and of her exploitation as an entertainer.[21]

Critics see Maggie the character and Maggie the woman as central to the play. Harold Clurman describes her as 'one of the most perceptively delineated women in all of American drama . . . Maggie is woman, redemptively sensual, intuitive, captivating, tormenting and tormented'. And for Clinton W. Trowbridge, Maggie is 'Miller's most fully realized and completely human figure of pathos'.[22] But Miller continues to deny Maggie's status in a play which 'is trying to recreate through one man [Quentin] an ethic on the basis of his observation of its violation'. *After the Fall* 'really is a play about the awareness of a man who sees what human nature is'. He wants to see Maggie as an incidentally feminine example of what Willy Loman had begun to represent – 'the push toward personal success that dominates America now [1966] more that it used to'. 'Maggie is obsessed by success, consumed by what she does. It's a jail. A prison which defines her, finally. She can't break through.'[24] Miller's theory attempts to shift the focus of the play away from Maggie the character, the person, to the theme she embodies: the success which instead of giving freedom of choice becomes an oppressive way of life. Once more Arthur Miller's theory depersonalises his play; once more the theory doesn't seem to square with a text which is explicitly about love and crucially about varieties of heterosexual relationships.

Whatever conflicts and obsessions have shaped Miller's theory, whatever theories and experiences have shaped *After the Fall*, in this play it is no longer 'sheer process itself' that fascinates Miller. Or 'how things connected'.[25] But how *people* connect. Miller insists that the play is not 'about something'[26] It is. It is about violence, choice, a fall into existential knowledge; about the impulses that generated concentration camps; but above all, about love. Enactments of love constitute its action; the exploration of the concept of love is the play's theme, and that theme is treated realistically and not abstractly; the word itself is the play's motif.[27] And anyone who saw the poignant performance of Frank Langella (television's Dracula!) as Quentin in the 1984–5 New York season will have seen how well *After the Fall* works when it is perceived and played as a love story. Conventionally, its central character Quentin has been discussed and portrayed as a self-referential man of severe limitations; a cold and selfish individual who can't feel appropriate guilt, sorrow, love; who can't feel for others, who can't understand, then, and therefore blames everyone except himself. But Langella and Miller have created a passionate man who is self-critical, not self-centred, who is ashamed of his inability to love consistently and unselfishly and greatly; who despairs of his failure to make his flawed practice match his high standard of perfectibility; who forces himself 'to face the worst thing I could imagine – that I could not love'.[28]

On the highest of the stage's three levels Miller sites 'the blasted stone tower of a German concentration camp. Its wide lookout windows are like eyes which at the moment seem blind and dark; bent reinforcing rods stick out of it like broken tentacles.' (11) The action on the two lower levels of the stage is generated by the operation of Quentin's mind. People from his past and present stand, lie, groan, gesture as he recalls and contemplates them. The initial starkness and dominance of the tower is undeniable; but as the play progresses the tower becomes first background and then another manifestation of the theme which is foregrounded on the two lower levels and on the rest of the stage. The theme is human relationships. For, as Miller says, the tower clearly expresses 'human separateness and its ultimate consequence'. He adds: 'In this play the question is, what is there between people that is indestructible?'[29]

What is indestructible for Quentin is the memory of the women he has loved and who have loved him. The most naive of men, he cannot understand that emotions can be ephemeral, that attitudes can change, that love can turn to hate, that love doesn't necessarily accommodate honesty. Most of all, this man, who wakes every morning hopefully as if starting life again, feels guilty at having life when others are dead.

In what is to become the pattern of the play, Quentin's opening speech is punctuated by references to women. 'Maggie died'. 'Mother died.' 'I met a woman' (Holga, the shrewd, chastened, compassionate survivor of all that Nazi Germany implied about the human race). He can't rest comfortably in these memories because they involve failed relationships, and in spite of the best intentions, in spite of loving, he has somehow contributed to those failures. A fourth woman, Felice, now appears briefly. Felice is peripheral in the action of Quentin's life, though she is to prove important for an understanding of it. Her calm, undemanding love for him – 'I'll always bless you' (16) – leaves him at this stage in the play bemused and envious.

Next the play appears to return to old Miller formulae. Quentin's brother enters and there is a sketch of the relationship between two sons and their father. But it is noticeable that it is not the mixture as before. The two brothers are not significant rivals; indeed, the rivalry of *Salesman* seems deliberately denied. So is the role-casting of fathers by sons as in *All My Sons*. When, a couple of months after Quentin's mother's death, his father seems to have resumed a normal life, Quentin is a little surprised and a little disappointed, but no more than that. There are denied echoes of *The Price* here. Quentin's father, like Victor's, goes bankrupt; and although Mother's first reaction is like Mrs Franz's – 'I should have run the day I met you'; 'I ought to get a divorce'; 'You are an idiot!' (29) – unlike Mrs Franz she makes the adjustment to her husband's reduced circumstances and her deepest regret is that Quentin takes her not unnaturally bitter words as her inflexible and final judgement.

John Proctor's agonies in *The Crucible* are undercut here, too. When Quentin admits to his first wife Louise that he has been attracted to another woman, he doesn't see why he should feel guilty. He's done the right thing: resisted the impulse to consummate the extra-marital sexual attraction. He's been honest and faithful. Isn't that love? He reacts indignantly when she's still judgemental. 'How much shame do you want me to feel? I hate what I did . . . I felt like nothing.' (48) But Louise cannot forgive, and Quentin cannot understand.

Miller proceeds to underline the ironic connection between

honesty and naivety. Quentin exhibits both those qualities yet is, in Miller's portrayal, less than admirable when he addresses the question of those subpoenaed for the McCarthy hearings. As he says to Mickey: 'But why couldn't you just tell about yourself?'(41) Following this speech, Maggie enters and lies down on the second platform. It is not a random association though Quentin takes some time to register the significance of the connection he is making. Maggie is later to enact Quentin's advice and tell about herself. 'You said we have to love what happened, didn't you? Even the bad things?'(94) And so, on their wedding night, she tells him why she went into analysis. Because she was 'with' two men on the same day.

Poor Quentin cannot practice what he preaches, and tries to conceal his disappointment at his average jealousy with a holier-than-thou spiel. Which doesn't convince or hold water. 'Sweetheart – an event itself is not important; it is what you took from it. Whatever happened to you, this is what you made of it.' 'The past' he says, 'is holy and its horrors are holiest of all'(95). The formula rings hollow; earlier he had given similar advice to Felice and had regretted it. 'Honey, you never stop loving whoever you loved. Why must you try?'(14) He then adds 'why do I make such stupid statements . . . These goddamned women have injured me'. He has to learn that his insufferable idealism is injuring them. And himself. He has wanted to believe in marital fidelity – his own – and that of his friend's seductive wife Elsie, who flaunts her nakedness before him as she changes out of a wet bathing suit in his bedroom. 'I tell you I didn't believe she knew she was naked! It's Eden! . . . Well, because she was *married!*'(32) Holga tries to teach him an appropriate cynicism, a realistic uncertainty.

HOLGA.   But how can one ever be sure of one's good faith?
QUENTIN.   (surprised). God, it's wonderful to hear you say that.
           All my women have been so goddamned sure.
HOLGA.   But how can one ever be?
QUENTIN.   . . . (kisses her gratefully). (23)

But he's still obtuse, and doesn't understand why Holga's words make him recall his mother's. 'When you grow up, I hope you learn how to disappoint people.' Quentin in the present responds: 'What the hell has this got to do with a concentration camp?' (25) The answer – that Quentin can't yet make – is everything.

Gradually, though, Quentin comes to debunk his Christ-like pretensions. 'What the hell am I trying to do, love *EVERYBODY*?' (83) He views the word love with increasing suspicion. Why 'is it that I'm looking for some simple minded constancy that never is and never was?' (46) 'Why do you speak of love', (80) he says to himself bitterly, denying the tenderness, the self-abnegation, the protectiveness – all aspects of love – in his relationship with Maggie (whose suicide seems to him to demonstrate his unquestionable failure to love). These are all aspects of loving which are tradition-ally associated with women and Quentin cares for Maggie like a woman. 'Dear', he calls her. He is mother, nurse and maid to her. And so, although most of the play's statements about love emanate from Quentin, Miller thus cleverly manages to avoid any notion that in Quentin he is writing about how men – as opposed to women – perceive love. He goes so far as to put Quentin in another traditional female position – on a pedestal. 'Adored again', (73) he groans.

In this deliberate, painful re-enactment of his attempts at love – so different from the memories which flood in on a helpless Willy Loman – it is the relationship with Maggie that brings Quentin's greatest self-awareness. He finds himself in the position of his first wife Louise, whose assertion of an independent identity within or without marriage has bewildered him. In Act One he's found it difficult to face up to her capacity to distance herself from him.

QUENTIN.   What's wrong with praise?
LOUISE.   Quentin, I am not a praise machine. I am not a blur
          and I am not your mother. I am a separate person . . .
          It's no crime. Not if you're adult and grown up. (49)

In Act Two Quentin's words could be Maggie's and Louise's Quentin's. Then Quentin says to Maggie: 'We are all separate people. I tried not to be but finally one is – a separate person. I have to survive too, honey'. (111) The tragedy of Maggie is that she can't make Quentin's compromise. She remains deeply romantic; she can't emancipate herself from the idealistic notion that she and Quentin can devote themselves exclusively to each other. On the basis of a loving, committed premise, she takes him for granted, as he has taken Louise's unquestioning devotion as read. Maggie can't accept the inevitable egocentricity of love that Quentin sorrowfully articulates.

QUENTIN.   (through a sudden burst of tears) Maggie, we . . . used
            one another!
MAGGIE.   Not me, not me! (113)

The emotions and the intellects of Maggie and Quentin take them to
different extremes: Quentin to the extreme of patient rationality,
Maggie to the extreme of impatient irrationality. Contemplation of
Maggie turns Quentin from a man of impossible hopes into a man
of viable practices; and arguably, contemplation of Marilyn Monroe
turned Arthur Miller from a playwright who attempted to transcend
human relationships into a writer who confronts them.

After the Fall confronts and does not resolve. It begins and ends
with the word 'Hello'. The first 'Hello' is tentative and is addressed
by Quentin to The Listener, his *alter ego* in this process of self-
examination. The last 'Hello' is addressed to Holga, and is spoken
by a Quentin who has acquired a good deal of self-knowledge and
some human wisdom. But if Quentin believes he knows, 'and even
happily, that we meet unblessed; not in some garden of wax fruit
and painted trees, that lie of Eden, but after the Fall', (120), Miller
does not imply happily ever after. Quentin is denying Felice's
blessing love; there is already a hint that in spite of herself Holga
will adore Quentin. But Quentin has found a theory which
illuminates and renders tolerable his human practice. If Maggie had
subscribed to the theory her suicide would have been unnecessary,
and so Quentin's philosophy is to a degree affirmed. And that death
– Maggie's, Marilyn's – is what leads Arthur Miller, to a degree still
evasive, to acknowledge indirectly that a Maggie or a Marilyn, a
woman, can be as significant and tragic a figure in the Miller oeuvre
as Willy Loman and company. The acknowledgement came in an
interview in which Miller said of *After the Fall*:

> There's nothing like death . . . There's no substitute for the
> impact on the mind of the spectacle of death. And there is no
> possibility, it seems to me, of speaking of tragedy without it.
> Because if the total demise of the person we watch for two hours
> doesn't occur, if he walks away no matter how damaged, no
> matter how he suffered . . . [30]

In theory as well as in practice then, Miller for once indicates that he
has decided to deal equally with men and women, and not to
subsume women under the heading Man.

An examination of the work that follows *After the Fall* shows Miller returning to the themes of that play: the place of sex in love; the desire to be loved uncritically; the dark suspicion that self-love always prevails; the inevitable failure of heterosexual relationships. But old habits die hard. Miller's theory still fails to suggest that he is writing love stories, albeit increasingly sombre ones. In *Elegy For A Lady* 'the Man' and 'a Woman' [italics mine] talk about nothing except varieties of love; yet the Author's Note describes this play as a passionate voyage 'through the mask of illusion to an ultimate reality . . . The unreal is an agony to be striven against and, at the same time, accepted as life's condition'.[31] There is still the tendency in Miller to describe his plays in the abstract terms which no longer seem relevant; perhaps because he finds the pursuit of love unremittingly problematic. 'How much of each of us is imagined by the other', he wrote in 1986; 'how we create one another even as we actually speak and actually touch.'[32] That grudging and tentative play-title, 'Some Kind of Love Story', accurately expresses Miller's reservations about the theory and the practice of love. [33]

Notes

1. Arthur Miller, Introduction to *Collected Plays* (1956), quoted in Robert A. Martin (ed.), *The Theatre Essays of Arthur Miller* (New York: Viking Press, 1978) p. 143.
2. Miller, *Death of A Salesman*, in Harold Clurman (ed.), *The Portable Arthur Miller* (New York: Viking Press, 1971) p. 132.
3. Miller, 'The Family in Modern Drama', (1956), in Martin, op. cit., p. 73.
4. Miller, *Incident At Vichy*, in Clurman, op. cit., p. 339.
5. Miller, Introduction to *Collected Plays*, loc. cit., pp. 122–3.
6. Ibid., p. 119.
7. Ibid., p. 117.
8. Ibid., p. 129.
9. Robert A. Martin and Richard D. Meyer, 'Arthur Miller on Plays and Playwriting,' *Modern Drama* xix, 1976, p. 378.
10. Miller, *The Price*, in Clurman, op. cit., p. 441.
11. Ibid., pp. 354, 359.
12. Ibid., p. 442.
13. Ibid., p. 423.
14. Ibid., p. 437.
15. Introduction to *Collected Plays*, loc. cit., p. 132.
16. Ibid., pp. 155–6.
17. Miller, *The Crucible*, in Clurman, op. cit, pp. 157, 189., 194, 196, 207.

18. Miller, *A View From the Bridge* (Harmondsworth: Penguin Books, 1971) pp. 45, 48, 69, 84, 85.
19. Miller, 'The Shadow of the Gods' (1958), Martin, *Theatre Essays*, op. cit., p. 178; Martin, ibid, 'Introduction', p. xviii.
20. Miller, *The Creation of the World and Other Business* (New York: Viking Press, 1973) pp. 14, 88.
21. *Life*, 7 Feb. 1964, quoted in Martin, op. cit., p. xxxii.
22. Clurman, op. cit., p. xxii; Clinton W. Trowbridge, 'Between Pathos and Tragedy, *Modern Drama*, x, 1968, p. 232.
23. Martin, 'Arthur Miller and the Meaning of Tragedy', Interview, *Modern Drama*, xiii, 1970, pp. 37, 38.
24. Olga Carlisle and Rose Styron, 'Arthur Miller: An Interview,' 1966, in Martin, *Theatre Essays*, p. 279.
25. Miller, Introduction to *Collected Plays*, loc. cit.
26. Miller, 'Foreword to *After the Fall*, 1964, in Martin, op. cit, p. 255.
27. Christopher Bigsby, 'The Fall and After – Arthur Miller's Confession', in Dorothy Parker (ed.), *Essays on Modern American Drama* (University of Toronto Press, 1987), comments usefully on what the play has to say about universal love.
28. Miller, *After the Fall* (Harmondsworth: Penguin Books, 1964) p. 116. All subsequent quotations are in textual parentheses.
29. Carlisle and Styron, op. cit., p. 289.
30. Carlisle and Styron, ibid., pp. 266–7.
31. Miller, 'Author's Note', *Elegy For a Lady* (London: Methuen, 1984) [iv].
32. Ibid, [v].
33. Miller's recently published autobiography, *Timebends* (London: Methuen, 1987), reinforces this essay's reading of Miller's attitude to his work. *After the Fall*, for instance, is still not so much about Maggie/Marilyn *per se* as about 'the complex process of denial [to which the individual contributes] in the great world' (p. 527).

9

'Not Avoiding Injury': Robert Lowell

JOHN A. WARD

At first it seems odd to describe the process of poetry as negatively as Robert Lowell does in the final poem of the volume named *The Dolphin*; the last eight lines of the poem titled 'Dolphin' read:

> I have sat and listened to too many
> words of the collaborating muse,
> and plotted perhaps too freely with my life,
> not avoiding injury to others,
> not avoiding injury to myself—
> to ask compassion . . . this book, half fiction,
> an eelnet made by man for the eel fighting—
>
> my eyes have seen what my hand did.
>
> (*TD*, 78)[1]

Injury to others and injury to oneself are peculiarly the product and problem for the autobiographical poet. But Lowell is proud of the accomplished poetic artifact; the only disadvantage is that he cannot ask 'compassion' and expect to get it.

Indeed, compassion was not forthcoming, but critical acclaim was: *The Dolphin* was awarded the Pulitzer Prize for poetry in 1973. Apparently, as he had in 1946 with *Lord Weary's Castle*, Robert Lowell had again fashioned a unitary volume of poems that expressed his own peculiar vision and successfully conveyed his view of his experience to a wide reading public. Although they interpret the volume very differently, Vereen Bell and Steven Gould Axelrod acknowledge the tendency of the series of sonnets in *The Dolphin* towards a plot, an implication that the love relationship chronicled in the volume has regenerated the poet and made the creation of the sonnets possible. Axelrod, who reads the volume as a single extended poem, puts the case positively, referring to the love

of Lowell for Caroline Blackwood: 'The progress of their love – her
giving birth to a son, his tormenting decision to divorce Elizabeth
Hardwick and marry her – became the basis for *The Dolphin*,
published in 1973. In this complex, beautiful, and deeply original
poem, Lowell achieved the artistic renewal he sought'.[2] Bell wisely
resists: 'But the *booklike* [italics mine] linearity of such a progression
cannot be accommodated by the form of real life'. Once again the
poet's awareness has subjected him 'to the incoherence of irreso-
luteness and ongoingness'.[3] The temptation to see such a regeneration may indeed be unwarranted, as Bell argues, but the volume
proposes a structure or plot familiar to a collection of love sonnets.
As a result, the nature of the love relationship described and the
effect of the love on Lowell's art is in question; does he affirm or
violate the integrity of his former and current loves by treating them
in detail and by name in his verse?

By introducing into that volume privileged material, letters and
statements by wives and children, Lowell provoked a critical
disagreement as lively as that between Axelrod and Bell on the
degree and effect of love's regenerative effect in *The Dolphin's*
sonnets. Whether the verse affirms or denies love's power to
regenerate, many readers are startled by Lowell's use of the real
names of his characters and his incorporation of their remarks in
extensive, albeit selective quotation. Reviewers as unlike one
another as William Pritchard and poet Adrienne Rich share this
response to *The Dolphin* and indicate that in this volume Lowell has
again, as he had in *Life Studies*, broken new ground in the use of
autobiographical and private material. Pritchard is mildly and
indirectly critical, concluding that 'one should feel uneasy about
this, should say at some point, yes Lowell has gone too far; you can't
turn life into literature twenty minutes or a year later',[4] but Rich is
outraged, referring to the final poem and injury done to self and
others: 'this is bullshit eloquence, a poor excuse for a cruel and
shallow book . . . it is presumptuous to balance injury done to
others with injury done to myself'.[5] Interestingly, both critics
change the pronouns awkwardly, Pritchard to the more impersonal
'one' and 'you' avoiding a direct attack on Lowell, whereas Rich
shifts the pronoun, in effect to imagine taking the blame herself,
appropriating Lowell's self in her sentence. Both pronominal shifts
remind us that charges of violation of privacy are familiar to Lowell
criticism; the critic is reluctant to see the new candour as requiring a
harsh reaction, whereas the poet can imagine herself making this
kind of autobiographical verse and is horrified. The issues of

naming and affirmation are, I believe, linked and even indistinguishable: Bell may be able to locate and articulate Lowell's distinctive kind of nihilism with particular clarity in his remarks on *The Dolphin* because Lowell seems to violate and invalidate love in this volume more clearly than ever before by making it so mercilessly and blandly public here.

The lover who describes erotic and amatory experience in verse has always faced the technical and moral dilemmas that are outlined above. Sidney and Donne and Yeats all confronted the question and addressed it with indirection or anonymity, protecting while celebrating the beloved, and thus proving the power of art to immortalise the love. Shakespeare's dark lady is dark still and Pasternak's Lara is famous in her fictive form, not as the love of his life. Pasternak puts the case for reticence most succinctly, and suggests that the problem is as much a self-absorption that borders on morbidity as a violation of confidence:

> The reason for his revision and rewriting was his search for strength and exactness of expression, but they also followed the promptings of an inward reticence that forbade him to disclose his personal experiences and the real events in his past with too much freedom, lest he offend or wound those who had directly taken part in them. As a result, his feeling, still pulsing and warm, was gradually eliminated from his poems, a romantic morbidity yielded to a broad and serene vision that lifted the particular to the level of the universal and familiar.[6]

Lowell, the confessional poet *par excellence*, breaks new ground, skirting the boundaries established by this tradition, trying to make private experience both unique and exemplary, providing details (places, names, comments, direct quotations) to demonstrate that his feeling is still pulsing and warm. Can Lowell both name and love – can he describe his own experience and honour its details without exposing his beloveds – children and lovers – to the scornful or curious scrutiny of the public? Or does he care less about such exposure than he does about candid revelation? In "Dolphin", the poet admits having

> . . . plotted perhaps too freely with my life,
> not avoiding injury to others,
> not avoiding injury to myself—

(TD, 78)

Rich is troubled by the implicit equation between the costs the poet pays for publishing his private experiences and the costs his intimate associates pay for his so doing; when injury has been done, where has love gone?

In *Life Studies* and *For the Union Dead* Lowell managed to describe in detail without naming. In the latter volume, particularly, Lowell's love relationships seem crucial to the structure of the volume and its accomplishment. In *Life Studies'* 'Man and Wife' and ' "To Speak of the Woe that is in Marriage" ' Lowell is just as confessional and specific as he frequently is in *The Dolphin*, but ultimately more successful; at least, in these earlier volumes he is not subject to the charges made by Rich and Pritchard. 'Water', 'The Old Flame', 'The Public Garden', 'Night Sweat', and others in *For the Union Dead* make allusions to particular people clearly enough for those in the know to identify them, but in *The Dolphin* the names used ('Lizzie', 'Harriet' and 'Caroline') explicitly make those people characters in Lowell's poetic fiction. Whether a significant portion of the reading public knew enough to invade the privacy of those names is only part of the question; Elizabeth Hardwick, Harriet Lowell and Caroline Blackwood must have felt exposed and knew that their experience and remarks were forever to be part of a public record, a record that sometimes abused them and left them no recourse but silence.

Thus I argue that when Lowell names in *The Dolphin* he shows us that he has lost confidence in the subtle, intimate, trusting pull of the beloved to help him out of mania into life and writing; the old intimacy and implication are gone, replaced by a sometimes coarse candour. The familiar shape of affirmation in the sequence of poems is still there, but it is wholly unconvincing. Lowell goes beyond the boundaries of the confidentiality and transformation so carefully established in *Life Studies* and *For the Union Dead* and uses names because the authenticity of erotic and loving experience is beginning to escape him, or has become too fragile or ironic to capture in verse. The volume of sonnets dedicated to love and restoration fails to present the reader with the poet as lover or the disabled man seeking love and health; it shows us instead Lowell trying to supply in artful lines a version of loving experience that proves love is powerless to save him, lost in life and writing. Indeed, it may show that he knew and wishes to demonstrate that love is and was powerless to save – a powerful revision of the tendency of a sequence of sonnets on love.

Let me describe my own response to *The Dolphin's* acts of naming – to its techniques of weaving in materials that readers and friends can readily identify, given the public's knowledge of Lowell's life. Although anyone acquainted with the highlights of Lowell's career can make the connections, Ian Hamilton's *Robert Lowell: A Biography* has made the act of identification much easier. We are now more surely aware of the violent but predictable swings of Lowell's mental 'health', and aware as well of the fact that he frequently associated the discovery of a new love with incarceration in hospital and the determination to be free and creative again. The cycle is perhaps clearest in the episode with Ann Adden, underlying the experience of 'Waking in the Blue' in March of 1958; elaborating the pattern the opening section of *The Dolphin* candidly describes mental instability ('*The hospital*. My twentieth in twenty years') and the hope for love's cure ('dolphin kissing dolphin'). What surprises is the section entitled 'Hospital II' in which we hear the irritated voice of the abandoned wife, clearly at a distance, clearly critical, speaking authentically, in her own voice. 'Voices' is apparently Elizabeth Hardwick speaking as she must have on earlier occasions. Earlier, her irritation (see Hamilton's account of her reaction to Ann Adden's relationship to Lowell) was out of bounds, not the stuff of Lowell's narrative. Now Hardwick's language and actions are placed before us, distinguishing between 'your real friends' and 'That new creature', asking for explanations: "Why in the name of Jesus" '.

My first reaction was shock at the trivial and conventional tones of these complaints, as if the language of the abandoned wife was too familiar to admit of poetry. My second reaction was my suspicion that by including this material Lowell was trivialising the person he had offended, turning her into a stock character but pretending to protect her integrity by seeming to quote her. The pretence was not enough, and when paragraphs like this one were produced as part of reviews, Elizabeth Hardwick was reportedly furious. Hamilton notes:

> For Hardwick, of course, these weeks of publication were acutely painful; her conduct, and her suffering, had been set up for idle public comment – the humblest of hack reviewers was entitled to muse on the half-fiction characters of "Harriet" and "Lizzie" and to ask which bits of letters were "real" bits, which burst of scolding dialogue was "fact", and so on.[7]

In his seventh chapter, titled with the final line of *The Dolphin* ('My eyes have seen what my hand did'), Vereen Bell makes an attractive case for the necessity and even fairness of including Hardwick's words: 'Lizzie's insistent presence in the book keeps alive the poet who finally puts the book together, and he concedes this readily'. But he is careful (or callous) enough to name her 'Lizzie' not Elizabeth Hardwick, maintaining the distance that Lowell creates in his half-fiction, and accepting the pseudo-intimacy that Lowell has created between reader and character. This argument depends on the assumption that the production of the verse is understood to be all in all by all participants. Once Elizabeth Hardwick has become the symbol or 'projection of the poet's dream'[9] named Lizzie, she can represent emphatically that 'other' who holds the poet's pseudo-regenerative love relationship up to appropriate scorn. But once the reader recognises the familiar, even sordid triangle, which the poet compares to the 'common novel plot' it is hard to feel that the end justifies the means.

Of all the poems in *The Dolphin* 'Records' presents the reader with the problem of the volume most clearly. How should one value these statements? Are they artful, crafted, and true enough to comprise a sonnet worthy of a place in a volume which won the Pulitzer Prize? Who wrote or compiled the quoted material? Under what circumstances was that material transmitted and authorised for publication? By using another's words does the poet expose his source to ironic subversion or invite the charge of plagiarism? Even the reader unfamiliar with Hamilton's biography suspects that these lines are excerpted from an angry letter from the Lizzie character. Can Lowell make poetry from words and images produced entirely by his wife, an accomplished author in her own right?

At least the poet titled the poem; as a result Lowell invites his reader to do what Lowell did when he first read the letter, to equate the sounds and memories embedded on the disks with other methods of transcribing reality, letters, poems, even thoughts. In addition, the last lines suggest that a poet is at work, as the speaker stops accusing 'you' (Lowell), and imagines a couple, a 'someone' who at first seems to be the new beloved and a man whose 'mysterious carelessness' vanquishes love:

> you doomed to know what I have known with you   1
> lying with someone fighting unreality—   1
> love vanquished by his mysterious carelessness.   1
>
>   (*TD*, 31)

At first, I assigned the pronomial roles this way: 'I' (line 12) as 'Lizzie' recalling lying with 'someone' (line 13) who is Lowell whose carelessness eventually destroyed their love (line 14). But the author of the original letter added another dimension with the predictive 'you doomed' (line 12). This phrase proposes a second simultaneous pronomial assignment: Lowell is soon to be 'lying' in bed as he has been lying by misrepresenting reality (line 13) in the company of another 'someone', who is herself fighting his tendency to produce fictions ('unreality'), and thus herself liable to suffer from his 'mysterious carelessness' as had her predecessor 'Lizzie', the author of the letter. The ambiguity of these roles is useful, for it illuminates the speaker's past position as well as it defines the accused's present state and future prospects. In both versions, Lowell seems bravely to accept the responsibilities of his mis-conduct by quoting the letter, but he has the final word insofar as he refutes the 'unreality'charge by honest self-critical quotation, even as he gives the author of the letter the space to say her piece and be 'admired' as (referring to my phrase used above) 'the poet at work'.

The complexity here *is* artful as it portrays the woman as both abandoned and abandoner. She can be perceived herself as the poet capable of defining the man's fault, recriminating, at the same time that she takes responsibility for closing off the relationship, challenging the man to test her hypothesis: this new love is to be 'doomed' as the last love was. Nevertheless, the nature of her words makes it easy for us to dismiss her. The casual quality of the woman's language, the repetitiveness and exaggeration, make the poem's statements seem deliberately trite in tone and common-place in content. She plays records, all her records; her heart seems to break a thousand times, but rather than not read his letter she'll have it break a thousand times.

'Her' lines are not finely tuned, spare, emphatic, rhythmic or whatever else poetry at its best might be; they do not allude to other poetic statements in any clear way. Lowell may allude in line 13 to earlier lines describing lovers in bed (such as 'in one bed and apart' in 'The Old Flame' or in the final lines of 'Man and Wife') throughout his career. The poet's craft is in part that of allusion as illumination; at least we may credit Lowell for creating both the original and the tendency of his readers to search his *oeuvre* for glosses. When we do search, however, we find instances (as my comments on ' "To Speak of the Woe that is in Marriage" ' will show) in which the woman is given a more authentic voice.

Elsewhere in *The Dolphin* the Lizzie character speaks in other

moods, two poems later contradicting her anger and resentment at
such false communication saying, 'I wish / I had your lovely letter
in my hand . . .' ('Communication'). And later ('In the Mail') she
says 'I long to see / your face and hear your voice, and take your
hand'. If it is hard in this sonnet sequence to conjure up a specific
shape for the poet, his mood and goal, it is equally hard to find a
consistent adversary in the Lizzie figure. Part of the problem surely
is that this figure is both pleading and complaining, two un-
pleasant, if sometimes necessary activities. But only rarely (as in
the 'old fashioned tirade' of 'Man and Wife') does her voice have
real resonance, nasty intonation and rich allusiveness. The image
of the woodchuck in 'In the Mail' is one notable exception, where
the woman as quoted moves from sentimentality – 'I long to see /
your face' – to the more appropriate image of a scruffy woodchuck
who weighs a ton and munches with 'your familiar . . . aspect'.
(*TD*, 41)

Here the woman seems to recall the skunk of 'Skunk Hour' ageing
gracelessly. Another fine passage in the woman's voice is in the
second part of 'Exorcism' where Lowell catches the explosive
rhythm of 'Don't you dare' as if it were an iamb – 'donchDare' – to
begin the penultimate line:

> *Don't you dare mail us the love your life denies;*
> *Do you really know what you have done?*

(*TD*, 41)

The automatic sign-off ('Love, Cal') concluding letters written
home while he pursues his new love is suddenly offensive to the
woman, who takes over the narration of this poem in italicised
lines. She senses the connection between his formulae and the story
he tells of discovered love. By contrast, his words are suddenly
vulgar ('one man, two women, the common novel plot') and he later
confesses in the 'Plane Ticket' section of 'Flight to New York' (*TD*,
72) to be replicating the triangle in Ford Madox Ford's *The Good
Soldier*, in which the man, Colonel Ashburnham, is the sentimen-
talist uncontrollably in love with a mindless girl. In these poems
Lowell seems to have created a genuine dialogue with the woman.
However, I conclude that this character is generally reduced to play
a part in Lowell's love story, and the part has got some – but not
many – good lines, certainly not enough to give the volume balance,
the balance of life or lively struggle. When the reader recalls that

this figure is a real person, the imbalance seems deliberately, even malevolently personal as well as technically intended.

If Bell is right, that the plot is not finally the progression of a successful love, and if I am right, that the apparent dialogue between man and wife is virtually a monologue, then *The Dolphin* may be only another volume in a series of efforts at self-fashioning, the poet ironically creating a new self out of the debris of his life, not even pretending to have accomplished his end. What this volume lacks is the authentic sense of threat or power in opposition; there is none of the pro-creative, challenging interaction that has character-ised earlier work. Elizabeth Hardwick is reduced to 'Lizzie', (while Harriet Lowell has become a parody of the grasping child, caught between separating parents) and illness itself no longer has the threat it once did, now that appropriate drugs have been found. Lowell has reduced the narrative of his life to meaningless play, with no stakes and no costs. The ninth section of 'Marriage' entitled 'Heavy Breathing' is relevant as a confession or at least as an explanation for Lowell's conduct, as poet and lover in *The Dolphin*. Initially he denies he is writing their life, for

> the fiction I colored with first-hand evidence,
> letters and talk I marketed as fiction—
> but what is true or false tomorrow when surgeons
> let out the pus, and crown the circus to see us
> disembowelled for our afterlife?
>
> (*TD*, 59)

Lowell might answer the rhetorical question that closes this sonnet by saying that all is equally true and false, as long as all is written, all poetry. Nonetheless, when he refers earlier to *their* book, he is misleading, for his experience is both shared and uniquely under his control as he writes. As long as Lowell presents his views, as in *Life Studies*, the fictions and facts are his, and so is the blame or credit. But this sonnet is loaded with the first person plural, and the people who share possession of that evidence, letters and talk are to be as disembowelled as the poet. Lowell's awareness of that threat is what pricks his conscience; is why he conflates the 'mine' with the 'ours'; is why he knows that although the burns are only superficial, yet they wound, will fester, require surgeons, and draw crowds, and that only he, having disembowelled himself re-peatedly in his lifetime, will feel no particular pain; will feel that all distinctions between fact and fiction are too arbitrary to matter. He knew that by naming he had crossed a boundary that other poets and lovers respected and feared; Lowell was always interested in exploring the outer limits of what his art could touch, describe, expose – 'a new frontier' (the phrase he used in the fall of 1957 in 'The Old Flame' anticipating John Kennedy's well-known challenge) – and in *The Dolphin* he scorned the limitations others wisely feared.

It was not always so. In *Life Studies* and *For the Union Dead*, Lowell wrote some powerful and affecting love poems without naming. Such poems serve both to describe the significance of the love of and for the beloved in Lowell's life and writing and serve the structure of the volume. They help the book-maker, the poet-architect, the lover-creator to accomplish something greater than the accumulation of statements, ideas and images in these volumes. Jean Stafford and Elizabeth Hardwick have both provided inspiration for these poems, yet are in the text only for the most determined of biographical readers and even then remain elusive. Consider the pair of poems that take the reader of *Life Studies* to the climactic and final 'Skunk Hour': 'Man and Wife' and ' "To Speak of the Woe that is in Marriage" '. The speakers of these poems (the man speaking first, the woman with the last word) achieve a partial, painful and somewhat distanced coupling, both in bed and in verse. These two poems testify to the paradox of simultaneous dependence and autonomy; the opposition between man and wife, a pair in agony, prepares us for a reading of 'Skunk Hour' that is neither simply hopeful nor absolutely desperate.

'Man and Wife' opens with two couplets:

> Tamed by *Miltown*, we lie on Mother's bed
> the rising sun in war paint dyes us red;
> in broad daylight her gilded bed-posts shine,
> abandoned, almost Dionysian.

(LS, 87)

The first line consists of a pair of trochees leading to three iambs, emphasising the power of the drug (Miltown, a tranquilliser frequently prescribed in the fifties) to create a conventional calm. The second couplet closes with a very fluid line, suggestive that the 'rising sun' has the power to render regular and graceful this bedroom landscape (as long as it is 'abandoned'; without the couple present!). Technique suggests order and harmony while the subject is separation and discord: an effective ironic start to a poem whose use of rhyme and metre contribute significantly to its ironic effects. The enforced and drugged calm of the first lines gives way increasingly to an apparent disorder, but rhymes in the first stanza link ideas and experiences ('glass' leading to 'pass' and 'mouth' finally to 'South' completing the tense scene of the remembered Village encounter).

The brief second stanza, without apparent or delayed rhyme, leaves the reader with a specific vision of the couple in bed together, yet far apart. With similarly productive tension in opposition, Lowell is both vague about the identity of the woman and precise about her loving invective, whose effect is as natural as the Atlantic Ocean, an effect uncontrolled and uncontrollable, but preferable to being 'Tamed by *Miltown*'. Invective now and tirade then define the beloved and her continuing love for the poet, but she is, unlike their friends the Rahvs, unnamed and 'still all air and nerve'. She is not explicitly given credit for bringing him back from mania: the crucial phase is 'as if you had', but her loving power and his appreciative response signal restoration.

In 'Man and Wife' and the poem that follows as a complement, '"To Speak of the Woe that is in Marriage"', Lowell has all his wits and craft about him. We seek the same complexity and craft in *The Dolphin* and miss it, or create it because we will it to be there: Axelrod for instance, finds a crucial couplet in the opening lines of the first poem and on the basis of that discovery, concludes that Lowell the sonneteer means to emphasise the power of love:[10]

> Any clear thing that blinds us with surprise,
> your wandering silences and bright trouvailles,
>
> (*TD*, 15)

If we sound the final 's' in "trouvailles," we may create the rhyme; Lowell tempts us to find the rhyme, but forces us to half-Anglicize the French when we do so. Is this gambit playful or careless? Does Lowell signal with such duplicity that he is aware of the lack of integrity in such a poem, in such a collection of poems? The reader does not have to work so hard or speculate so ingeniously in *Life Studies*, for Lowell has done the construction with care. The woman narrating '"To Speak of the Woe that is in Marriage"' is created in a sonnet made up of a series of couplets, a formal choice ironically referring to her husband's disintegrating form in the preceding poem ('Man and Wife'). He starts with a couplet closing with a feminine ending without the characteristic attendant double rhyme ('open' and 'happen'); a truly tricky device announcing that this poem, composed as it apparently is of quotations, will be artful. The relevant lines are:

> "The hot night makes us keep our bedroom windows open.
> Our magnolia blossoms. Life begins to happen."
>
> (*LS*, 88)

Conventional assignment of emphasis and syllabic divisions are subordinate in these lines to the conversational power and integrity of her voice; so the sixth line tempts us to abbreviate 'screwball' by syncope to create a regular pentameter line, and we might do so if we imagine the line exploding with her venomous emphasis. But the regularity of the line is no virtue in itself and the next line invites both possibilities: by syneresis to make 'monotonous' into 'monot'nous' and thus get pentameter, or to leave the eleventh syllable where it is and hear her dulled sensibility in the alliterated line:

> This screwball might kill his wife, then take the pledge.
> Oh the monotonous meanness of his lust . . .
>
> (*LS*, 88)

Either way, Lowell is inviting us to create the speaker's identity fully. We discover in Hamilton's biography that these lines are in fact derived from comments made by Elizabeth Hardwick, but they do not depend for their authenticity on our ability so to identify them. This sonnet is the 'tirade' or 'invective' that revives the poet in 'Man and Wife,' and the sonnet's title, derived from Chaucer's Wyf, reminds us of the rightness of her position. The woman speaking is no shrew, no bitch, no adversary; she sees the man's self destruction, and it draws her final comment. The poem prepares us for a last image of the man's violation or abuse of the woman, but we get instead the man, not the woman 'gored' and 'stalled'. Chaucer's Alyson, like the woman here, beats her man with a book, but in this poem Lowell is wise enough to allow Elizabeth Hardwick anonymously to strike him, and he takes the blow like a man.

The impression created by these two poems is of honest and artful play, a mature struggle between worthy and committed lovers. The woman is not repetitive, nor predictable. She does not stoop to clichés: she sees the 'swagger' not the 'stagger' in the drunk. This sonnet in contrast to 'Records' in *The Dolphin* shows us the abused wife in full and impressive control, and because she is more Alyson than Elizabeth Hardwick, the reader is empowered to see the general, as well as suspect the particular, significance of the portrait. Furthermore, as in *For the Union Dead* where the marital poems take the penultimate position in the volume and prepare us to read the last poem ('For the Union Dead'), in *Life Studies* we are now ready to see both sides of the final images of the poet as he is presented in 'Skunk Hour'. Placed as they are, 'Man and Wife' and ' "To Speak of the Woe that is in Marriage" ' suggest that some kind of marital strife as well as honest respect and love for the spouse is crucial to Lowell's writing. The image of the mother skunk rooting in the garbage is related to the preceding images from the natural world, the stalled elephant and the Atlantic waves, both placed at the close of their respective poems. But the image has more to do with the sexual politics of those poems. Lowell looks at the skunk as distinctly 'other' and admires its tenacity and unconcern; it seems to combine a concern for its offspring and a disregard for the approval of the world. It proceeds on its way naturally, suggesting the woman's relentless attention to her family and the poet's outrageous unconventionality, an impossible coupling of contraries, but the fantastic ideal of the volume nonetheless.

In *For the Union Dead* topics of sexual and by implication marital relations predominate structurally. 'Water', the first poem in the volume, sets the issue before us with the woman dreaming, anticipating Lowell's imagery in *The Dolphin*, that she is a mermaid. By trying to pull off the barnacles from the timber of a wharf-pile, the imaginary figure seems to yearn for the conditions of an ideal pre-history as well as guarantee the painful self-laceration that characterises all marital and love relationships in Lowell's poetry. As we turn to the next poem in the volume, 'The Old Flame', we are prepared for a closer look at the painful past history of that love, and we are not to be disappointed. But if we become curious about the biographical basis for this poem and we turn to the version of this poem in *Notebook* and review Hamilton's biography, we discover that Lowell is probably conflating in these two opening poems experiences with three women, giving the reader the impression that they are a single continuous sequence. Lowell's friendship with Elizabeth Bishop is the ostensible topic in 'Water'; the home mentioned 'belonged' to Lowell and Jean Stafford; the phrase 'ghostly imaginary lover' alludes to Elizabeth Hardwick's first novel *The Ghostly Lover*. 'The Old Flame' is thus emphatically an amalgam of many experiences, and any interpretation based on Lowell's life must be made very cautiously; equally, any one of the three women must have felt the public had no part in her private encounter with Lowell. Of course 'Your old voice / of flaming insight' takes us back to the 'tirade' and 'invective' of 'Man and Wife' and 'poor ghost, old love' is repeated later in 'Old Love' in the third section of 'Hospital II' of *The Dolphin*, clearly by now an exclusive reference to Elizabeth Hardwick. Between the indefiniteness of the allusions in 'Man and Wife' and the specificity of allusion in 'Hospital II: 3' lies the power of 'The Old Flame'.

The indefiniteness of reference allows Lowell to use specific past experiences with three women to introduce an implicit plot in *For the Union Dead*, a plot which Steven Gould Axelrod has usefully analysed.[11] Briefly, in the opening poems Lowell asserts a kind of control; gradually, in the middle of the volume, loses his sense of control and connection, and then makes a successful appeal for help and connection in the last pieces of the collection. Characteristically, the final poems in this sequence, 'The Flaw' and 'Night Sweat' (like 'Man and Wife' and '"To Speak of the Woe that is in Marriage"'), are a conscious pair both in form and allusion, and together they demonstrate that Lowell has emerged from solipsism into relationship; from despair to trust. These poems are heavy with allusions to Elizabeth Hardwick but do not name her, and by that indirectness manage to contribute more effectively to the volume which began with questions of marital relations.

In 'The Old Flame' Lowell asked his 'old love' to speak with her old voice of flaming insight presumably to help the poet see the critical distinction between 'the best' which the new folk have apparently accomplished with the old house and the painful past in which they were together 'awake all night', 'in one bed and apart'. The reader is at first puzzled, for the old agony and the scrubbed new cottage seem to have nothing to do with one another. We expect a bitter sneer at the New England kitsch which now covers their dilapidated place, but doubt after hearing the description of their life that Lowell could be ironic.

Health to the new people,
health to their flag, to their old
restored house on the hill!
Everything had been swept bare,
furnished, garnished and aired.

Everything's changed for the best —

(*FUD*, 6)

This jumble of private hell in the past and the public image of the
new folks' heaven is a deliberate attempt by the poet to articulate
his flawed or bifurcated sensibility; after all, the clichés of colonial
style on the scenic tourist road along the Atlantic all the way up to
Maine are often mocked, as in 'Skunk Hour' when Lowell described
the 'fairy decorator' at work in his shop. Lowell needs to hear the
beloved's voice for his private salvation and he needs its authentic
inspiration to see the public world more clearly.

An answer to Lowell's plea for help emerges in 'The Flaw', when
Lowell discovers a formal strategy: in a sense, a message from a very
old-fashioned muse. The entire poem is composed of five six-line
stanzas and a final couplet, all in pentameter lines. Lowell set the
poem up on pages 66 and 67 of the volume so as to set apart the final
fourteen lines on page 67, two six-line stanzas and the couplet, a
final sonnet that appears surprisingly as an almost separable unit.
In this sub-set of 'The Flaw' Lowell seems to be playing with a
notion of formal determinism, that is, the inevitability of the sonnet
form as a comment on his relationship to and understanding of his
beloved.

I feel that Lowell's use of the sonnet form in these poems is an
indication that he is in control of his artful world and communicat-
ing effectively with his beloved. The idea of coupling in couplets
was ironically proposed in '"To Speak of the Woe . . . "' and is
raised again in the thirteenth and fourteenth lines of 'The Flaw'.

Old wives and husbands! Look, their gravestones wait
in couples with the names and half the date —

(*FUD*, 66)

In a curious way, the effect of getting this couplet at this time is to
raise and then postpone the possibility of a sonnet; one feels the
tentative conclusion in these lines, and then one is rushed along to
complete the stanza. The 'sonnet' on page 67 concludes with

> Dear Figure curving like a questionmark,
> how will you hear my answer in the dark?
>
> (*FUD*, 67)

There is no clear sign that the lover hears and responds, except in the way Lowell forms the poem and completes the conversation in the next poem 'Night Sweat'.

If it seems a little too ingenious to see 'The Flaw' as a pair of sonnets divided by four lines, 'Night Sweat' is more obviously composed of two sonnets. The first is a conventional English sonnet, three *a b a b* quatrains and a couplet, almost too restrictive for Lowell the violator of conventions. The second is less constrained, although rhymed, ending with two lines that do not rhyme, although they have their rhyme words at a distance. The final seven lines begin:

> My wife . . . your lightness alters everything,
> and tears the black web from the spider's sack,
> as your heart hops and flutters like a hare.
> Poor turtle, tortoise . . .
>
> (*FUD*, 69)

As he does here, with 'spider's sack' and 'your back' (the last words of line 14), Lowell delayed the rhymes in 'Man and Wife' to suggest the divided but related nature of the couple in that poem; now his use of the sonnet form and delayed rhyme suggests a closer relationship. Furthermore, his assigning her the nicknames turtle and tortoise, ordinarily associated with Lowell himself (see 'Caligula' and 'The Neo-Classical Urn' in this volume) suggests that the transference and interaction has already been accomplished; that she heard his answer in the dark, Instead of naming her, he uses his own nicknames and thus confuses any attempt at identification, as he had early in the volume, by conflating experiences with three different women. The sonnet tradition of alluding to, but not exposing, the beloved is upheld and extended in *For the Union Dead*.

For the Union Dead is a volume with a purpose: Lowell seeks an authentic contribution or response from outside of himself and his increasingly directionless sensibility in order to write poetry. That contribution, that response, can be seen in both the beloved's tones and the forms of the sonnet. More and more frequently late in his career, Lowell employed the sonnet form, presumably because it embodied an authentic authority against which or within which Lowell could weave his verse. But failing to allow his lovers privacy, integrity and autonomy in these later sonnets (in the *Notebook* volumes, *Lizzie and Harriet* and *The Dolphin*), Lowell lost his grip on a resource he had found in *Life Studies* and *For the Union Dead*. The sonnet sequence in *The Dolphin* displays very little rhyme, uses a good many names, and varies the metre so endlessly that no norm is implied against which variants can be measured; by loosely employing the sonnet form while ignoring most of its technical possibilities, Lowell seems to proclaim that the sonnet form, however loosely employed, is a sufficient counterpoise to his own disorderly tendency to experiment with 'unreality'.

I infer that he finally decided that in disembowelling himself it was acceptable, even unavoidable, to disembowel others, as long as he did so within the confines of the honourable sonnet form. As previously mentioned, the verb 'disembowelled' appears in 'Heavy Breathing', the ninth section of the series entitled 'Marriage' in *The Dolphin*; there Lowell seems to blame such an act of dissection jointly on the 'surgeons', but would have to admit that he has invited their scrutiny. James Boswell two hundred years earlier seems to have been similarly ambivalent, wishing to preserve himself both for and from posterity, imagining himself to be safe within the conventions of another form, the private journal. Frank Brady, Boswell's biographer, quotes Boswell in his journal describing his wife's uneasiness about leaving a public record of private experience: 'My wife, who does not like journalizing, said it was leaving myself embowelled to posterity – a good, strong figure. But I think it is rather leaving myself embalmed. It is certainly preserving myself'. Brady continues, quoting Gray's 'Elegy':

> 'Ev'n from the tomb the voice of nature cries.' He had no doubt that, whether embowelled or embalmed, what would be preserved was the genuine James Boswell, so far as he could be known: he would be emBoswelled.[12]

A gifted poet, Robert Lowell was also gifted in the sense that he was lovable and often loved by those who saw his weaknesses ever so clearly. He 'Lowelled' himself in his last volumes, injuring others and himself as only he could, having violated the rights of his beloveds to express their love for him in their own fashion, unamended or distorted by his versions and revisions.

Notes

1. The works by Robert Lowell cited in this essay are *The Dolphin* (New York: Farrar, Straus & Giroux, 1973), hereafter *TD*: *Life Studies* (New York: Farrar, Straus & Cudahy, 1956), hereafter *LS*: *For the Union Dead* (New York; Farrar, Straus and Giroux, 1956), hereafter *FUD*.
2. Steven Gould Axelrod, *Robert Lowell: Life and Art* (Princeton University Press, 1978) p. 214–5.
3. Vereen M. Bell, *Robert Lowell: Nihilist as Hero* (Cambridge, Mass: Harvard University Press, 1983). p. 195.
4. Cited in Ian Hamilton, *Robert Lowell. A Biography* (London: Faber & Faber, 1982) p. 432.
5. Ibid.
6. Boris Pasternak, *Dr. Zhivago* (New York: Pantheon Books, 1958) p. 453.
7. Hamilton, pp. 244–9.
8. Bell, p. 201.
9. Ibid., p. 198.
10. Axelrod, pp. 218–9.
11. Ibid., pp. 140–4.
12. Frank Brady, *James Boswell. The Later Years, 1769–1795* (New York: McGraw-Hill, 1984) p. 148.

10

Debate in the Dark: Love in Italian-American Fiction

ROBERT VISCUSI

Italians, according to stereotype, make great lovers. Like most stereotypes, this one is true but not true enough. It leaves out something important in the interest of rendering its object relatively harmless. Thus, if one says the poor are shiftless, one is unlikely to want to add why it is that they cannot find decent jobs. Women are hysterical if you refuse to listen to anything they say except with their bodies. And so on. Italians are great lovers to people who would rather not think of them as economic or political agents. This is a peculiar and, in Italian history, a profound reality. The lay theology of heterosexual love, though its early development took place elsewhere, reached a spectacular pitch of elaboration in thirteenth and fourteenth-century Italy precisely as a way of endowing with effective agency forms of feeling that had no other avenue of expression. That is, the great new language of love one finds in Dante and Petrarca and Boccaccio is most clearly seen as a way of legitimising the dignity of the uxorious burgher against the systematic linguistic and ritual exclusion long practised by a powerfully homosexual priestly hierarchy. The medieval church was a club of men who preached salvation and lent money.[1] The Trecento poets found a way of identifying women with apocalyptic fulfilment (Beatrice in Paradise), ships and armies (Laura beyond reach), and Fortuna, the atavistic fertility goddess of Italy (every other woman in the Decameron).[2] The innovation was so successful that Italians have never forgotten it; never ceased to cherish and sanctify this among all their literary traditions, because their war against the corporation of monks has never ended. It is not impossible that Italians are great lovers because their priests are very rich.

155

This tradition, which thrives in folklore (and always has) no less than in high literature, has served Italian migrants to the United States of America very well. In America, the Italians encountered two priesthoods: the Irish Catholics, no less homophiliac than the priests encountered in Italy, and the married clergy of the various protestant sects. Italian Americans have had very little difficulty resisting inducements to affirm the Irish Catholic clergy, who lack the Franciscan poetry that sometimes distinguishes Italian priests.[3] Arguably, too, the protestant clergy carry a virus of apocalyptic homosexuality, no doubt inherited from Martin Luther, that can make them very tiresome indeed; that they have had a dreadful effect on the affectional life of Americans is the thesis, more or less, of Professor Fiedler's five-hundred page pamphlet, and to some extent he is right. But it is equally true that bourgeois artists have fought a long hard and mostly successful battle against this fundamentally feudal and monastic tradition in interpersonal relations – a struggle very fully recorded, it seems to me, in the pages of *The Scarlet Letter* and *The Ambassadors*. In the still-young tradition of Italian-American fiction the struggle, indeed, *qua* struggle, scarcely exists at all. Italian migrants came to America quite fully convinced, both by experience and by anticlerical folk tradition, that apocalyptic or homosexual religion was a dangerous thing and that love and marriage had profound economic, political and emotional values. In Italian-American fiction, the question is not much whether men shall love women. The question is rather, in this new country, so suddenly and so miraculously escaped as they find themselves from bishops and barons alike, which woman shall they marry. This problem is obviously a practical one in any situation. But in America, it also becomes a theoretical question, because for Italians, as for most American immigrants since the Civil War, the problem is not priests but outsiders. The mass migrations of the late nineteenth and early twentieth centuries made ethnicity into a vast field of inquiry. At first, it interested mainly the agents of social control: the immigration officers, social workers, police, politicians.[4] But as the migrants left behind them second and third generations of increasingly prosperous English-speaking college-bred descendants, ethnicity became, as theology had once been, the loom upon which the poetry of love was woven.

All Americans are racists, runs another stereotype, to which one must add that Americans are of all races. No American race, properly speaking, has seemed to exist since the Civil War, and it may be that it is the profound desire to breed such a people that has produced this universal preoccupation which we find moving through the language of even the most impassioned lovers in the United States. More likely, however, it is the simple material desire of poor people to plant their seed where it will most richly flourish. Certainly, in Italian-American fiction the question that often moves at the heart of the matter is shall the hero (or heroine) marry dark or light? Almost always the latter. But the argument is carried out in terms of the former: one re-examines the mates within the tribe before moving outward. A hard saying, this, requiring examples. Since (another stereotype, truer than most) nobody seems to read Italian-American fiction, I am choosing these examples not only to unfold my meaning but also to offer the reader entry into a literary tradition that remains quite literally in a different sort of dark than the one I have in mind.[5]

The first thing to know about this tradition is that all of its concerns, perforce, are diplomatic.[6] That is, in a world where the reality of other peoples is ubiquitous and pressing, a tradition of narrative must find ways of dealing with the complex foreign relations that are going to constitute a large part of the texture of daily life. This need will make itself felt in many pursuits but in none will it press so sharply as in love and marriage. Of course it is dangerous to attempt too authoritative a statement about such things, but it certainly is possible and useful to outline recognisable way-stations in a progress that by now many millions of people have made. In drawing this, as in any outline, one needs a principle of abstraction and a principle of development. My principle of abstraction is this: Italians regard themselves, in the racially-coded rainbow of American skins, as a dark people. The principle of development is that in the debate of exogamy, the search is for a partner adequately light, a search that inevitably ends, in most instances, in the choice of a non-Italian mate. As is always the case, too, you cannot hear the voices of children without hearing the voices of parents.

Exogamy is about avoiding incest. This old truism of anthropology takes on vivid coloration in the wild confusion of American ports of entry in the twentieth century. Most immigrants, not only Italians, have lacked not only the language of the country but any real tradition of learning a foreign language.[7] Mass migration meant the entry of what were in effect whole nations – tens of millions of the very poor, often illiterate or at best little schooled, and almost always trailing long xenophobic traditions across the dust of Ellis Island and into the murk of Mulberry Bend. These places, of course, notoriously enforced an intense interculturalism only dreamt of on drunken afternoons in the hopeful corridors of UNESCO. Jews, Italians, Poles, Lithuanians, Irish, Germans, English, often lived in the same tenement blocks, shopped in one another's stores, infected one another with lice and influenza in the crowded public schools.[8] Indiscriminate intimacy became, as it has remained, one of the more striking features of American civil society. Little wonder then, that immigrant cultures tended to select those marks of their own distinction that could be protected from this ceaseless cement-mixer and to endow them with striking virtues they had never possessed before: every European who comes to America has a chance to observe the high sobriety which often accompanies the very mention of certain totemic foods – borscht, latkes, collard greens, ravioli, sauerbraten. Food, however, has proved easier to preserve than many subtler essences. Italians, Germans and Japanese, for example, were induced by the turns of geopolitics to forget a great deal about their political and historical traditions. Marriage has proved particularly difficult to manage. Catching mumps from someone at the age five is a natural prelude to falling in love with the same person ten or fifteen years later. What all of this means is that the step of marriage, always difficult enough to require assistance from wise elders, became for many people in this situation a formidable enigma.

For of all things lost in the ocean, the sense of generational continuity appears to have been the one most persistently afterwards sought in vain. In the choice of a mate, one inevitably reflects, relives, expresses, opposes or suffers aspects of the desire of one's parents. The resolution of this transmission of libidinal force can be as easily comic as tragic. Shakespeare's families go in both directions, and so, within a narrower range, do those of Jane Austen. To the ordinary uncertainties of this passage, which give love stories much of their interest, is added, in Italian-American fiction, the complication of racial and social ambitions that are often enough not especially well understood by any of the participants to the transaction. There is among the possibilities, to begin with, the parental will so intensely perplexed by the complexity of the extratribal world that it aims to keep its children entirely to itself.

And some of the children simply go under. Such is the fate of the hero of *A Circle of Friends*, an office-worker so tied to his mother and his sister in the Bronx that his only alternatives of escape are the church and the pornography parlour.[9] The character of Fredo in *The Godfather* is such another, 'a child every Italian prayed to the saints for. Dutiful, loyal, always at the service of his father, living with his parents at age thirty'.[10] Fredo, when he finally does escape, only gets as far as Las Vegas prostitutes who delight him with baroque variations that even Puzo, a writer not given to maidenly fastidium, refrains from describing in any detail. Such lost souls in general have not drawn powerful interest from writers of fiction – hardly surprising, given the absence of conflict and the predictability of their sentimental careers. As objects of literary attention, they are hard to sustain because they live almost entirely within a discourse of proverbial lore – the 'circle of friends' is a parody of popular notions of Dante, and the description of Fredo speaks for itself.

I

Love, like so much in literature, becomes interesting when it undermines those preconceptions that most readily find expression. Thus it is that the complex emotional strategies developed by those who resisted maternal and racial enclosure have produced some striking works of fiction. Among these, I am going to take as paradigmatic the hero of Joseph Arleo's remarkable novel *Home Late*.[11] This work, published in 1974, has been unjustly ignored, and I suspect that most readers of this essay are not going to find a copy of it easily, so that its action is worth a brief resumé. Michael Bianchi, aged thirty-three, son of Italian immigrants, began his career as a painter, married a wealthy blonde girl from Connecticut who saw him as an attractive nonconformist, and became (to her dismay) a successful advertising executive. The novel opens directly after the death of his father and mother (in that order). It appears that these deaths have left their son in a chamber of echoes, where one sees him reconstructed along his parents' misalignment. His father had not liked Michael's marrying 'out' – the girl was too different. The mother, however, had always felt herself too good for her husband: she came from a family that had owned land in Italy: she had encouraged her son to study painting in Florence; she had been pleased with his great American success. Now, as his mother is dying, Bianchi has an affair with a childhood sweetheart, someone his mother had despised as unworthy of him. Eva enters his life as the *revenant* of the stereotypically Italian (dark, passionate) and stereotypically maternal, and much of the conversation about her emphasises the heroic expanse of her bosom. Michael has made her pregnant, has been discovered by his wife, his mother has died, and in a drunken confusion he has come to hide in the empty house of his parents.

> The third morning, on his hands and knees, wearing only underwear so as not to soil and crumple the clothing he had brought with him for the day it became necessary to dress again, he oiled the mahogany table in the dining room, slits of sunlight cracking through the blinds he'd drawn first thing to secure the secrecy of his presence there, grateful for the smell of polish on his hands and knowing it would linger regardless of how thoroughly he washed, that smell more redeeming than the waxy smoke of candles lit in prayer. (7)

This chamber of fetishes and totems, we may say, represents in the emotional economy of the hero the body of his recently-deceased mother. Its aromas and its darkness find adequate echoes in the object of Michael's current affections: Eva the once-scorned is now living with her mother because her husband is in Vietnam. She is childless and desperately wants to be a mother. Michael, not meaning to, enables her to fulfil this ambition. He also gives her, as she asks, a screen-test at his advertising agency. When the test is made Michael's colleagues, accustomed to the boyish figures of the pale models they usually see, spend all of their film getting Eva to take off her clothes for what they claim is going to be a brassière ad. At the screening, which has the air of a stag party, Michael starts a fight with the photographer and in the process loses his job. The action of the novel investigates his way of resolving the total impasse that results. Will he save his career, return to blonde Carole in Westport, escape his mother's ghost?

He will. Sort of. In fact, there is no full emotional escape possible. Eva represents in effect the mother-as-object, but Carole represents the object of the mother – standing, as she does, for all his mother wished of him. Michael's escape, such as it is, amounts to an affectional askesis that leaves him 'adjusted' but more than a little numb. He must, in the end, accept the spoliation of his mother-goddess in the screening room. Really, he has no choice. Eva, the girl of his adolescent dreams, is no more an appropriate companion for this college-bred, Florence-trained, well travelled burgher than is the black prostitute with whom we also see him go to bed one trying morning. Our hero, that is, finds in the usual inferential labyrinth of wandering husbands, that he loves the object he has married because he is himself the object of the love that married her. Further, he discovers that while he has been indulging himself, his wife has likewise had an escapade with a fashionable gymnastics instructor called Pino. Michael's way of dealing with this revelation merits citation:

> He wrote his name and underlined it, and under it he wrote "Carole." They were in relation to one another, parts of a whole number. He drew an equal sign beside their name and forced himself to continue "Pino" over "Carole," equal sign, "Eva" over "Michael." It was a balanced equation, a diagram of past months, and each fraction had been reduced to zero.
>
> (221–2)

It is worth emphasising that this final balancing is the working-out of purposes that had crossed in the marriage from the start: Michael, rejecting the dark Eva, had fulfilled his pretentious 'aristocratic' mother's purpose in choosing a 'white' girl from the upper reaches of Connecticut aristocracy (*Bianchi*, whites), and he had revised this choice, as it were, in parody when his mother died, this time choosing to mate with Eva, the unfulfilled mother rejected by the unfulfilled mother herself; Carole, who had thought she was marrying a romantic Italian painter, found instead she had chosen a man who aspired to precisely the status of the father she thought she was escaping, and she had parodied her original choice in her adultery by choosing Pino – as basic, as physical in his way as the chthonic Eva in hers. The characters thus play out the brutal implications of a decision taken originally on the basis of crude stereotypes but lived out, as one expects, in the blunt discomfort of the blatant error.

Arleo's novel is certainly not alone in the grimness with which it views the predicament of its hero as the instrument of parental will. A similar algebra of stereotypes moves the hearts of the characters in *The Godfather*. Michael Corleone marries Kay Adams precisely because she is not like the women of his tribe:

They were not impressed with her. She was too thin, she was too fair, her face was too sharply intelligent for a woman, her manner too free for a maiden. Her name, too, was outlandish to their ears; she called herself Kay Adams. If she had told them that her family had settled in America two hundred years ago and her name was a common one, they would have shrugged. (17)

In this case, it is not the mother's but the father's purpose that the youth unconsciously carries out; his father who wants his family to become an American dynasty. When the courtship is interrupted by Michael's murder of a police captain, the hero finds, in his hiding-place in Sicily, a different sort of wife:

She had a crown of ringleted hair as purple-black as the grapes and her body seemed to be bursting out of its skin.

. . .

She was all ovals – oval-shaped eyes, the bones of her face, the contour of her brow. Her skin was an exquisite dark creaminess and her eyes, enormous, dark, violet or brown but dark with long heavy lashes shadowed her lovely face. (333)

Perhaps it is a sobering thought that prose of this quality sells books in the millions, but part of the reason it does so is precisely what we are investigating here: the goddess in question – Apollonia as she is called – never rises for an instant out of the steamy murk of cliché in which we first encounter her hopelessly swimming, and it is her very adherence to the iron codes of stereotype that creates her appeal for readers who recognise in her, as in Michael Corleone, the protagonist of an affectional allegory only too familiar to them. Apollonia represents, much as Eva does in *Home Late*, the Italian-American boy's act of independence: Michael pointedly marries her without asking his father's permission, because in fact she is, from his father's point of view, precisely the wrong wife for him. Framed in grapes and smelling of camellias, Apollonia is the oleograph on a can of olive oil. She is *Italy* as designed by the architect of the Victor Emmanuel monument. She is Destiny, Mother (see also the fallopian romance of Guiliano in Puzo's recent disaster *The Sicilian*, where the gangster actually travels through a tunnel to visit his maternal mistress[12]), and she is above all and in every nosegay of hyperbole, *Dark*.

Michael Corleone marries her; but as the numerous readers of the novel do not need to remind the myriad viewers of the movie, Apollonia accidentally dies at the hands of assassins who aim to kill her husband. Thus the labyrinthine purposes of the Godfather, as befits the designs of a divinity, are served by his enemies, so that Michael is free, when he returns home, to marry the girl who will best further the Family's progress. How much this tacitly fulfils the Godfather's ambitions is best seen in a passage in which he specifically alludes to the famous apology of John Adams, who said that his generation made war so that its children could be mathematicians and their children poets.

> We have been fortunate here in this country. Already most of our children have found a better life. Some of you have sons who are professors, scientists, musicians, and you are fortunate. Perhaps your grandchildren will become the new *pezzonovanti*. None of us here want to see our children follow in our footsteps, it's too hard a life. They can be as others, their position and security won by our courage. I have grandchildren now and I hope their children may someday, who knows, be a governor, a President, nothing's impossible here in America. (292–3)

Puzo offers two ways of considering the consequences of Michael Corleone's choice. In this novel, Kay Adams accepts her role in the clan, produces sons, and prays for her husband's soul. In the film *The Godfather II* she rebels; aborts a son; leaves her husband. Both of these are plausible results, because neither of them requires that one suppose anything like tenderness, intimacy, moral community between the married lovers. A woman may, or may not, choose to enjoy sleeping with her father-in-law's totem.

Thus it emerges that in Italian-American fiction love has presented itself as a dilemma. To the ordinary interplay of youthful desire and parental ambition have been added the innumerable complications of a world of bewildering social heterogeneity and the subtle but unmistakable traces of the American racial palette, where white sits over black as mountains over the sea, always and everywhere. And you may find this dilemma expressed in the subtler discourses of Gilbert Sorrentino or Helen Barolini every bit as clearly as we have seen it in the blunt allegory of Joseph Arleo or in Mario Puzo's boiling pot.[13] Nonetheless, this is not the end of the story. Dilemmas do not only make victims, they also make heroes.

II

Heroic love in Italian-American fiction is the discovery, or perhaps
the invention, of Pietro di Donato. His most important works –
Christ in Concrete, This Woman, and *Three Circles of Light*[14] – all have
at their core a definitive tragedy in the life of the author, who was
twelve years old when his father, a bricklayer, died in the collapse of
a scaffolding and was buried in freshly-poured concrete. The loss of
the father at this crucial point in the son's development becomes, in
di Donato's fiction, the basis for challenging, questioning, suffering, enacting – all on a conscious and fully represented plane – the
will of the father, simultaneously definitive and dubious, that
moves through so much of Italian-American fiction. Di Donato's
imagination moves directly to the level of ritual terror in imagining
his situation. A few lines from the father's death scene:

> He shouted wildly. "Save me! Save me! I'm being buried alive!"
> He paused exhausted. His genitals convulsed. The cold steel
> rod upon which they were impaled froze his spine. . . . "Air!
> Air!" screamed his lungs as he was completely sealed. Savagely
> he bit into the wooden form pressed upon his mouth. An eighth
> of an inch of its surface splintered off. Oh, if he could only hold
> out long enough to bite even the smallest hole through to air! He
> must! There can be no other way! He is responsible for his family!
> He cannot leave them like this! He didn't want to die! This could
> not be the answer to life! He had bitten halfway through when his
> teeth snapped off to the gums in the uneven conflict. The
> pressure of the concrete was such, and its effectiveness so
> thorough, that the wooden splinters, stumps of teeth, and blood
> never left the choking mouth. (20–1)

The indecent clarity of this scene initiates a circle of anguish, fury,
guilt, and passion that does not cease in di Donato's fiction, but it
also effectively breaks through the possibility of any self-censor-
ship: a writer who has thus castrated and cut the teeth and tongue
out of his own father is free to do anything.[15] Primary among his
capacities is the force that allows him to dramatise the paradoxes of
love in the immigrant world with a directness one does not find
elsewhere. Later in the same novel, for example, at a wedding scene,
a bricklayer named Master Fausta announces a theory of love over a
suckling pig: ' "Before all the world I declare this pure love, but what

a love! for the naked little angel who lies in roasted beauty under these very eyes."' (245–6)

Kissing the suckling's mouth, he claims to love it with all the sincerity of his golden heart. When the women shriek and ask him why, he hisses in response, '"Bee . . . cause love wishes to *devour*!"' Nor is this the end of the matter. Di Donato never omits his consummations:

> Luigi with long knife cut into the suckling and revealed the luscious meat beneath the crisp candied-like brown surface. The ohs and ahs were ecstatic, and Fausta only warming to his theory of "love" plucked a fig from the suckling's eye and before eating held it up and said: "Perhaps I am taken up as fool or lying one, but tell me veritably, has that creature of my wife such a fig that I may eat?" (246)

The complicated joke suggests a marriage bed, not merely full of diversion, but positively teeming with furies. The implication is richly fulfilled, even too much so, in di Donato's subsequent works. *This Woman* records the marriage of the son of the same martyred bricklayer. The young man chooses a spectacularly beautiful, extravagantly *pale*, redheaded widow. To be sure of possessing her, he insists upon making love to her on her husband's grave. Even that is not enough for him: he exhumes the corpse and beats it to a foul jelly. In *Three Circles of Light*, we follow the early sentimental career of the same hero. It turns out that the sainted father, the Christ in the concrete, while sponsoring a brood of eight children with his Italian wife, had maintained an affair with an 'American' woman who had an inadequate husband. The son, who inherits the responsibility of feeding his brothers and sisters, also feels obliged to live inside the old man's body. He is initiated by an Italian goddess of love called Stella – dark, perfumed, abundant, married. But in the end he follows the racial imperative to seek outwards. In a recent manuscript, di Donato goes once more across the ground of this marriage 'out', and even across the territory of his writing it all down: '[Paul] wrote about [his father's mistress], and in his fiction laid her the way his father did'.[16]

Di Donato dramatises a condition acutely felt in much of Italian-American fiction. The Italian peasant family sharply sacralises the will of the parent. Its proverbs and its gods have woven for this family a powerful consonance of heavenly fathers and mothers.

Obeying the dictates of these numina, whatever it may exact in Italy, creates in the heterogeneity of American life impossible contradictions and, often as not, leaves in its wake haunted children who become, as lovers, hopeless wanderers. Probably the best evocation of their dilemma is Gilbert Sorrentino's *Aberration of Starlight*.[17] Sorrentino adapts the obsessive repetitiveness of the *nouveau roman* to the recollections of the son of one of these 'mixed' marriages, a boy whose father was Italian and whose mother was Irish: socially, temperamentally, sexually, these parents played out a series of irreducible misunderstandings that left both of them and their son in an affectional limbo that the boy revisits continually during the course of the novel, going over the same events again and again without ever arriving at any emotional resolution except a certain bitter resignation.

The only novel I know successfully to exorcise the greedy departed is the recent *Ghost Dance* of Carol Maso.[18] She dramatises the problem, as it were, at its roots:

> My grandfather lifts his ax. When it is poised above his head, my father, just a boy, freezes the scene. He is afraid to watch the ax drop, for my grandfather is not chopping wood as one might expect. My father pulls himself from the bed and moves closer to the window. He rubs his eyes to be sure and then he sees it: his father is cutting down the beautiful tomato plants, grown from seed, hacking them down to the ground. Earlier that season they had put up stakes together for those fragile plants to hold on to.
>
> Is this what my father means when he says there are things it is better to forget? Is this what he is forgetting – his own father out in the garden chopping the tomato plants into pieces, insisting that they are Americans now, not Italians? Did his father announce that there will be no more Italian spoken in his house? No more wine drunk with lunch, as he burned the grapevines? Did he tell his wife there would be no more sad songs from the old country? How much she must have wept, hugging her small son to her breast! (74)

What is particularly right here is not merely the image of destroying the chain of generation, by now a tradition in Italian-American fiction, but the use of the interrogative mode. The narrator can perfectly well speculate what it means, can place here 'they are Americans' in such a way that the pronoun refers to the slaughtered tomato plants, but cannot *know* 'what my father means'. The action of the novel fully explains her confusion. The father, a brilliant mathematician, goes to Princeton, does incredibly well, but when he meets Christine, a beautiful Vassar girl who is also a poet of 'genius' (but we never see a line of her production, so that we must take it entirely on faith), he entirely obliterates himself in his devotion to her. Their children – the narrator and her brother – grow up under a lacy fog of opulent inattention, where the father, who becomes some unspecified variety of wealthy stockbroker, never discusses his work at all but spends all his time listening to classical music, waiting on, and for, his increasingly dotty wife. She disappears every year for months on end and, when home, passes most of her time 'working' on her poetry: on the occasions that she does condescend to speak to her children, she does so in a metaphorical jargon that appears to derive from the manuscripts of the schizophrenic in Carl Jung's *Symbols of Transformation*.[19] The children, not surprisingly, generally do not know precisely where they are, much less what they want from life, but instead spend enormous amounts of emotional energy imitating their father's hopeless veneration for this distant, splendid object. The only emotionally sound person in the whole family is the grandfather who, having given up being Italian, finds that he can only be American by going the whole distance and having himself initiated into an Indian tribe. He learns there, among other things, the ritual which gives the novel its title, wherein one scatters black and white cornmeal to persuade the ghosts of the newly-dead neither to return nor to seduce the living into their world of shadows.

This ritual provides the novel with its resolution. The mother, the world-famous poet Christine Wing, dies in an automobile accident. Afterwards, it emerges that her long annual absences were passed in the company of Sabine, a Parisian chanteuse who had been her lover for twenty-five years. The narrator, whose own sexuality is as uncertain as everything else, finds herself soon enough in bed with this same famous woman:

"I will see you again," I whispered. I was losing sight. She touched me gently and the silenced deepened. My mother was calling us from far off. Her voice came nearer as we kissed long and deep. Her voice moved into my mouth. "Sabine," I said. For a moment she was with us, in me, or I in her, in the center of that darkness where she was still alive, and we talked to her. "I love you," Sabine said. "I've missed you so much, Christine."

She was warm and safe and she put her great arms around us in the dark. "Oh, Mom," I said. "I love you." (253)

It is very reassuring to find, at the end of this novel, the narrator and her brother picking up the bags of black cornmeal and white cornmeal and passing these substances four times round their heads. ' "Good-bye, Mom," we say, looking up to the ceiling, looking up to the sky, "Goodbye." ' (275)

And good riddance. Maso has performed the extraordinary feat of enabling one to see a domineering parent entirely from within the eyes of an enchanted daughter whose utter passivity before her imagination of the mother's will gradually, gently, irrefutably paints the tortured, sensitive, talented poet as a monster – a lifelong ghost, whose final passage merely clarifies what had been her identity, such as it was, all along: the object, not only of her own mirror-fantasies, but equally of the disconnected desire of her powerful but hypnotised husband. His stunned and stunning silence, his rapt helplessness, more than anything else points our eyes back to the holocaust in the tomato patch, the death of the vine, the rooting out of the paternal palate and the paternal tongue: 'there will be no more Italian spoken in this house'. So the family is a chain of broken links, the grandfather who deprives himself of his own speech, the father who yields up his own strength, the daughter who must summon up the force of a lifetime simply to announce that she is not her own mother.

III

Italy – that leg, that foot, that branch, that root, that materpatria – has not provided its emigrants with a portable chain of generation. Its only modular culture, prepackaged for easy travel, has been that of its Church, which vaunts itself mother and head of all churches. But this culture, *purtroppo*, does not well serve the purposes of a bourgeois form like that of the novel or that, *a fortiori*, of Italian-American life itself. Even in so attenuated a form as the *dolce stil nuovo*, medieval Italian Christianity does not suffice to the exigencies of the American situation. John Fante has devoted an entire novel to demonstrating the impossibility of loving in America either as an Italian Catholic or as an Italian-American Dante. *Ask the Dust* very elaborately displays how you cannot put a circle around a Beatrice in a city like Los Angeles, which has no walls, and that in any case you cannot idealise a woman when you do not have the slightest idea who, coming as she does from another place and another people, she may be.[20] Even Jesus is not much help. 'Almighty God', the hero prays one day, 'I am sorry I am now an atheist, but have you read Nietzsche?' (22)

The last hope of the bourgeois artist, perhaps, is bourgeois Italy itself – that changing hive of *alta moda*, of moonlit piazzas, of serious cousins. Helen Barolini has written what remains, after almost a decade, the first and only investigation of this promising, more or less Jamesian, situation: a heroine who leaves her successful country-clan Italian-American parents in upstate New York and finds an extraordinary husband and an extraordinary lover in Italy.[21] The husband is a poet, the lover a novelist – thoroughbred Italians of the best kind, the best stock; but neither relationship flourishes. Her husband loves her, but she loves the lover, who merely makes, as it were, the best of it, enlisting her help in his campaign for the Strega prize, getting her pregnant and not wanting the baby. She dies in a car crash, and her place at the centre of the story is taken by her daughter Tina, a thoroughly confused if serious person, who cannot decide whether she is Italian, like her Venetian father, or American, like her restless mother, or, God forbid, Italo-American, like one of the tourist boors she snubs in Piazza Navona; but she resolves her problems at last by marrying a Cape Cod Wasp whose family home has been inhabited continuously since 1670:

> Tina's room had a handsome maple bed with a fishnet canopy and a cross-and-crown coverlet that was old and faded and beautiful. At the foot of the bed stood an old sea-chest used by a Jowers sea-captain on some trip to the ends of the earth. There were hooked and braided rugs on the floor and a child's Chippendale chair by the fireplace. The room was papered in a reproduction of an early style. Everything was right. It was the equivalent of the fine Italian hand among the old families of the Veneto. Both were seafaring families, both had accumulated wealth and possessions and pride; but her father's family had

been on the decline since the First World War and their
possessions decimated, the style become faintly seedy. The
Jowers family, however, were still enjoying their New World
vigor. (411)

The placid gaze of the young fiancée at all these earnests of solid
possession does not very gloriously imitate a poetry of love.
Nonetheless, she is portrayed in the novel as a lover. And a
Dantista, no less, frequently citing some appropriate line or two at a
sunset or a party. Barolini does not hesitate to sacralise the girl's
equal attachment to fine old families and houses and rocking chairs.
These, and the the complex algebra of race and geography they
crystallise, appear before the girl and the reader as the solution of
the complex of ancestral and parental wills that have produced the
contradictory situation of young Tina, who is no less American than
Italian, and no less Italian-American than either.

In the end, when one considers this tradition, one sees, as Barolini
suggests, how much its dialogue of love expresses itself through
objects. The confusion of voices is so great, the passion of
intermarriage and integration so overpowering, that any lucid
eloquence of language has been, and perhaps yet remains, impossible. When parents and children do not speak the same language,
they learn to communicate through bedposts and quilts, houses
and trees, deeds and dollars. It would be a mistake to dismiss this as
not love. It is, at root, what love in its most rudimentary form must
remain: the generational will that does not stop at the boundaries of
the tribe and does not pause in Babel. It accepts the confusion of
desires but it produces its children. It is not the height, but it is the
basis, of any possible civilisation. It is beginning to explore the
plausible elaboration of its own beauty but it has not yet, perhaps,
come far enough from the moment of terrible necessity that
produced its definitive migration and that has produced as well, the
most unforgettable moments in its literature. It might be best to end
with one of these moments. In Mario Puzo's *The Fortunate Pilgrim*,
Lucia Santa, the mother of an immigrant family, struggling to put
bread on the table, depends strongly upon the earnings of her
daughter Octavia, who works as a dressmaker.[22] But Octavia wants
to go to school and become a teacher.

Unexpectedly, shamefacedly, Octavia had said, "I want to be happy", and the older woman became a raging fury, contemptuous – the mother, who had always defended her daughter's toity ways, her reading of books, her tailored suits that were as affected as a lorgnette. The mother had mimicked Octavia in the perfect English of a shallow girl, *"You want to be happy,"* And then in Italian, with deadly seriousness, "Thank God you're alive."(17)

Octavia, in the end, is happy. She marries a Jewish poet and spends her childless life reading books. The mother, the fortunate pilgrim of the title, is never happy or even content, but she raises her family and leads them out of the slums to the Promised Land of Long Island. And that painful journey, for this migrant people, still remains the most resonant image of love. Great struggles and great contradictions reside in this love: Lucia Santa's children more often than not hate her for her determination, for her desire to move ahead. They often fail her or themselves. But in the end she gains her point, and the pilgrimage proceeds. It is a pilgrimage mostly without God, mostly without priests, mostly without a theology. They are not going to heaven. They are on their way to a modest middle-class suburb, with their harried sons at the steering wheel and their blue-eyed daughters-in-law trying to placate their blond grandchildren in the back seat.

They know, these matriarchs and patriarchs, what pain they have inflicted. They have lived in agonies of doubt. But their ghosts, when they have died, have not repented. For they remember where they began and what they left behind. To them, love has not been a song, but the stone foundation of a three-bedroom house, and the well fed discontent of their grandchildren has been music enough. At the beginning, we reflected briefly upon the relationship between the monastic theologians and the Trecento Florentines. At the end, we might draw a parallel between the monastic theologians and the theoreticians of the left. These have never ceased to be shocked that exploited peasants, set loose in the chaos of American life, have not made a revolution, have not wanted to express their class solidarity with the children of black slaves. It appears to have been too much to ask of them. They came to America with the project of having enough to eat. That gained, they wanted to see that their children would have a solid insurance against starvation. This has been their project, this their love. That it has not been able to overcome its own overpowering desire to feed its children, that it has accepted a certain racial guilt as the price of its headlong marriage with the best and the worst of American life, that it has in short never forgotten its ancient poverty in its passion to set down roots in the richest soil, perhaps does not deprive the impulse itself of a certain stark brilliance.

Notes

1. For the place of the church in medieval economy, see Jean-Christophe Agnew. *Worlds Apart: The Market and the Theatre in Anglo-American Thought, 1550–1570* (Cambridge University Press, 1986), which provides, pp. 1–57, an extraordinary summary and development of modern thought on this question from Marx and Simmel down to Cipolla and LeGoff.

2. See, for example, G. Mazzacurati, *Forma e ideologia: Dante, Boccaccio, Straparola, Manzoni Nievo, Verga, Svevo* (Naples: Liguori, 1974).

3. See Rudolph J. Vecoli, 'Prelates and Peasants: Italian Immigrants and the Catholic Church'. *Journal of Social History*, 2 (1969) 217–68.

4. The most important work in this long tradition remains Nathan Glazer and Daniel P. Moynihan. *Beyond the Melting-Pot: The Negroes, Puerto Ricans, Jews, Italians, and Irish of New York City*, 2nd edition (Cambridge, Mass.: MIT Press, 1970), a work which not only brings up to recent date the preoccupations of social engineers but suggests by its very title the flattening field of heterogeneity into which each of these groups found itself cast.

5. There are in fact but two book-length studies on this subject: Rose Basile Green. *The Italian-American Novel: A Document of the Interaction of Two Cultures* (Rutherford, N. J.: Fairleigh Dickinson University Press, 1974), and William Boelhower, *Immigrant Autobiography in the United States: Four Versions of the Italian American Self* (Verona: Essedue Edizione, 1982).

6. See R. Viscusi, '*De Vulgari Eloquentia*: An approach to the Language of Italian American Fiction'. *Yale Italian Studies*, I, 3 (1981), 21–38, for a discussion of the diplomatic imperative in this literary situation.

7. A classic study of this problem is Leonard Covello, *The Social Background of the Italo-American School Child* (Totowa, N. J.: Rowman and Littlefield, 1972).

8. The best portrait of this social world is that of Pietro di Donato in the 'Tenement' Chapter of *Christ in Concrete* (Indianapolis: Bobbs-Merrill, 1939) pp. 127–70. For the effects of this way of life, see Glazer and Moynihan (note 4, above), and Michael Novak, *The Rise of the Unmeltable Ethnics* (New York: Macmillan, 1973).

9. Lou D'Angelo, *A Circle of Friends* (Garden City: Doubleday, 1977).

10. Mario Puzo, *The Godfather* (New York: Putnam's, 1969), p. 17.

11. Joseph Arleo, *Home Late* (New York: Warner Paperback Library, 1974).

12. Mario Puzo, *The Sicilian* (New York: Simon & Schuster, 1984).

13. For Sorrentino and Barolini, see below, notes 17 and 21.

14. Pietro di Donato, *Christ in Concrete*, loq. cit.; *This Woman* (New York: Ballantine Books, 1958), *Three Circles of Light* (New York: Julian Messner, 1960).

15. Some readers may find this enthymene abrupt. The middle terms may be followed in R. Viscusi, 'The Semiology of Semen: Questioning the Father', in Rocco Caporale (ed.), *The Italian Americans through the Generations* (New York: The American Italian Historical Association, 1986) pp. 185–95.

16. Pietro di Donato, 'The Venus Odyssey', unpub. ms, p. 109.

17. Gilbert Sorrentino, *Aberration of Starlight* (New York: Random House, 1980).

18. Carol Maso, *Ghost Dance* (San Francisco: North Point Press, 1986).

19. 'The Miller Fantasies', in Carl Jung, *Symbols of Transformation*, 2nd. edition, trans. R. F. C. Hull (Princeton University Press, 1956), Bollingen Series, xx, pp. 445–62.

20. John Fante, *Ask the Dust* (New York: Stackpole Sons, 1939); for this interpretation, see R. Viscusi 'The Text in the Dust: Writing Italy across America', *Studi emigrazione*, 65 (1982) 123–30.

21. Helen Barolini, *Umbertina* (New York: Seaview Books, 1979).

22. Mario Puzo, *The Fortunate Pilgrim* (1964: reprinted London: Heinemann, 1971).

11

'I Want You': Enigma and Kerygma in the Love Lyrics of Bob Dylan

RICHARD BROWN

> The quest which has distinguished our fiction . . . is the search for an innocent substitute for adulterous passion and marriage alike. Is there not, our writers ask over and over, a sentimental relationship at once erotic and immaculate, a union which commits its participants neither to society nor sin – and yet one which is able to symbolise the union of the ego with the id, the thinking self with its rejected impulses?[1]

Fiedler's remarks, which were compelling to many and infuriating to others, have been sidestepped in much subsequent criticism of American writing, its aspirations and developments. They may in some ways best be understood as products of the intellectual mood of their times, both in the unmistakable ring of those decades of mass youth culture and in the sense that they may remind us of a mode of academic criticism which welcomed the interpretative freedom or flair of a critic like Fiedler, attached neither to theoretical principle nor to traditional notions of scholarly propriety. This kind of 'freedom' we may now distrust, or see as inevitably enslaved to the ideological prejudices of its time; but we may come to regret its absence. And if the slightly dated ring of Fiedler's remarks reduces their value as accounts of *Moby Dick* or *Huckleberry Finn*, might it not suggest an application to the mass popular writings of the time?

Youthful Greenwich Village night-club truth teller, spokesman for the oppressed racial minority or the victim of false justice, hero and symptom of a morally alienated youth, Cassandra of the nuclear holocaust, folk, rock or blues musician, beat poet, professional orphan, country and western singer, puzzle, persistent self-

174

portrayer and self-betrayer, Pied Piper, 'born-again' and then 'grown-up again' Christian, Bob Dylan has written songs that have been and may continue to be seen as among the most valuable expressions of the feelings and interest of young people in that time. And as the times have changed so, famously, has Dylan's commentary on them.

Throughout his writing there has been a kind of consistency in producing lyrics on the subject of love which may be thought of as a central theme of his songs. The oeuvre is full of aphoristic (though hardly Snoopy-like) definitions of love from the early, highly sceptical 'Love is Just a Four-Letter Word' to the 'Love is all there is, it makes the world go round' of 'I Threw It All Away' on *Nashville Skyline* (1969), the 'True Love Tends to Forget' of *Street Legal*, or the 'love that's pure' which 'hopes all things' and is opposed to 'water'd down love' in the song of that name on *Shot of Love* (1981).[2]

To be sure Dylan's oeuvre and sensibility hardly conform to Fiedler's most sensational and most controversial proposition: that the romantic searching in American literature conceals the 'evocation of a delicate homosexuality'.[3] Male figures and male relationships are of course important to Dylan; why should they not be? One could mention the importance of his early attachment to artistic fathers like the folk singer Woody Guthrie whose political consciousness survived from the hungry 30s to the early post-war period, or of that embodiment of American popular machismo Johnny Cash in the period of Dylan's 'conversion' to country and western style music in the late 1960s. The cameraderie and male-bonding of the folky popular music scene of those days is captured in 'Bob Dylan's Dream' on *The Freewheelin' Bob Dylan*. When Dylan reaches for an example of the strained, passionate, destructive relationships that have characterised his creative life in 'You're Goin' to make me Lonesome when you Go' on *Blood on the Tracks* (1974) he reaches for the all-male relationship of Verlaine and Rimbaud. Then there is that teasing gender-bending squib 'Jet Pilot' from 1965, released on *Biograph*. The new-Fiedlerian may observe Dylan's 'born-again' fulminations against homosexuality and conclude that something is indeed here repressed.[4] But, taking into consideration the prominence of material relating to gender transgressions in long traditions of popular and theatrical spectacle (not to mention its obtrusive revival in the so-called 'Glam-Rock' tendencies of the early 1970s), Dylan's oeuvre is recognisable for the consciousness and consistency of its interest in heterosexuality: its fascination with a variety of female types as desired or reviled objects of erotic interest and for its sustained attention to modern love from a male point of view.

Fiedler's interpretative panacea has its relevance here but that relevance consists more in its description of symptoms that I quoted above than in its hypotheses concerning their causes. Dylan's lyrics interest us not for any latent homosexuality they may conceal but in their exploration of a male sexuality that has a spontaneous passion and vigour while retaining subtlety, intelligence, honesty and intimacy. At their best Dylan's songs have a truth to the heart's affections rather than to received moralities, which is all the more immediate for the alternatingly incisive, parodic, or comically managed 'deliberately iggerunt' vernacular idiom in which they are often composed.[5]

The attractions of Dylan's lyrics have long been touted in the marketplace. Their claims to be 'poetry' have long been discussed and no one could wish to hear more on this theme. It may be hard these days not read Dylan's adopted stage name as a callow exploitation of the potentially dangerous myth of 'poet as hero' in one of its most potentially dangerous forms. And yet his are lyrics which have quite understandably recommended themselves to more serious elements in the audience for popular music and now stimulate a growing body of serious literary-critical considerations.[6]

Dylan's writing to date seems to fall most conveniently into five distinguishable phases and I shall be treating his love lyrics as they appear in each of them. Briefly, I take these to be a first period in the early- to mid–1960s, up to and including the first *Greatest Hits* album in March 1967; a second period associated with his 'discovery' of the country and western style of popular music in the late sixties and culminating in *New Morning* in 1970; a third period including the four important mature recordings up to *Street Legal* in June 1978; the controversial 'born-again' Christian material at the turn of the next decade and the latest, the fifth phase beginning with *Infidels* in 1983. Dylan's succession of new styles and images of 'other sides', even within the first of these marked 'periods' has led him and his views to be familiarly tagged as an 'enigma': a useful term in being confronted with the variety of moods, stances and attitudes in these songs, but one that should not be allowed to obscure the eager questioning of thought and the significant element of teaching or 'kerygma' that these songs also often display.

I

During the first of his creative phases the range and variety of Dylan's love songs soon becomes apparent with such uncompromising statements of devotion as 'Love Minus Zero No Limit' and 'She Belongs to Me' sitting alongside strikingly venomous and bitter 'hate songs' like 'Positively 4th Street' (albeit not directly concerning a sexual relationship) or the 'Ballad in Plain D' that unashamedly pays off the old score of an argument concerning Dylan's girlfriend Suze Rotolo and her sister with whom he was staying in a Greenwich Village flat at the time.

'Ballad in Plain D' is the most painful, awkward and therefore also one of the most intriguing of these early songs: its language labouring towards but never achieving metaphorical polish (the lost love is described at one point as a 'magnificent mantlepiece' that he held in his 'grip'), while its feelings and autobiographical origins remain painfully raw and undisguised. Ballad-like retrospective formulae – 'I once loved a girl . . .' – do little to distance material which centres on emotional disaster: 'I gagged twice, doubled, tears blinding my sight / My mind it was mangled, I ran into the night'.

The song strikes us as something that is quite out of the ordinary decorum of romantic feelings yet it retains some elements of that structure of feeling. Hating (the 'parasite sister') and loving (the 'creative one' with 'sensitive instincts') are after all conventionally separated and parting is presented as a conventionally painful experience ('I think of her often . . . ').[7]

The aphoristic moral lesson that concludes the song (and comes uneasily in some ways since the singer has clearly made such a mess of his own experience) conservatively warns us that there may be no such thing as 'freedom' in love, since 'even birds are chained to the skyway'. In other songs though, parting is not treated like this and it is partly the songs of this other type that mark Dylan out as a new talent: one as determined to penetrate to truths behind the romantic myths of love as he is to expose the social truths disguised behind myths generated by self-interest and corrupt power.

Characteristically it is the moment of the lover's departure that gives Dylan the occasion for writing, and the message to his lover is a harsh but clear one: it was good while it lasted but in the words of one of the best known of these songs, 'It's All Over Now Baby Blue'. As in 'One of Us Must Know' there is a need to try to explore the frayed ends of relationship. Love comes to an end in these songs; it may be painful or hard to understand but perhaps these are relationships (like the encounter in Bertolucci's *Last Tango in Paris*) where 'we never did much talkin' anyway'. The moral may not be heavy but a light one and the advice an easy-going 'don't think twice it's alright'. When it's all over, as Dylan's lover-persona says in another of these songs, 'Most likely you'll go your way and I'll go mine'.

Like any serious writer, Dylan is always 'thinking twice' about the same situations, offering different shades and different articulations each time he returns to them and it is perhaps this which helps the songs add up to something more than just jiltings, to something more like a sustained exploration of certain emergent conventions of love. He may need to offer a course in demystification to get his message across. He may have to explain that the stereotype of the romantic lover 'who will promise never to part', however ardently desired by his partner, is simply not available: 'It Ain't Me Babe'.

He may himself be the abandoned party coming to terms with being 'Temporary', and presumably also vulnerable, 'like Achilles', or suddenly finding himself alone again in a world full of strangers where 'something has changed' and 'she just acts like we never have met'. In these situations Dylan's early lover-persona is not the one to deny himself the satisfaction of a little bile. Nor is he above exploiting the emotional vulnerablity of the moment of departure (or using the threat of departure) as a strategy for procuring something that is not going at all but its opposite: 'If you've gotta go, go now. Or else you gotta stay all night'.

There's little that is dressed-up, dignified or disguised here. The idiom artfully recreates moments of apparently raw emotion, and taken together the songs evoke a modern, urban, youthful world, where social and familial authority and power seem neither desirable nor even perhaps possible, where impressions and relationships are emotionally unreliable or philosophically uncertain, where each individual is fundamentally lonely and where the world seems new and radically unfamiliar every morning. Little is more suggestive of a world in flux than the omnipresence of present participles (with those distinctive apostrophes marking the elided 'g') in Dylan's idiom.

The world of these songs is a world where the overarching coherence implied in the very word 'Goodbye' makes the word seem inadequate, and where one needs to be honest enough to oneself and to others to say 'fare thee well'. Of course Dylan can be more conventionally lyrical and nostalgic in this period too, in such undeniably central songs as 'The Girl from the North Country'. Such songs serve to defend the lover-persona against charges of callousness, naivety or irresponsibility. It can be a 'Restless Farewell' where the lover is forced into a dangerously abject moral posture of self-excusal, pleading that 'ev'ry girl that ever I've touched, I did not do it harmfully' or less convincingly, that 'ev'ry girl that ever I've hurt, I did not do it knowin'ly'. At his strongest Dylan's early lover-persona is interesting and distinctive precisely because he seems to know what he is up to and because this knowledge offers some way out of the emotional pains that may themselves be a conventional imposition. As he explains 'To Ramona', 'It's all just a dream, babe, / A vacuum, a scheme, babe, / That sucks you into feelin' like this'.

Christopher Ricks has praised the undeniably powerful folk-ballad-like 'Boots of Spanish Leather' as Dylan's greatest love song.[8] The eponymous boots may indeed by one of Dylan's purest images in the Tennysonian or Eliotic 'objective correlative' manner, but is this really Dylan's distinctive contribution to the songs of this period? 'Boots of Spanish Leather' has the advantage of being a song that stands out, but perhaps it stands out because its moment of separation is posited on a future reconciliation, because its longing is less typical of this world of 'freewheelin' ' relationships of the sincere but fleeting Kerouacian variety. Such relationships may be experienced as mysterious, difficult and disorienting, as in 'Fourth Time Around' (or indeed the Beatles' 'Norwegian Wood' whose air of melancholy mystery it seems to translate into free fantasy); but their mysteries can still seem more real than the romantic clichés they supplant.

A built-in ambiguity of the second person pronoun is the stock in trade of the popular love song. The lover addresses a 'you' who is the fictional beloved but the 'you' who is also addressed (and who actually listens, after all) is the singer's audience, whose affection the songwriter no less ardently desires than that of a mistress. That Dylan's love songs often seize upon the moment of separation in a relationship is no less appropriate in these terms, since his career as performer has been characterised by a repeated turning away from disappointment of his audience. And this is an ambiguity which Dylan consciously exploited on the famous occasion of the

Newport Folk Festival of 1965 where he sang 'It's All Over Now Baby Blue' to announce his first departure of style and taste from the folk/protest to electric rock modes.[9] For lover and for audience there are lessons about self-reliance and the unreliablity of convention or established myth that are given out.

There are of course songs which welcome or invite new lovers as well as those which announce the transitoriness of old ones in this period of Dylan's writing. In such songs women are 'Rainy Day Women' (though these may stand for anything that gets you 'stoned') or they may be the powerfully obsessing complex figures described so memorably in 'Visions of Johanna' and 'Sad-Eyed Lady of the Lowlands'. But the prevailing atmosphere is one where the list of complex ulterior motives that may bring people into contact and conflict has to be exorcised for the lover to focus on the essential 'All I really want to do / Is baby be friends with you'. There's no point in making promises or pledging undying love in these situations, Dylan freshly observes in 'Pledging my Time' since 'If it don't work out / You'll be the first to know'. Of these songs few are more typical of his direct and exuberant style of wooing, or combine elements of enigma and kerygma more successfully than 'I Want You' released on *Blonde on Blonde* (an album whose songs have been said to be 'all about women').[10] The song shows a mastery of its apparently casual form that made it one of Dylan's occasional popular 'hit' singles and it is neatly balanced between the directness of the repeated refrain and the mystery and interest of the material in the stanzas.

The song begins unexpectedly and ambiguously, portraying the world in images as a deathly, guilt-ridden place where the prevalence of a melancholy music seems to promise inevitable failure in love. All its ills seem to be attributable to the frustrated sexual desire of the older generation of 'all my fathers', (this is surely the 'true love' that is referred to here) and indeed may be curable by its satisfaction. The sanest attitude is that of the 'chambermaid' in the penultimate stanza (who prefigures the second best Louise in 'Visions of Johanna'), a kind of prostitute, or at any rate someone who can accept sexual desire frankly and openly and give affection without jealousy: 'she knows where I'd rather be but it doesn't matter'. The final stanza offers a familiar scene of petty bickering between the lover-persona and the 'dancing child with his Chinese suit' who seems to be some rival. Love is portrayed as a more destructive force than the sentimentalised convention would allow. The lover has done something that 'wasn't very cute', an action that is explained (if not justified) in the final return to the refrain 'because / I want you'.

Its lesson is clear enough and fits with the redefinition (or culmination) of romanticism that we may see as characteristic of the modern post-Freudian situation. Against the conventional 'I love you' Dylan poses that most incontrovertible of modern realities, the reality of sexual desire: a redefinition that might seem all the cheekier when we remember the extent to which a belief in the conventions of romantic love was essential to the popular songs culled from the musical comedies of the 1940s and 1950s and performed by the smooth, stylish singers of the Frank Sinatra and Bing Crosby generation that immediately preceded Dylan. We remember too the extent to which the term love survived as a panacea in the songs of such contemporaries as John Lennon and Paul McCartney.

Dylan's songs draw on a tradition distinct from that of Rogers and Hart, George Gershwin or Irving Berlin. It's a tradition which can be traced in the repertoire of songs he did not write but chose to perform in the early years of his career and has its roots in the blues. The Dylan of the first album recording gathered a reputation for being death-obsessed in his material but alongside the three 'death songs' there are at least as many rambling or urban blues and as many songs again that deal with love. These include the traditional prostitute's lament 'The House of the Rising Sun' a complaint against 'that kind of woman makes a man lose his brains' in 'You're No Good' and Eric von Schmidt's good-humoured 'Baby Let me Follow You Down' with its infectiously gleeful promise that 'I'll do anything in this Godalmighty world / If you'll just let me come home with you'. Despite the 'VD Blues' songs that he performed in this period, we remember the spirit of his performance of 'I'm Going to Get You Sally Girl', whose enthusiasm alone persuades us that he really will.

Dylan's position on the low-life sexual world of the blues is obviously ambiguous: on the one hand regretting the sexual exploitation of victimised women associated with prostitution (it is notable that he retains the female persona of the original unlike the successful Eric Burden and the Animals version) but on the other hand attracted to a freedom from respectable bourgeois ideals of chastity, fidelity and euphemism. The whores and gamblers of this socially realistic world are the figures who develop into the gallery of surreal grotesques who inhabit later songs.

It is the *idées reçues* of love that undergo interrogation here, whether in songs that refuse the term love altogether or else those whose low-life settings seem to protest against the dominance of a commercially tainted and conventionalised ideology of romantic love in the respectable suburbs. Even in a song like 'Love Minus Zero No Limit', whose title seems to imply some superogatory devotion to this very ideology, where images of ice and fire suggest a tradition reaching back to Petrarch and where the contrast between the 'silence' and vulnerability of the lover and the 'violence' of the world outside seem highly successful reworkings of romantic convention, we can still see Dylan's characteristic distance from the world where 'People carry roses / and make promises by the hours'. He loves his love precisely because 'Valentines can't buy her'.[11]

So highly-raised is our awareness of the evils of sexual possession that we might heed no further than the title of 'She Belongs to Me'. But to do so would be to miss the playfulness of tone throughout the song and the deliberate jokiness of that statement as a title for a song which celebrates a completely self-possessed woman who has 'got everything she needs', who is 'nobody's child' and who turns out to be a 'hypnotist collector' to whom you may be only a 'walking antique'.[12]

II

Undoubtedly a changed note enters Dylan's work with the albums that followed *Blonde on Blonde* and it is a change which can I think most clearly be charted in relation to the love songs. The powerful new development of a surreal or semi-mythic narrative in the title song and in 'The Ballad of Frankie Lee and Judas Priest' make *John Wesley Harding* a very special album but the flavour of the next two albums is foreshadowed in the two love songs that close the second side and (some have said) seem out of place on it; 'Down Along the Cove' and 'I'll be Your Baby Tonight'. Both seem emptier than material that has gone before. We may suspect a whole range of ironies from a 'truth-telling' lyricist in a song which begins by advising 'Close Your Eyes' but, by comparison with the subtle and deceptive songs we have been discussing, these songs both seem to be and are straightforward declarations of a relatively unproblematic love. 'That mockingbird's gonna sail away' says Dylan both to a beloved and to an audience who have come to admire precisely that 'mockingbird' element in his song.

The use of steel guitar as background accompaniment gives a clue to what was to follow in *Nashville Skyline* (1969) and *Self-Portrait* (1970), where Dylan appropriates not only the style but also the structures of feeling, the exaggeratedly sentimental and domestic romantic idealism, of such songs: precisely those things that had led him to jibe at the 'country music station' in 'Visions of Johanna' that 'there's nothing, really nothing to turn off'. 'To be alone with you' remains the lover's ambition but it is no longer one that is problematic, illicit, or at odds with some implied social convention. On the contrary 'Everything is always right / When I'm alone with you' and 'Night-time is the right time / To be with the one you love'. Neatly elaborated imagery of night and day ties together songs which have a relaxed, confident expectation that 'Tonight I'll be staying here with you'. Love turns problematical night into easy cheerful day; he would 'Love to spend the night with Peggy Day'.

The songs of departure no longer make tentative explorations of raw feelings; they rest content with conventional attitudes and explanations: 'Oh I miss my darling so / I didn't mean to see her go'. The fidelity and reliablity of the beloved becomes possible and indeed necessary, perhaps even at the expense of the kinds of truth that were held dear in earlier songs: 'so darlin' I'm counting on you, / Tell me that it isn't true'. The songs evidently reflect a change in Dylan's own circumstances and it is a change that is easily traceable to his secretive marriage to Sara Lowndes on 22 November 1965.[13] Suddenly the angry beat poet was saying that he wanted to attend the Isle of Wight Festival of 1969 because of the associations of the place with the most established and public voice of Imperial England, Tennyson.

It was a change that gradually but inevitably manifested itself in the songs whose close relationship to autobiography and confession was not breakable and it was a change that seemed to require not only a more 'sincere' and straightforward love lyric but also and more problematically an almost complete inversion of the relationship with cultural tradition that had characterised the early songs. Dylan's 'Self-Portrait' of 1970 offers a characteristically jokey refusal of the kind of retrospection that would have restated, summarised and confirmed what had gone before. It represents a trauma or crisis of *guilty* retrospection which rejects that past, prompted by a sense that things are different from how they seemed. Instead of offering Dylan in his own words, the album put together uncon-vincingly nostalgic pastiche versions of songs by others, including the 1940s Rogers and Hart 'Blue Moon' that seemed to be the epitome of everything the early songs were striving to be unlike.

A song from *Nashville Skyline* has most come to typify that change. The song, 'I Threw It All Away', claims that 'Love is all there is' and its paternal lesson ('take a tip from one who's tried'), makes the case against an immature emotional carelessness. It's no wonder that a song which says of love that it 'makes the world go 'round' has come to be discussed in terms of the problems of the writer in the modern world in relation to cliché. Christopher Ricks's recent essay makes the provocative point that in a modern situation where everything has already been said it may not be possible to avoid the cliché entirely, a fear that is confirmed by the apparent impossibility of ever talking about cliché except in cliché. The task of the writer may then be defined as one which needs to re-animate or re-invigorate the cliché.[14] The argument is an important one and has its analogies in recent attempts to reassess the allusiveness of such classic Modernist authors as Eliot, Pound and Joyce, who centrally redefine the authorial stance in relation to his or her writing, occluding the authorial and making the literary text a veritable tissue of quotations, cross-references and allusions to the familiar or the unfamiliar.

No doubt such interpretations of these songs are as valid as they are attractive and there is a line of filiation between the Dylan who indentifies the convention of the norm in order to attempt to evade it and the Dylan who adopts the language of the norm with an extravagance that seldom seems far short of self-paraody. Is this special pleading? No doubt there is a danger of too easily justifying a betrayal or conformism here. Yet the pattern of an artistic development which, on the Yeatsian model, is one of stark 'vacillation' between contraries is not so odd as it might at first seem. We cannot quite escape the fact that the doctrine as well as the simplified manner of these songs has an appeal that also asks to be recognised and we should not omit to ask whether Dylan's distance is always apparent, even in these attempts of a non-mocking univocal tone (perhaps especially in them).

The album *New Morning* released in 1970 represents something of a culmination of this phase of Dylan's writing, though his use of an innovative style of piano accompaniment and reliance on fresh, new material of his own equally suggests that a further 'New

Morning' has arrived. Love is the positive term that the younger Dylan had distrusted; now it is a transcendent ideal. 'True love can make a blade of grass / Stand up straight and tall.' It can 'cure the soul, it can make it whole'. An affirmative notion indeed which may or may not suffer a kind of reduction from the conditional ending 'if dogs ran free'. The love songs on the album are among Dylan's most sincere celebrations of monogamy, for example 'Sign on the Window' with its concluding idyll: 'Marry me a wife, catch rainbow trout, / Have a bunch of kids who call me 'Pa' / That must be what it's all about'. It may be churlish to ask why Dylan doesn't write that *is* what it's all about or why he doesn't offer as full and sophisticated an account of marital bliss as of pre-marital turmoil. 'If Not for You' which Dylan has said was written 'thinking about my wife' is as total a statement of marital commitment as 'I Want You' was of extra-marital desire. It is a charming song. Some of its ideas are fresh and lively (if not for you 'I couldn't find the door / Couldn't even see the floor') but it soon resorts to the homely impact of the familiar phrase: 'I'd be lost if not for you', and to repetition. The final rather unobtrusive link to the single-line refrain is the most interesting line. 'Anyway it wouldn't ring true', we are told. 'It', presumably, is the admittedly conventional formulae that abound in these songs. And again there is the reinforcing prominence of that conditional 'if'.[15]

Kerygma seems to have triumphed over enigma in the moralising of some of these songs, yet the puzzle remains that the lessons seem less deeply felt, less arduously learned than those of the earlier phase.

III

Whether we think of it as a period of stylistic experimentation, a phase which prophetically foreshadowed the 'end of the 1960s', a loss of direction, a period initiated by Dylan's much-rumoured motor cycle accident, a period of disagreement between Dylan and his recording company about musical direction or a period of marital seclusion in the Woodstock house with Sara; this period is overshadowed by the songs on the four mature albums of the mid 1970s *Planet Waves* (1974), *Blood on the Tracks* (1975), *Desire* (1976) and *Street Legal* (1978).

Musically the albums represent a development less from the

officially released material of the previous albums and more from
the officially unreleased, but more assured, Electric Rock based
material that Dylan had been working on with The Band throughout this time and which had been available in the so-called
'Basement Tapes'. The lyrics, too, have a new-found toughness and
a return from sentiment, naivety and cliché to a more subtle and
exploratory imagery. In the cheerful uxoriousness of 'Wedding
Song' we no longer hear that love makes the world go ' 'round' but
have the more interestingly modulated and more precise 'Ever
since you walked right in, the circle's been complete'. On *Planet
Waves* it seems possible to admit that love may sometimes go wrong
once again. 'Dirge' begins dramatically 'I hate myself for lovin' you
and the weakness that it showed'. It works through powerful
images of human self-destructiveness and returns to a notion of
truth that would not have been out of place in the early songs: 'The
naked truth is still taboo whenever it can be seen'. In 'Going, Going,
Gone' a relationship is at an end. We hear the conventional lesson –
'Don't you and your one true love ever part' – but the *idée reçue*
comes in quotation marks from the voice of 'Grandma'.

'On A Night Like This' may be a reworking of 'To Be Alone With
You' but here the scene-setting is more vividly particular and there
is an attractive atmosphere of transient (or at any rate extra-marital)
pleasures in the 'pretty miss' and the 'touch of bliss' she brings.
Love songs like 'Tough Mama', 'Hazel', 'You Angel You' and
'Something There Is About You' celebrate fresh feelings of love and
desire and it is a love based not on familiarity but precisely on the
fact that 'Somethin' there is about you that I can't quite put my
finger on'.

In *Blood on the Tracks* these tendencies develop: the album title
punningly implying a kind of emotionally painful confessionalism
(though perhaps also that familiar melodramatic heroine tied down
in front of a railway train). 'You're a Big Girl Now' is a return to the
songs of parting that characterised the 1960s, preaching an emotional independence and maturity (while still feeling the 'corkscrew
to my heart'). Once again the romantic cliché is returned to its
quotation marks 'Love is so simple, to coin a phrase', and the lover
seen in a process of 'learnin' '. 'You're Going to Make Me Lonesome
When You Go' implies that there is going to be a parting.
Relationships may be fleeting, difficult, back 'on the road' like that
in 'Tangled Up in Blue' and the language and imagery is that of
motion and flux, of tangles and twists, of 'Buckets of Rain' and of

'Idiot Wind'. 'Tangled Up in Blue' contains a puzzling reference to 'an Italian poet / From the thirteenth century' in which Dylanists have sometimes tried to see a reference to Dante but might rather, perhaps, see Petrarch since the point seems to be to explore the experience of quoted love conventions when 'every one of them words rang true' (as if the lyrics of 'If Not For You' were written by Dylan himself 'from me to you'.[16]) The album's centrepiece, the long narrative 'Lily, Rosemary and the Jack of Hearts' is set in the Dylan dream world of whores and gamblers that he had not visited since *John Wesley Harding*, and Dylan allows himself more or less straight blues songs, from 'Meet Me in the Morning' to 'New Pony', on *Street Legal*.

The title of *Desire* confirms Dylan's return to his true subject, the joys and disasters of which have provided his earliest and best material. It represents the culmination of a period of tension for him in his own marriage which was to end in divorce the following year. 'Well, now that Dylan and Sara are having problems, maybe he'll start writing some better songs', a journalist wrote and the autobiographical background can easily be traced.[17]

Dylan's imagery of affection had played upon a contrast between the violence of an external 'social' world and the vulnerability of the private self: its desire for shelter. 'Love Minus Zero' ended with the lines 'my love she's like some raven / At my window with a broken wing'. 'Let the four winds blow', he says in the more secure and more cliché'd 'On a Night Like This', 'around this old cabin door'. It ceases to be the lover who has the power to give this 'shelter'. In the tempestuous imagery that returns in *Planet Waves* he is still more likely to be the recipient of or seeker for a maternal shelter. In 'You Angel You' the avian wing has not only been healed but has now become the healer. 'You've got me under your wing', Dylan purrs contentedly, in a return of the metaphor to the cliché. *Blood on the Tracks* is full of shelter and storm. The 'big girl' puts him 'back in the rain' while she is 'on dry land'. And there is the delicious invitation. '"Come in," she said, "I'll give you shelter from the storm."'

Shelter may be offered and the offer may hang there tantalizingly even after 'something's comes between us' as it does in this song. In 'Oh Sister' however it is just this shelter that is denied and Dylan sheds persona again (or takes on the 'confessional' rawness of 'Ballad in Plain D') to register the painful reaction to a conventional romantic expectation or a trust that has, once again, led to disappointment. As in the song 'Abandoned Love' from this same period, we see indeed a raw note of matrimonial breakdown. The term 'sister' is used with searching uncertainty ('Oh Sister, am I not a brother to you / And one deserving of affection'). Images of the sister as lover and the lover as sister are extended by this homespun Sunday-school idiom ('am I not'; 'deserving of') hinting further at a specifically Christian duty of obedience and self-sacrifice. The gap that has opened up in this lover's conception of the world is one that he must resort to; an appeal to some higher or transcendent form of justice to heal or to revenge: 'Our Father would not like the way you act / And you must realize the danger'.[18]

But the best of these songs won't be reduced to that level: the traumatised period of self-hating self-portraiture seems to have given way to a more profound kind of self-knowledge (and whereas he may still 'hate myself for loving you') that allows Dylan to return to his material with a new subtlety, maturity, awareness and control.

It has often seemed tempting to think of Dylan's best known love songs as a spiralling series of oppositions. There is the accomplished, urbane, powerful and dominant 'artist' of 'She Belongs to Me' against the quietly knowing, vulnerable, essentially innocent woman of 'Love Minus Zero' on *Bringing it All Back Home* (1965). On *Blonde on Blonde* (1966) the public, ideal but absent and unattainable Johanna in the restless, irritable, symbolic, 'Visions of Johanna' contrasts with the softly melancholic 'Sad-Eyed Lady of the Lowlands', misunderstood by all except the tentative and thoughtful lover who speaks in this literary and allusive song.

More self-consciously and more deliberately, a subtle dichotomy re-appears on *Desire* between the 'mystical child', 'Isis' and, named for the first time, the autobiographical 'Sara'. Though Sara too is referred to as 'mystical wife' in the song, it is the contrasts in manner between mythic and realistic that initially separates the two songs.

In 'Isis', while retaining the Western or 'road-movie' dream landscape of such earlier songs as 'Frankie Lee', Dylan takes much of what he needs from the Egyptian myth. The mysterious atmospheric name of the last pagan goddess of that mythology; the idea of the bride as both sister and wife and as 'throne' or 'seat' of Osiris; and the idea of Osiris as a pacific songster on a world-conquering quest, all seem relevant here. In the myth Osiris dies but his dismembered corpse is annually reconstituted and reborn through 'Isis' flooding the Nile. In Dylan's version it is only the companion of the quester who dies (though the quester 'was hopin' that it wasn't contagious'). The idea of eternal return is conveyed in the Escher-like narrative scheme, in which the travellers are set to return on the day before they set out.

The lover's quest that takes him away from his beloved could easily be interpreted as Dylan's search for self-knowledge through creativity. It is a quest that of its nature is doomed to ultimate failure: a failure that is easily compensated for by the unfading promise of return and regeneration. Such desires are not mutually exclusive or incompatible: the song concludes that both desires are the same: 'What drives me to you is what drives me insane'.[19]

In the comparatively realistic mode of 'Sara' we are given rare and convincing glimpses of Dylan's children. As well as Sara's name we have for the first time a direct gloss on an enigmatic earlier song, when he tells us about writing 'Sad-Eyed Lady of the Lowlands' for her: an enigma solved. The song is a kind of family photograph album of memories, though the impression of such simplicity is deceptive since the happy beach of the opening turns to an empty one at the end and since the song belies its apparent realism and clichéd domestic conventionality with a number of allusively mythic threads.

Sara is a 'Glamorous nymph with an arrow and bow' a chaste Diana, at the end of a song in which typically, enigmatically, she has been a 'Scorpio Sphinx', a 'mystical wife', and a 'Radiant jewel'. More particularly she is, or has been to him, a sweet virgin angel: the paradoxical virgin/mother of the Christian myth to set against the sister/wife of the pagan myth in the other song. The children are immersed in myth too. They are 'hearin' about Snow White': a story which in its Grimm version starkly reinforces an ideal of romantic happiness against twin anathemas of orphanhood and external malice but in its more familiar Disney version became a hymn to the chaste, vacuum-cleaning housewife of American suburbia. Dylan's song is a kind of 'Scorpio Sphinx': a mystery carrying the sting in its final plea, 'Don't ever leave me, don't ever go', that proves the fragility of the myths that have gone before.[20]

IV

The description of Sara as a 'Sweet virgin angel', however distanced, and the new moralistic notes of marital retributiveness that start to

enter the work give an indication of the next radical shift of
direction that Dylan's writing took at the end of the 1970s: greatly
expanding the gospel element in his earliest gospel/blues material
to provide a new message for the 'born-again' Christian movement
that became popular in California at that time. Dylan's sense of
justice and morality and his allusive range had always been
immersed in a Christian tradition but he had taken a critical or
innovative stance in relation to that tradition. Even the adoption of
romantic cliché in the *Nashville Skyline* to *New Morning* phase
retained a populism that resisted this kind of tradition. Now
Dylan's preaching insists on the Christian solution to life's enigmas
and his songs about love modulate accordingly.

In a rare statement of his 'views' on love and marriage made
while publicising his partly autobiographical film *Reynaldo and
Clara* in 1978 (the year after his divorce) Dylan says, 'in my case, I
first got really married and then got really divorced. I believe in
marriage. I know I don't believe in open marriage. Sexual freedom
just leads to other kinds of freedom. I think there should be a
sanction against divorce'. He retains his suspicion that conventions
of romantic feeling are an entrapment: 'Women use romance and
passion to sweeten you up. A man is no more than a victim of that
passion.' But freedom has become a dirty word again.[21]

Angels make their appearance throughout the work from sexy
'junk-yard angel' of 'From a Buick 6' to the equally worldly angel of
the song 'You Angel You' on *Planet Waves*. The angel in 'Precious
Angel' on *Slow Train Coming* may be 'the queen of my flesh' but it is
the 'light' of her message – the necessity of faith and the inevitablity
of divine retribution – that the 'blind' lover praises. Love songs like
'I Believe in You' appeal not to the ambiguity of pronouns in the
popular song tradition but to the analogous ambiguity in the *Psalms*
or the *Song of Songs* between love of human and divine objects.
Women have become a danger and the singer seeks only a 'God-
fearing woman', who is 'One I can easily afford'. It is Satan who
whispers 'when ya get tired of the Miss so-and-so I got another
woman for you', though perhaps Dylan's true complaint emerges in
the complaint against those who 'trust their wives'. On the vacuous
album *Saved* (1980), personal affection as well as erotic licence have
been banished. The only woman worth bothering with is the
'Covenant Woman', who the singer does not claim to love (God's
love is the only kind mentioned) but of whom he says he can 'trust
you to stay where you are'.

Not the least remarkable thing about Dylan's preaching is the way that it remains instructive whatever its stance. Indeed as it changes it intensifies. His amazing and acceptable capacity for self-contradiction is again in evidence in the third and last of the 'gospel' albums *Shot of Love* (especially if we take all of the songs from that period; a fuller picture has emerged through the release of contemporary material on *Biograph* (1985). Songs like 'Shot of Love' itself and 'Water'd-Down Love' now insist on using the word love as a metaphysical cipher for religious self-discipline and commitment. Yet 'Heart of Mine' restores the heart as the seat of contradictory and problematic human affections of the 'Trouble' which, in the song of that name, seems once again to have a cause but no easy cure. In 'The Groom's Still Waiting at the Altar', the image of Christ as bridegroom, from *Songs of Songs* and *Revelation*, governs the marital metaphor; and yet the song offers a fragment of human love-story with a Claudette who could not (in real as well as metaphorical senses) 'Be respectably married or running a whore-house in Buenos Aires'. Unreleased at the time, 'Need a Woman' starkly contrasts *eros* with the *agape* of 'need a shot of love'. 'Caribbean Wind' isn't shy in its biblical allusiveness (it begins 'She was the rose of Sharon from paradise lost'). However, Dylan's Bible is a repository not of doctrine but of an enigmatic imagery which once again preaches the lesson of a fundamental emotional storm 'Fanning the flames in the furnace of desire'.

V

'Been so long since a strange woman has slept in my bed.' Nothing more clearly announces the return of an interest in erotic love and the arrival of a fifth phase of Dylan's writing than his first line of 'I and I' from the album *Infidels* (1983). Dylan's fascination with the post-Romantic, post-Whitmanesque, self-contradictory self can be seen in the way that no less than fourteen of his songs begin with the word 'I', by far their most common first word. Love songs investigate the relationship between this 'I' and some 'you' who may be seen through the more or less distorting prism of desire. In the Jamaican patois made suddenly popular by Bob Marley in the early 1980s 'I' can mean 'you', and 'I and I' 'You and I': a formula which had an evident appeal for this aspect of Dylan's interest.

It is a puzzling song whose refrain repeats the vision of a world where people mete out to one another a Medusa-like injunction against the invasion of their privacy: 'no man sees my face and lives'. Dylan's 'Christianity' has more often than not a strong Old Testament flavour, not least here where he looks into 'justice's beautiful face' to learn and apparently to accept the morality of 'an eye for an eye and a tooth for a tooth'. Christian love is supposed to forgive but 'True Love' according to Dylan on *Street Legal* is not so ambitious, it 'Tends to Forget'.

In 'I and I' Dylan uses biblical imagery for its sensuous ambiguity rather than for any pre-digested doctrinal message, calling on the illicit love of David and Bathsheba. This woman 'in another lifetime' may have been married to 'some righteous king who wrote psalms beside moonlit streams'. The song deals with a fleeting relationship and leaves the singer 'still pushing myself along the road, the darkest part'. Satan still stalks *Infidels* and he is perhaps an even more interesting character than he has been on the previous three albums. In 'Man of Peace' he is the seducer who 'knows just where to touch you, honey, and how you like to be kissed', and seems fatally attractive, not least since his ambiguous or enigmatic appearances seem to echo the enigma of the 'Jokerman' who appears in what is clearly one of Dylan's best songs ever, included on this album. It is Dylan's lover-persona who is the stronger party again, asking the girl not to 'Fall Apart on Me Tonight', albeit because he himself feels that he might not be able to 'handle it'.

Many of the Christianised formulations of experience remain on *Empire Burlesque*. The lover cannot be trusted to show love since 'my love may be only lust'. Yet that admission does represent a certain kind of trust, the trust in one's own experience and feelings implied in the song's prescription 'Trust Yourself', which is as opposed as could be to the admonitions offered in 'Trouble in Mind'. 'I'll Remember You' and 'Emotionally Yours' are brimming with romantic sentiment but there is a tough new 'hate song' on the album 'Seeing the Real You at Last' and a return to Dylan's youthful scepticism in the powerfully retributive song in which we are instructed that 'It won't matter who loves who / You'll love me or I'll love you / When the night comes falling from the sky'.

In the most recent of these phases Dylan has returned to the kind of search defined by Leslie Fiedler as in the mainstream of American literature: an attempt to explore or reconcile opposing forces of ego and id, the 'thinking self' and the body, sin and society, the innocent and the erotic. The songs of this latest phase seem to recognise opposing moods and ideologies of love and to allow them a kind of co-existence. The varieties and apparent contradictions of Dylan's songs have, as we have seen, led him to be described as a kind of artistic enigma. The love songs themselves explore the enigmatic, mysterious and contradictory experience of desire. But as well as their mysteriousness, the songs cultivate a kind of didactic or instructive manner. They may be offering a strategy for living and loving in the uncertain world of fleeting youthful passion. They may temporarily clothe themselves in the clichés of sentimentality that they had seem to defy. They may return again to the mystical and seer-like; frantically counsel self-abnegation, and yet again turn back to a recommendation of sceptical emotional self-reliance. The appetite for teaching seems not to reduced in face of the contradictoriness of what is taught.

I have tried to suggest that the strongest strain is in the earliest and latest of these phases, where the richness of the song's language is at its most powerfully exploratory and where the experience is most freshly recreated. But parody, quotation and cliché are never far from the centre of what makes these songs work, and we cannot yet know in what new or unexpected areas this dynamic, vacillating talent will resurface.

Notes

1. Leslie Fiedler, *Love and Death in the American Novel*, 3rd edition (Harmondsworth: Penguin Books 1984) p. 339.
2. Reference is made throughout to Dylan's principal album recordings, all of which have been made with CBS with the exception of *Planet Waves* (Island Records, 1974). Texts of the songs are all discussed as they appear in *Bob Dylan: Lyrics (1962–1985)* (London: Jonathan Cape, 1987).
3. Fiedler, p. 338.
4. Robert Shelton, *No Direction Home: The Life and Music of Bob Dylan* (Harmondsworth: Penguin Books 1987) p. 484.
5. Shelton, p. 400.
6. Aside from Shelton's thorough and valuable critical biography one should mention essays by Frank Kermode and Stephen Spender in *Esquire* magazine in 1972. For the published proceedings of a recent academic conference on Dylan see Elizabeth Thompson (ed.) *Conclusions on the Wall* (Manchester: Thin Man, 1982). Some of the valuable body of critical work by Dylan's most distinguished academic critic

Christopher Ricks may be found in *The Force of Poetry* (Oxford University Press, 1982).

7.   *Lyrics*, p. 142.
8.   Shelton, p. 214.
9.   Ibid., p. 302.
10. Richard Goldstein in *The Village Voice* (September 1966), quoted in Shelton, p. 327.
11. *Lyrics*, p. 167.
12. Ibid., p. 163.
13. Shelton, p. 325.
14. Christopher Ricks, 'Clichés', in op. cit., pp. 356–68.
15. *Lyrics*, p. 285.
16. Shelton, p. 441.
17. Quoted in Shelton, p. 460.
18. *Lyrics*, p. 382.
19. Ibid., p. 378.
20. Ibid., p. 390.
21. Shelton, pp. 473–4.